# Intelligence for Economic Development
## An Inquiry into the Role of the Knowledge Industry

# Intelligence for Economic Development
## An Inquiry into the Role of the
## Knowledge Industry

EDITED BY
Stevan Dedijer & Nicolas Jéquier

BERG
Oxford/Hamburg/New York
Distributed exclusively in the US and Canada by
St. Martin's Press, New York

*025.063*

*I 61*

First published in 1987 by
**Berg Publishers Limited**
Market House, Deddington, Oxford, OX5 4SW, UK
Schenefelder Landstr. 14K, 2000 Hamburg 55, W.-Germany
175 Fifth Avenue/Room 400, New York, NY 10010, USA

© Stevan Dedijer and Nicolas Jéquier 1987

**British Library Cataloguing in Publication Data**

Intelligence for economic development: an
  inquiry into the role of the knowledge
  industry.
  1. Information theory in economics
  I. Dedijer, Stevan   II. Jéquier, Nicolas
  338.4'7001            HB133
  ISBN 0–85496–520–3

**Library of Congress Cataloging-in-Publication Data**

Intelligence for economic development.

  Includes index.
  1. Economic development—Information services.
2. Industry—Information services.   I. Dedijer,
Stevan.   II. Jéquier, Nicolas, 1941–
HD76.2.I58   1987          025'.063389          86–32250
ISBN 0–85496–520–3

Printed in Great Britain by Billings of Worcester

# Contents

# Figures

**Table**

# Preface

## Lewis M. Branscomb*

Over a decade and a half has passed since the Secretary General of the Organisation for Economic Co-operation and Development (OECD) chartered a group of experts, led by Dr Pierre Piganiol, to explore the role of scientific and technical information in policy formulation at the highest levels of government and in other sectors.[1] Like many of its member nations — the industrialised countries of the Western world — the OECD was in the process of defining the issues and activities in information policy and the organisational structures that could best deal with them. The Piganiol group focused attention on the fact that the purpose of information policy was to foster the taking of intelligent decisions. Information for policy was at least as important as policy for information.

Since that time, countries in all stages of development have come to recognise the crucial role that information resources and processes play in national life and development. With the rapidly developing importance of information-managing technologies, particularly communications and computers, attention has increasingly focused on the development of the information technology infrastructure including the collections of information to which this technology can provide access. While vitally important in every society, the facilities and institutional arrangements for the manipulation of information occupied centre stage in policy discussions. Debates about access began to push into the background the proper concern for the intelligent use of information.

This is perhaps best illustrated by the prominence of access in

---

*The author is Vice-President and Chief Scientist of the IBM Corporation.

1. This report was published under the title *Information for a Changing Society*, OECD, Paris, 1971. For a summary and review of this report, see Edward L. Brady and Lewis M. Branscomb, 'Information for a Changing Society', *Science*, vol. 175, no. 4025 (3 March 1972), pp. 961–6.

discussions of the concept of a new World Information Order, at the expense of emphasis on the need for all countries, especially those in the process of rapid development, to generate the indigenous capability to determine what information they require and to be able, not only to make intelligent decisions on the basis of it, but to put those decisions into practical effect in a productive manner.

This book may well prove a milestone of great importance in resetting international thinking on this point and focusing it on the correct objective: strategies for development that emphasise the resources, institutions and processes required for intelligent decisions. All nations have this requirement, of course. Leaderships in developing nations may frequently be more motivated than those of industrialised countries to organise programmes and policies to foster knowledge-based strategies for national development.

This is, however, equally needed in highly industrialised countries whose complex economies require a highly effective use of available knowledge about alternatives and their consequences. Very few countries make efficient use of available information. Wrong decisions, in my opinion, much more frequently arise from the failure to use information that was, in principle, available, than are caused by current limitations in human knowledge.

Given the immense cost of research to acquire new knowledge, it is startling that financially-pressed budget-makers in governments do not place a higher priority on the processes and institutions for making intelligent decisions based on all available knowledge and experience. Such a policy, correctly implemented, would not only help set priorities for national programmes of research but would also provide a more understandable and persuasive basis for justifying these public investments. This argument would seem to apply with even greater force in developing countries.

Because this book focuses both on information products and information functions — that is, decision-making capability — its authors have chosen to use the word 'intelligence' to identify the capability whose role in development they wish to study. This is a somewhat daring and, perhaps to some, a confusing decision, for the word 'intelligence' has many connotations that may divert the reader's attention from their central point. However, because so much attention in the discussion of the information society, the development of informatics and the World Information Order focuses on data, information or even knowledge as assets that exist separate from the people and institutions that create and use them, a new concept is needed to deal with the capability into which this knowledge is fed.

In the first chapter, there is an excellent definition of intelligence as it is used in this study, drawing an analogy from the psychological meaning of intelligence, as a mental attribute of human individuals, extended to social organisations such as industrial firms or nations. Thus, intelligence becomes the ability for such institutions 'to acquire new information and knowledge, make judgements, adapt to the environment, develop new concepts and new strategies, and act in a rational and effective way'. Intelligence, as a basis for a knowledge acquisition or research strategy, can thus be understood in this light.

There are three very important issues as one develops strategies for the use of the knowledge industry to strengthen intelligence for development that I believe will require additional study and debate.

First, the importance of government policy at a high level, focusing on such strategies, is likely to result in policies for implementation that are highly centralised and largely placed within government institutions. This will surely frustrate the development goals described in this book, for the ability for every economic entity to make intelligent decisions is critical to the execution of successful development. In past years we have seen many examples of developing countries that acquired the best world experts to participate in their central planning, with the result that excellent plans were drawn but never implemented. Any government can engage the assistance of the world's experts. It is much more difficult to develop the intellectual traditions, the independence of thought and action and the education levels that link every decision-maker to the world's knowledge and experience. I doubt that any government information policy can achieve this objective in the absence of a very broad base of social, economic and political development.

My second concern, which is, in a way, in contrast with the first one, is that many developing countries find it politically extremely difficult to exploit their opportunities and capabilities, when only a fraction of the society can participate at the world level. Very small countries, such as Singapore, have demonstrated the possibility of establishing at the world level both the informatics technology and the institutional capability to participate at the world level with respect to information access and use. Few developing countries would be able to adopt policies that permit a Singapore to exist when the rural areas badly require their own informatics development, but at a different level. To participate effectively in the world knowledge network, there must be a functioning node in the country through which the knowledge and experience can be diffused and adapted to local institutions and capabilities.

My third concern is the need to integrate the strategy for intelligence in development with the strategy for education. I found it striking that this book devotes as little space as it does to the role of educational institutions in the generation of the capability the authors correctly seek.

In many countries, the educational process approaches this task very inefficiently and with marginal effectiveness. Politically, education is viewed primarily as a means for sustaining and propagating national culture and traditions, and for imparting a set of skills required for the people to find useful work. In highly industrialised countries, the educational system does indeed play a major role, both in the analysis of alternative choices for the society and for individual institutions, and also in the training of professionals for just such roles. Even so, there is extensive dissatisfaction among those professionals with the ability of the democratic political process to deal rationally with objective facts and come to correct decisions.

This situation is far worse in developing countries where the educational institutions are at best weakly connected to national decision processes and economic activity, and at worst are seriously alienated politically from the government and leadership groups. Yet there is no institution in any country as well suited to the enhancement and diffusion of the capability for rational thinking as educational institutions. If the educational establishment is also permitted to play a major role in publicly financed research, the natural concomitant of graduate and professional education, their effectiveness in the intelligence needed for economic development will be even greater.

I can only hope that this volume will stimulate the thinking that can reverse the trend from the 'fixed pie' mentality that has dominated international discourse on economic development for the last decade, and return it to a recognition that the world's knowledge is shamefully underutilised and the capabilities of all nations to better themselves could be radically improved with a proper priority placed on education, research and intelligent illuminated decision-making. If this re-focus does not take place, a strong case might be made that another United Nations Conference on Science and

Technology for Development might be convened in the hope that, this time, a more substantive and constructive approach to international co-operation in the application of human intelligence to development might be achieved.

CHAPTER 1

# Information, Knowledge and Intelligence: A General Overview

## Nicolas Jéquier and Stevan Dedijer

This book seeks to explore one of the most complex issues facing the developing countries today, namely how to deal with the information revolution and the explosive growth of the knowledge industries in the Western industrialised countries. In the last forty years, practically all the world's dependent territories and colonies have achieved political independence, and the last fifteen years have witnessed innumerable attempts on the part of developing countries to acquire a greater degree of economic independence. Today, however, the sources of power are not so much control over territory, natural resources or industrial production, as control over information, technology and knowledge.

The central role played in the economies of the industrialised countries by the production and utilisation of 'knowledge' or 'information', taken in their widest sense, can now be documented with the help of a number of different indicators, such as total employment in the communications sectors, the size of research and development expenditures, enrolment in higher education, the growth of information-related services or annual investments in information hardware. These efforts to quantify and understand the knowledge industry are in some ways similar in scope and originality to the attempts made in the 1930s to measure the overall flow of goods and services in national economies and construct the first macro-economic models, and it is now conventional wisdom to view highly industrialised societies as 'information economies'.[1]

1. The pioneering studies on the knowledge industry are Fritz Machlup, *Knowledge and Knowledge Production*, Princeton University Press, Princeton, 1981, as well as his earlier book *The Production and Distribution of Knowledge in the United*

1

The knowledge industry in these countries has been growing rapidly under the combined impetus of competitive market forces, direct and indirect government support, strong social demand and constant technological innovation. Its dynamism, however, is not so much the result of deliberate policies as the manifestation of deep and still little understood changes in the values, aspirations and collective goals of advanced industrial societies.

The challenge facing developing nations is that this expansion of the knowledge industry is taking place for the most part in the highly industrialised countries. An indirect indication of this can be found in the relatively small overall size of the knowledge infrastructure in the developing countries. With over 70 per cent of the world's population, these nations, taken as a group, account today for some 20 per cent of world trade and around 11 per cent of world industrial production. However, they have less than 7 per cent of the world's telephones and other telecommunications infrastructures, less than 6 per cent of the world's computers, and account for only 5 per cent of the world's scientific publications and some 3 per cent of research and development expenditures world-wide.

Most of the world's knowledge is produced and consumed in the highly industrialised countries and plays a central role as a resource, or production factor, in their economies. However, it is also recognised as a major resource for the developing nations, and one of the problems these countries must solve is how to gain access in one way or another to the knowledge produced in the industrialised countries that is relevant to their own development objectives. The other problem is to build up their own capability to produce and especially to absorb new knowledge in an effective way. The central theme of this book is that the effective absorption and utilisation of knowledge by the developing countries can be greatly facilitated by — and is indeed dependent upon — a coherent intelligence effort or, more generally, upon a development-orientated intelligence policy. Each chapter attempts to explore a certain number of facets of intelligence in the process of socio-economic development.

Part I examines the evolution of what can be called the intelligence function and puts the task of building up a knowledge industry and gaining access to information important for develop-

---

ment in a perspective somewhat different from that of information specialists, science-policy practitioners or development writers. Part II, which is devoted to five case-studies on the uses of intelligence, seeks to provide concrete illustrations of the general themes raised in the preceding chapters. Part III analyses some of the difficulties a developing country is likely to encounter in building up its development-orientated intelligence capability and proposes a number of guidelines for such a policy.

## The Ambiguities of Intelligence

The very idea that intelligence may be an instrument for development raises a number of difficulties that cannot be dismissed out of hand. One of these is semantic: what does one mean by 'intelligence', 'intelligence policy' or 'intelligence activities'? How do these concepts relate to 'knowledge', 'information', 'data', the 'knowledge industry' or 'information systems'? This difficulty is compounded by the fact that several basic terms have various connotations: in British usage, the word 'intelligence', for instance, has a somewhat broader meaning than 'intelligence' in American usage. Translation difficulties only add to the confusion. The French word *intelligence* refers almost exclusively to the intelligence of an individual, not to the information-gathering activities of a government agency or an industrial firm, while the term *renseignement* (like *Nachrichten* in German) is applied to the intelligence-gathering activities of national security agencies, and not to those of a private corporation or a social group.

The same semantic problem comes up when trying to define a term like 'information': does it simply mean organised data, in the computer science usage of the word, or should it be defined more broadly as any form of meaningful message? The problem of terminology will be examined in some detail at the end of this introductory chapter. For the moment, we suggest that 'intelligence' can be defined as the process whereby a society or an organisation acquires information taken in the widest sense, processes and evaluates it, stores it and uses it for action.

The use of such a concept as 'intelligence for development' also raises political and cultural problems. Psychologists and other social scientists use the term 'intelligence' to describe the capacity of an individual human being to understand his environment, develop

3

new concepts, draw inferences, make abstractions and use in an effective way all the relevant information provided by his five senses. But when intelligence is taken in a broader sense, it all too often evokes cloak-and-dagger activities such as espionage, illegal wire-tapping and the devious acquisition of secret information. This is perhaps most obvious in American usage of the word 'intelligence', and it may be interesting to recall here that in French, the only wider usage of the term *intelligence* is to be found in the expression *intelligence avec une puissance étrangère* (conspiring with a foreign power), which is tantamount to high treason. A final difficulty stems from the very novelty of this concept of 'intelligence for development'. There is a vast amount of literature on intelligence by psychologists and other social scientists, a smaller but much faster-growing number of books, articles and reports on machine intelligence and artificial intelligence as an outgrowth of the computer sciences, mathematics and systems analysis, and several hundred, if not several thousand publications on the intelligence-gathering activities of national security agencies or the uses of intelligence in the business world.[2] By contrast, there is practically nothing on intelligence as an instrument of development, and more generally on what can be called 'social intelligence', that is, the overall intelligence-related activities of a society.[3]

## Intelligence for Development: An Ongoing Activity

One of the themes running through this book is that the developing countries today are already carrying out a substantial amount of development-orientated intelligence work. In fact, while the terms

2. See, for instance, D. Blackstock, *National Intelligence: A Bibliography*, Center for Policy Studies, Washington, 1979; and W. Harris, *Intelligence and National Security: A Bibliography*, Harvard Center of International Studies, Cambridge, MA, 1979. Bibliographies on business intelligence can be found, for instance, in A. Huff, 'Business Intelligence: A Bibliography', University of Lund, Lund, 1976; L.M. Daniels, *Business Intelligence and Strategic Planning*, Harvard Business School, Cambridge, MA, 1979; and F.T. Pearce, *Intelligence*, Industrial Marketing Research Association, London, 1970.

3. See Stevan Dedijer, 'Social Intelligence for Self Reliant Development', University of Lund, Lund, March 1985. In this report, Dedijer points out that the term 'social intelligence' was first used by the psychologist E. Thorndyke in 1923, by the philosopher J. Dewey in the 1930s, by the social planner B. Gross in 1967, and by the students of enterprise strategy, H. Mendel and A. Mueller, in 1972. For a more comprehensive analysis of social intelligence as a synthesis of biological intelligence,

'intelligence for development' or 'intelligence as an instrument of development' are new, the concepts, activities, institutions and practices which underlie them are not. These activities, however, are generally not considered as a form of intelligence, even if in practice they conform rather well to what we mean by development-orientated intelligence. When a country like Jamaica, for instance, makes a consistent effort to gather all the potentially useful information about the aluminium industry, new technological developments in this sector and the history of the companies involved in bauxite mining and alumina processing, and then uses this information in its negotiations with foreign aluminium firms, it is in effect carrying out development-orientated intelligence work, even if these activities go under the name of 'market research', 'information gathering' or 'negotiation preparation'.[4] When South Korea or Taiwan scout the American scientific and technological community for highly qualified Korean and Chinese specialists who might eventually be encouraged to return home to newly established research centres or to act as consultants and advisers to local industrial firms, they are also in effect using intelligence as an instrument of development, even if these programmes are aimed primarily at reversing the brain-drain and building up an indigenous research capability. Algeria is basically doing the same sort of development intelligence work when one of its government agencies hires a large American consulting firm to look into the market prospects for natural gas in Western Europe, evaluate the effects of energy conservation programmes on the demand for oil and pick the brains of the world's leading energy experts.

## The Need for Information and Knowledge

These examples suggest that the scope and volume of intelligence work carried out by the developing nations is considerably larger than one might suspect. This development instrument, however, is probably still far from being used as effectively as it might be. One of the reasons is that intelligence, which is widely acknowledged as

---

human intelligence, artificial intelligence and governing intelligence, see Stevan Dedijer, 'The 1984 Global System: Intelligent Systems, Development Stability and International Security', *Futures*, vol. 16, no. 1. February 1984.

4. See Chapter 8 of the present volume.

a legitimate and indeed necessary tool to maintain national security, is not yet consciously recognised as one of the means for promoting economic and social development. The importance of a development-orientated intelligence effort is amply demonstrated by a few specific examples.

Take the case of a country like Guyana, for instance, which in 1976 extended the limits of its territorial waters to the now customary 200 miles; with a stroke of the pen, the area under its sovereignty was extended by some 50 per cent. The new territory most probably harbours important natural resources: it is attracting the international shrimp-fishing industry, it borders on the oil-rich offshore areas of Venezuela, and could well be among the richest sources of polymetallic nodules. But, as the Guyanese government report to the 1979 United Nations Conference on Science and Technology for Development (UNCSTD) stated, Guyana, with a population of 800,000, had neither qualified oceanographers or specialists in marine resources, nor a single oil-industry engineer.[5] What is more, not a single Guyanese student at home or abroad was studying these disciplines at the time.

This means that for the next 10 to 15 years, Guyana will be unable to explore, let alone exploit, the new resources lying at its doorstep without foreign help. Quite clearly, the country is in need of development intelligence on offshore resources: Guyana must try to acquire at the lowest possible cost and within a reasonable time the knowledge needed to exploit these resources and to negotiate with the foreign firms that are likely to participate in the work. It is worth noting that Guyana faces similar problems with its forest resources and mineral deposits: the country's 215,000 square kilometres are covered for the most part with tropical rain forests which remain largely unexplored and unexploited, and there are most likely large mineral deposits in addition to the bauxite which is already being worked. One inexpensive means of gathering intelligence about these resources is remote sensing (i.e. photography from orbiting satellites of the Landsat type), but more important is the capacity to interpret the information thus gathered.[6] The intelligence challenge facing Guyana is fairly typical of the problems

5. *Guyana National Report*, Ministry of Science and Technology, Georgetown, 1979.
6. The development of such a capability is discussed in detail in Chapter 11 of the present volume.

encountered by developing countries when they try to mobilise the knowledge, information and know-how vital to their long-range development efforts.

## Technological Intelligence

The Western industrialised countries are currently spending over 230 billion dollars a year on research and development. Many of the innovations coming out of the laboratories of American, European and Japanese corporations will most likely have a major impact on a number of key economic sectors in the developing nations. Take, for instance, optic fibres, the hair-thin glass wires that are beginning to replace copper wires and cables in telecommunications systems. This new technology has been progressing much more rapidly than anticipated by professional forecasters and could dramatically affect the export earnings of such major copper producers as Zambia, Zaïre, Peru and Chile. It is also raising serious doubts about the long-term economic viability of several large projects for the development of copper resources in a number of other countries. The intelligence problem here is not simply to monitor new technological developments taking place in the industrialised countries, but to try to evaluate their probable impact and, equally important to take the right decisions on the basis of information which is always incomplete and sometimes unreliable and which deals with future events whose probability is difficult to estimate. In other terms, what is required is a technological intelligence capability.

Another example which might be mentioned here is the potential impact on the economies of sugar-producing countries of recent developments in the field of artificial sweeteners and sugar substitutes. This problem could be illustrated with the help of a few pieces of information culled from open sources, and might serve as a way of illustrating the ways in which a development-orientated intelligence effort might function. The first of these items is the announcement by the Coca Cola Company in March 1980 that it would henceforth be using high-fructose corn syrup as a sweetening agent in all its non-diet soft drinks (low calorie drinks were sweetened with saccharin, following the banning of cyclamates). Two months later, a small article in *Business Week* magazine revealed that a recently established genetic engineering company in California had developed a process for transforming high-fructose corn syrup into crystal sugar.[7] The third item of information, which appeared in all the major American newspapers in August 1983, was that the US Food and Drug Administration had finally approved the sale on the American market of aspartame, a sugar-like protein developed a few years earlier by Searle and Company. The fourth item was the announcement by Coca Cola that it would shortly be launching a new range of low-calorie soft drinks sweetened with aspartame. Several journalists noted that other companies, notably Pepsi Cola, would almost certainly follow suit very soon.

Civil servants in the ministry of agriculture and even the head of state in a country that is totally dependent on cane-sugar exports no doubt stay abreast of developments in the field of sugar substitutes. But what about a country that has only recently begun to develop its sugar-cane plantations for the home market or for exports? What about the local development bank which is considering a number of investment projects, one of which happens to be a new sugar-cane plantation and sugar-refining plant? What about the senior officials in a planning ministry who have to deal with dozens if not hundreds of new projects in completely different fields each year and who by definition cannot know the details of every single industry or technology in the country? These are not idle questions. Sudan, for example, is planning to become a major sugar exporter: its Kenana project is the world's largest sugar-development project, with a planned output of over 300,000 tons of sugar a year. Tanzania, too, is planning to develop its sugar-cane plantations so as to become self-sufficient in sugar.

The planning agency or the development ministry that must take decisions about expanding sugar-cane plantations or establishing new refineries needs the capability to assess the probable long-term effects of sugar substitutes on their country's projects. In this connection, it is worth noting that the World Bank, which has financed several sugar development projects over the last decades, is now aware of the fact that these new technologies may affect the viability of its sugar projects. As early as 1976, it commissioned a series of reports by independent consultants, who cautioned the Bank not to

7. High-fructose corn syrup can be extracted from the starch of a number of crops, notably wheat, maize and cassava. Two of its main drawbacks are, or rather were, (a) the fact that it comes only in liquid form, which means it can only be used in drinks and confectionery, and (b) its instability, which makes it difficult to use in canned foods, which are likely to have a long shelf-life.

become involved in further financing in this field.[8]

This story of sugar substitutes points up some of the major difficulties to be overcome in building up an intelligence capability. First, a country must be aware that a problem does in fact exist. The reports commissioned by the World Bank suggest that this was true of the Bank but the same can probably not be said of Tanzania or Sudan, and it is worth thinking about the factors that can stimulate such an awareness. Second, a country must have the ability to assemble the relevant information from a wide variety of sources, perceive that a particular item of information is important and try to get an overall picture even though some pieces of the puzzle may be missing. Third, a country has to be able to assess all the available information, evaluate its importance and reliability, and make value judgements as to the likely impact of the developments which have thus been identified. Finally, decisions have to be taken on the basis of this information. Guyana's inability to explore its new offshore resources is a typical illustration of the need for intelligence about natural resources, while the sugar industry story clearly shows the need for intelligence about new technologies. But these are only two elements, albeit important ones, in a development-orientated intelligence effort. Another potentially important element is intelligence about multinational corporations.[9]

## Intelligence about Multinational Corporations

Subsidiaries of foreign multinational firms often account for a substantial proportion of industrial employment and exports in developing countries. Yet it is surprising to see how little many of these countries know about the multinationals operating on their territory. Little use is made of available sources of information on these companies, even though this information may be crucial to negotiations on such issues as future investment plans, local partici-

---

8. This analysis of prospects for high-fructose corn syrup can be found in three mimeographed documents: E.M. Brook, 'The Sugar Substitute, High Fructose Corn Syrup', The World Bank, Washington, September 1976; George T. Tsao, 'High Fructose Syrups', Purdue University, West Lafayette, IN, n.d.; Fred Gray, 'Sugar Substitutes: Their Competitive Position', US Department of Agriculture, Washington, February 1976.

9. On this point, see Stevan Dedijer, 'Multinationals, Intelligence and Development', paper presented at the International Conference on Informatics and Industrial Development, Trinity College, Dublin, March 1981.

pation in management or equity, technology transfer, pricing policies, employment objectives or subcontracting to local firms.[10] For this, the host-country negotiators need to understand the multinational's psychology, its motivations and strategy, its attitudes towards foreign markets and its long-term plans. This information is also essential if a good working relationship is to be established between host country and foreign firm.

The penalties a developing country may have to pay as a result of poor information about multinationals is clearly illustrated by the negotiations which took place in the late 1970s between India and a number of foreign corporations. India's objective was to get all foreign firms to conform to the new legislation requiring at least 50 per cent local equity participation in the Indian subsidiaries of foreign firms, and access by the Indian partner to the technology used by that subsidiary. Negotiations on this issue with two major foreign firms, IBM and Coca Cola, were notoriously unsuccessful. Both companies discontinued their operations in India, and it would seem that this proved extremely costly to India, even if it did encourage the development of an indigenous computer industry and stimulated the sales of locally-produced soft drinks (as well as illegal imports from Coca Cola's bottling plant in Nepal!).

What is interesting here is not only the fact that India overestimated the strength of its negotiating position (for both companies, the Indian market, despite its very large population, accounted for a very small share of world-wide sales and was thus not vitally important), but also that the Indian negotiators were apparently unaware of these firms' policies, practices and traditions. Anyone who has read an official company history of Coca Cola or articles published in *Fortune*, *Forbes* or *Business Week*, or who has talked even briefly to one of its competitors, knows that Coca Cola's unpatented, most closely guarded secret is its 100-year-old formula for the concentrate which has made the company famous. Any negotiation aimed at gaining access to this specific technology was doomed to failure from the start. Similarly, the Indian negotiators could have known from reading one of the company histories of IBM, any biography of founder Thomas J. Watson, or even the firm's annual reports, that this company has always insisted on retaining full ownership of its foreign subsidiaries.

10. See Rita Cruise O'Brien (ed.), *Information, Economics and Power. The North–South Dimension*, Hodder and Stoughton, London, 1983.

The reasons for this policy of IBM are largely managerial and technological, but probably also have much to do with the company's corporate identity, its internal value system and its history. What the Indian negotiators apparently failed to appreciate was that IBM's insistence on 100 per cent ownership of its subsidiaries was not a negotiating ploy — as it might have been with another company — but a non-negotiable issue. The intelligence problem in such a situation is to perceive which points are negotiable and which are not, and to judge whether a demand for local equity participation might reluctantly be agreed to by one foreign corporation, while for another — IBM in this instance — such a request would inevitably lead to closing down its manufacturing operations in the host country.

The example of India's negotiations with IBM and Coca Cola points to the need for intelligence about multinational corporations and for what might be called negotiation intelligence. The story of the sugar industry clearly points to the need for scientific and technological intelligence. What is also required is intelligence about foreign markets, which is vital if a developing country is to increase its exports, identify changes in consumer preferences, understand how foreign distribution systems operate and develop a network of commercial agents abroad.[11] Finally, a country also needs economic and financial intelligence to keep track of international capital flows, assess the evolution of interest rates and identify upturns and downturns in the world economy.[12] These different 'sectoral' intelligence activities can be viewed, somewhat schematically, as the building blocks of a development-orientated intelligence effort (see Figure 1.1), but it should be kept in mind that there is a considerable amount of overlapping. Effective intelligence work on multinational corporations, for instance, cannot be dissociated from intelligence on scientific and technological developments, and market intelligence depends heavily on economic and financial intelligence.

11. One of the international agencies that can help developing countries build up their foreign trade intelligence is the Geneva-based International Trade Centre (ITC), which was set up by the United Nations Conference on Trade and Development (UNCTAD) and the General Agreement on Tariffs and Trade (GATT).

12. In the same way, banks need intelligence about their borrowers. This is one of the reasons why over 100 leading international banks established the Institute of International Finance in 1983.

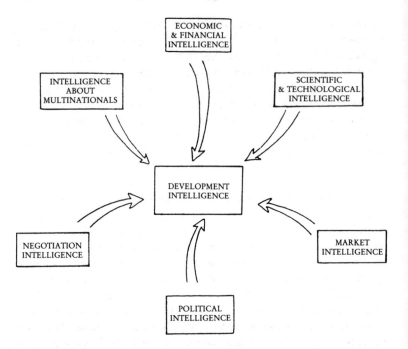

**Figure 1.1.** The components of a development-orientated
intelligence effort

### Data, Information, Knowledge and Intelligence

Any intelligence work, be it military intelligence, corporate intelligence, or what we have called development intelligence, calls for the acquisition and evaluation of very different types of information and knowledge. At the most elementary level, we find data, that is, sets of numbers, as they might appear in national statistical abstract, the balance sheet of a large corporation, the market projections made by a consulting firm, the print-outs of a computer used for seismological analysis or the electronic signals from a communications satellite. These data are often totally meaningless to the non-expert but very revealing to the specialists: the detailed accounts of an industrial firm will tell a lot to an accountant or a stockbroker, but are most likely not of much use to someone with no knowledge of accounting, finance or economics. Thus what is important is not sets of figures as such, but rather the information

12

content which can be extracted from them. These data can be represented in the form of 'bits' in a computer memory, sets of figures in a statistical table or the individual letters in a printed text. Their value as information, that is, as a meaningful message, depends on what can be called the absorptive and analytical capacity of the brain, the individual or the institution receiving the data. Information could thus be defined as data, taken in the widest sense, which have been received, processed and understood. This represents the next level of complexity in the 'information pyramid' shown in Figure 1.2.[13]

Several criteria can be used to evaluate the different items or pieces of information collected by an intelligence unit. One is its importance, or lack of importance, to the receiver. Another is its reliability: is it a verifiable or measurable fact, or does it deal with a probable outcome, a likely event, a possible fact? A final criterion is the distinction between quantitative and qualitative information: quantitative information may seem to be more reliable, but often the really important information is of a more qualitative nature. The next level of complexity in our information pyramid is 'knowledge'. Knowledge can be viewed as a stock of information which has been processed, analysed, evaluated and tested, and which is continually updated and enriched by the permanent confrontation between this new information and previous information stored in a 'memory' (the memory can be a computer memory, the human brain, or the experience of an institution). The final level of complexity is intelligence in the psychological sense of the term, namely the ability of an individual — and by extension of a social organisation such as an industrial firm or a country — to acquire new information and knowledge, make judgements, adapt to the environment, develop new concepts and strategies, and act in a rational and effective way on the basis of the informations thus acquired.[14]

As we noted earlier, one of the difficulties in dealing with such terms as 'intelligence', 'information' or the 'knowledge industry' is that each one can mean rather different things. 'Information', for

13. For a more elaborate version of this concept of an 'information pyramid', see F.T. Pearce's 'intelligence ladder' in Chapter 4 of the present volume.

14. This concept of 'intelligence', as applied to a country, is at the origin of the creation, in Venezuela, of the world's first and only 'Ministry for Development of Intelligence'. For a good overview of the problems and objectives of such an unusual type of government department, see the interview of Minister Luís Alberto Machado in *Science*, vol. 214, 6 November 1981.

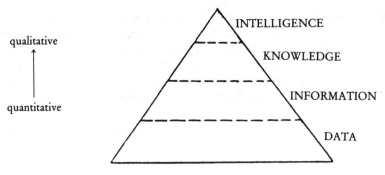

**Figure 1.2.** The information pyramid

instance, is often used as a synonym for 'data': computers and associated equipment, usually known as 'information systems', in effect process data rather than information. When talking about the 'knowledge industry', one is generally dealing with the whole range of activities of our information pyramid. It includes not only data processing (that is, computer systems) or the industries which serve as the basis for the transmission and diffusion of data, information and knowledge (such as telecommunications networks, the mass media or education), but also the services and industries that produce new information and new knowledge (for example, governmental and industrial research laboratories) or store knowledge and information (such as libraries or data banks).

The term 'intelligence' in turn can be understood in three different ways. It can refer exclusively to the upper layer in our information pyramid, namely the ability to make judgements and adapt to the environment in a coherent way, or it can refer to the information and data-gathering activities of a national security agency and, by extension (essentially in British usage), of an industrial firm or any other social organisation. In this second sense, intelligence is essentially a process of information acquisition, storage, analysis and evaluation. The third conception is a synthesis of the first two: it includes intelligence-gathering activities defined in the widest sense, as well as the higher level ability to make judgements, evaluations, inferences, and use this knowledge for action.

In all three conceptions, intelligence can be viewed as a set of complex processes, but it can also be understood to mean the result or product of an information-gathering activity, and is thus virtually synonymous with information. Unless otherwise specified, the term 'intelligence' in this work refers to the third definition, and not exclusively to 'information', or to 'intelligence' in the psychological sense of the word. It is, however, important to keep in mind that the terminology in this field is still far from being fully established, a problem which, it may be noted, was also typical of the computer industry in the 1950s.

The various chapters in this book focus, directly or indirectly, on intelligence as an instrument of development, that is, the intelligence activities carried out by developing countries to mobilise and use knowledge for development purposes. However, it is important to keep in mind that, aside from these development-orientated intelligence activities, there are also more conventional intelligence activities, related as in any other country to political priorities, security objectives and social imperatives. These wider intelligence activities form what some authors call 'social intelligence' and what others, notably Harold Wilenski, term 'organisational intelligence'.[15]

## The Intelligence System

The semantic and conceptual problems arising from the use of such terms as 'intelligence', 'information' or 'knowledge' are due in no small part to the frequent failure to distinguish between products and functions. Intelligence, for instance, can refer to the product of information-gathering work (as in the expression, 'We have intelligence that our competitor, company X, is planning to launch its new product on December 10') or to the information-gathering and analysis work itself ('Our intelligence about competitors is pretty strong'). In the same way, when talking about the 'knowledge industries' a distinction is not always clearly made between those sectors which produce knowledge (a research laboratory, for example), those which store knowledge (data banks, libraries, and so on), those which transfer or transmit knowledge (the educational system or a telecommunications network), those which evaluate and process knowledge (a governmental policy-analysis unit or an industrial firm's strategic planning division) and, finally, those which apply this knowledge to action. For this reason, it may be useful to look at information, knowledge and intelligence as a system, and see how its different parts fit together.

15. See Harold Wilenski, 'Organizational Intelligence', in *International Encyclopaedia of the Social Sciences*, vol. 11, McGraw-Hill, New York, 1973, as well as Dedijer, 'Social Intelligence for Self Reliant Development'.

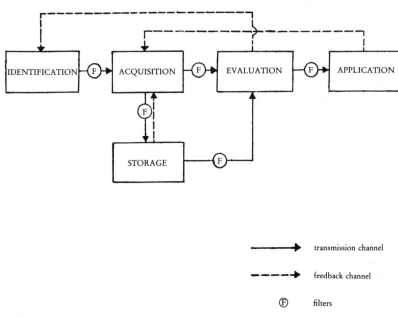

**Figure 1.3.** The intelligence system

A number of different models of such a system can be envisaged, since the idea is not to represent reality in all its complexity, but simply to provide a tool for understanding a particular structure or institution. The model of an 'intelligence system' shown in Figure 1.3. should be viewed with this in mind; its sole aim is to show some of the main functions or activities in the field of intelligence and to help identify some of the typical problem areas. The first of these problems is that of identification: how does an individual, an institution or a country identify the issues and trends on which its intelligence effort should focus? Much identification work is of a routine nature, in the sense that the problems to be studied are fairly obvious, the challenges familiar and the adversary well known. An industrial corporation, for example, knows who its principal competitors are and, among them, which could pose serious marketing or technological threats. In the same way, national security agencies devote most of their intelligence effort to a small number of clearly identified potential adversaries. In such cases, the problem of identification is rather minor, in the sense that it is dominated by obvious economic or geo-political constraints, and reinforced both by habit and by a long-standing familiarity with the opponent.

Problem identification may often be fairly simple, but history clearly shows that some of the biggest intelligence failures stem from failures in the identification process. Such failures tend to occur when the opponent, the threat or the challenge is totally new or unexpected, falling completely outside the normal frame of reference of the intelligence organisation or unit. Obvious examples are the failure of certain state security organisations to identify the threat presented by fundamentalist religious movements, or that of a good many firms in such mechanical industries as watch-making, sewing machines or calculating equipment, to identify the revolutionary change brought about by the advent of micro-electronics. In the political field, such failures can result in revolution and civil war; in business, they can lead to bankruptcy. Though it may be easy with hindsight to pinpoint the institutional, cultural, social or political causes of a spectacular failure to identify a challenge or threat, it is much more difficult to discern the factors that make for an effective identification capability.

Part of the difficulty stems from the fact that the process of identification is not as rational as corporate planners or heads of national security would like it to be; it is a rather intuitive, even artistic process, which calls for imagination, perceptiveness and sensitivity, as well as for an ability to sense nascent changes. Some of the largest consumer-orientated industrial firms, for example, now regularly scan the *New York Times* and other leading newspapers and magazines for the weekly list of best-selling books, or subscribe to the 'content analyses' of the national press carried out by specialised consulting firms.[16] This may seem rather irrelevant to a corporation's intelligence effort, but has in fact proved a useful if indirect way to identify some of the basic concerns of the public, which in the long run could affect the company's operations. Swings in public opinion are often captured, if not crystallised, by a best-selling book. In the 1960s the big car and chemical firms totally misjudged the new public concern for safety and environmental protection which had so aptly been captured in Ralph Naders's book *Unsafe at Any Speed* or Rachel Carsons's *Silent Spring*. This problem of identification is not, of course, specific to intelligence institutions and units alone. It can also be central to scientific research: what often distinguishes the Nobel Prize class of scientist from the more pedestrian researcher is the ability to identify an

16. See John Naisbitt, *Megatrends*, Warner Books, New York, 1982.

17

important research problem and make a correct evaluation of its 'solubility', to use Sir Peter Medawar's term.[17]

## Open, Grey and Secret Information

Another important box or 'problem area' in the system sketched in Figure 1.3 is the acquisition or generation of data, information and knowledge. This is the activity which is most generally associated with 'intelligence' in the narrow sense of the word; it is also the one which evokes espionage. To put matters straight, it should be stressed that espionage, which can be defined as the acquisition of secret information by illegal means,[18] represents only a very small part of the total information-gathering activities of a corporation, a national intelligence agency, or a country. By far the largest part of the information-gathering activities of any intelligence organisation focuses on 'open' information, that is, information which is openly available in print or from individuals. The fact that this information is freely accessible does not, of course, mean that it is without cost: the man-years of work involved in finding relevant open information, monitoring new information and developing appropriate channels of communication can be quite expensive. Confidential or secret information, by contrast, accounts for a very small part of the data, information or knowledge collected by an intelligence unit, although the public grossly overestimates its importance.

One of the reasons for this tendency to overestimate the importance of secret or confidential information is its frequent confusion with what can be called 'grey' information, that is, information

17. Peter Medawar, *The Art of the Soluble*, Methuen, London, 1967. For a good account of problem identification in the scientific field, see, for instance, the story of the discovery of the DNA molecule's structure in James D. Watson, *The Double Helix*, Atheneum, New York, 1968. On the uses of 'lateral thinking' in the identification of problems, see notably Edward de Bono, *The Use of Lateral Thinking*, Jonathan Cape, London, 1967.

18. Putting together open pieces of information or data may, of course, result in final information which can be considered as secret, but technically speaking such an activity cannot be described as espionage. The legality or illegality of the means of acquisition often depends on technical definitions: photographing a military objective from the ground is generally recognised as espionage, but photographing the same objective in even more detail from outer space is now more or less reluctantly accepted as a legal activity. In the same way, the definition of what constitutes secret information differs considerably from one country or culture to another: statistical data on foreign trade or industrial investment are considered secret in some countries, while in others they are openly available.

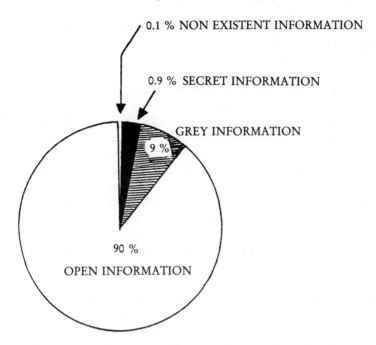

**Figure 1.4.** The different types of information

which is not published or widely diffused, but to which access can nevertheless be gained, provided one knows that it exists and has the adequate channels of communication. Information falling into this category includes xeroxed documents, preprints of scientific articles, rumours in business circles, project proposals submitted to a research-funding agency and discussions with well-informed specialists.[19] The balance between open, grey and secret information can be roughly broken down as follows: 90 per cent of all necessary information is open and freely accessible; 9 per cent is grey information; and 0.9 per cent is secret or confidential information (see Figure 1.4.). This is merely a rule-of-thumb indication of the relative importance of these three types of information. What should be kept in mind are the orders of magnitude: open information is at least ten times as abundant as grey information, and the latter in

19. One interesting effort to assemble grey information in the scientific field is that of the System for Information on Grey Literature in Europe, set up in the United Kingdom in 1984. For further details, see the brochure 'Your Passport to Grey Literature', The British Library Lending Division, Boston Spa, October 1984.

turn is at least ten times as abundant as secret or confidential information.

Grey information is more difficult and time-consuming to find, while secret or confidential information is often totally inaccessible, and its search involves a number of risks and penalties. In Figure 1.4 we have added a fourth category which often tends to be forgotten: non-existent information. This sometimes accounts for a far from negligible information-gathering effort on the part of an intelligence unit. The reason is not necessarily poor judgement: there is often no way of knowing that a particular piece of information does not exist, or at least not exist yet.

Secret or confidential information cannot remain secret for ever. Much in the same way as radioactive material decays over time, secret information gradually passes into the category of grey information, and then into the category of open information. This is what happens, for instance, with information about a company's technological innovations or its financial troubles: first known to a limited number of higher-level executives within the firm, the information gradually percolates down to personnel, then the rumour mill of industry observers, company customers and other interested circles (this is the stage of grey information), and finally hits the news and the stock-market.

## Information Overload and the Memory Function

Contrary to what is widely believed, one of the major problems facing any intelligence organisation is not the difficulty of acquiring information — be it open, grey or secret — but rather the danger of over-abundant information. The amount of information that can be amassed usually greatly exceeds the organisation's capability to process and use it, and this gap between processing ability and acquisition capacity tends to grow with time, largely as a result of the enormous increase in the volume of available information and the growing sophistication of acquisition techniques. This tendency to accumulate vast amounts of often obsolete or irrelevant information is one of the typical pathological syndromes of an intelligence organisation. In too many situations, decision-makers still find themselves without sufficiently reliable and reasonably complete information on which to base their evaluation of the problem at hand.

The process of information acquisition is closely linked with the system's storage and evaluation function. Storage is in essence the memory function of an intelligence system. It can take the form of computerised data banks, conventional libraries, the brain of an individual or the institutional experience of an organisation. The value and effectiveness of what is stored depends not so much on the quantity and the quality of information thus accumulated as on the ease and speed of retrieval: a book which has mistakenly been returned to the wrong shelf in a large library is as good as lost. This is, of course, one of the major attractions of computer systems: the storage capacity is practically unlimited, and the retrieval of information is almost instantaneous.

The quality and efficiency of an intelligence system also depends on two other elements sketched in Figure 1.3, namely the information channels, and the filters that can be found in the various channels. The faster the flow of information in the system, the more efficient the system is likely to be. This speed of transfer is conditioned both by the nature of the channel itself (transmitting information by mail for instance is much slower than its transmission by voice over the telephone, or by electronic means) and by the width or capacity of the channel. The processes of transmission, in turn, are influenced by the filters which exist at various points in the system. These filters may be 'natural': the greater the distance, the greater the amount of information that is lost or distorted. The filters may be also physical devices, as in a telecommunications network, where their function is to filter out the unwanted noises and interferences in the transmission process. But the most important filters in an intelligence system are of a social nature, as illustrated by the industrial firm that does not want to recognise the technological threat posed by a competitor, or the military intelligence unit that systematically blocks the further transmission of information about its adversary because it does not fit in with its evaluation of the enemy's capabilities or intentions.

The capacity of an intelligence system to acquire, store and transmit information is one thing. What is ultimately much more important is its capacity to evaluate the relevance and reliability of the information for decisions and action. The evaluation function is critical to the success of any intelligence effort; it is also at this stage that some of the most monumental intelligence failures tend to originate. The difficulty here, as with the identification problem mentioned earlier, is that good evaluation calls for complex skills

21

involving judgement, intuition and imagination. The relevance of any intelligence effort depends on its effective links with action. An industrial corporation which correctly identifies the technological threat from a competitor, which succeeds in gathering additional information and confronts this information with what it already knows (with the information stored in its institutional memory or its files), which makes the right judgement about the threat, but which ultimately fails to use this information in its long-term planning or short-term decisions, is in effect wasting its intelligence effort. The same is true of a developing nation which acquires computerised information systems, spends large amounts on education and develops its internal capacity to create new knowledge, but ultimately fails to use this knowledge to pursue its economic, social and political goals.

## The Emergence of Social Intelligence

Government agencies, industrial firms, political parties, trade unions, armies and political pressure groups are all involved in intelligence work. These activities, which consist in identifying problems, threats, opportunities or challenges, gathering vast amounts of information, data and knowledge, storing and evaluating this information, and using it to achieve the organisation's goals, are seldom consciously recognised as intelligence work. In an industrial corporation, scanning the economic and political environment in order to identify emerging threats, promising market opportunities or unusual technological challenges is an activity which goes under such names as market analysis, technological forecasting or long-range planning. In the same way, when a government department tries to develop better methods for assembling and storing the increasing amounts of information it needs in its daily work, it tends to think in terms of 'information systems' rather than in terms of intelligence activities.

Intelligence work is generally assumed to be an activity performed essentially by what is known as an intelligence organisation, that is, a national security agency concerned primarily with military and strategic tasks. National security agencies, whether they are dealing with external or internal security, with intelligence in the narrow sense (the gathering of information) or with counter-intelligence (countering the information-gathering activities of another country's security agencies), represent only the tip of the intelligence iceberg in any society. It is, however, the tip which has been the most widely studied and which tends to attract public attention. The high visibility of national security agencies has tended to divert the attention of scholars, journalists and historians from the ultimately much more important and far wider range of intelligence activities carried out by corporations, social groups, private institutions and government agencies.

What the present book tries to do is to look at intelligence activities within society and explore some of the main aspects of what might be called the intelligence function and its management. The implicit hypothesis running through the various contributions is that this intelligence function, which plays a central role in highly industrialised societies, is equally important to the developing nations and could, if properly used, help them to mobilise information and knowledge more effectively for development purposes. In this perspective, intelligence can be considered as an instrument of development.

This concern with the problems of intelligence in development should not, however, overshadow the wider problem: intelligence is not only an instrument for the world's poorer nations to master the new opportunities presented by the explosive growth of the knowledge industries, but is an important activity of any society, whatever its level of development. At the societal level, it is somewhat similar to the intelligence (in the psychological meaning of the word) of a human being. In the same way that psychologists or neurologists speak of a human intelligence, one could speak of the intelligence of a society, or 'social intelligence'.

Several authors in this book, in their investigation of the role of intelligence in the process of development, have in fact used this term of 'social intelligence'. For the moment, this is more an approach than a general theory or a complete system, and our hope is that the investigation presented in the chapters that follow will serve not only to launch the idea of 'intelligence for development', but will also pave the way for a study of 'social intelligence'.

PART I

# The Evolution of the Intelligence Function

In this first part of the book, five authors explore the place and role of the intelligence function in society. Such a function might be defined as the organisational capacity of a nation, a government, a corporation, or indeed any social organism, to acquire and use information in order to probe its environment, identify new threats and challenges, and respond in a creative way to new circumstances. One of the central preoccupations of the authors, who are all practitioners of intelligence and information, is that the capacity of any organisation to accumulate and store information usually vastly exceeds its capacity to analyse and evaluate this information, let alone to use it in an effective way. Another of their preoccupations is the inherent conflict between the need for openness, accountability and transparency on the one hand, and the need for privacy, restrictiveness and secrecy on the other hand.

Wilhelm Agrell's historical survey of intelligence activities at the national level ('The Changing Role of National Intelligence Services') suggests the existence of three big periods in the evolution of this national intelligence function. First was the classical or 'Elizabethan' age, marked by the invention of the earliest organised national intelligence agencies aimed at promoting the interests of the newly emerging nation-states of Europe. Second came the 'modern' period, which was marked in particular by the development, at the end of last century, of the first military intelligence agencies. And third is the contemporary period, characterised by the explosive growth both of the amount of information to be processed and of the technical means for acquiring information. In this last period, intelligence and national security have come to acquire a much wider meaning, and intelligence agencies are now increasingly concerned with developments in the world economic situation and with new trends in science and technology, and are in effect becoming major partners in the knowledge industry.

This new role of national intelligence agencies is further explored by William Colby ('Comprehensive Intelligence for Advancement'), who is among the first senior-level intelligence professionals to have supported the view that intelligence can be a major instrument in the process of economic and social development. Like other authors, Colby rightly considers that national intelligence agencies constitute an integral part of the knowledge industry. His analysis of the types of information gathered by intelligence agencies suggests that much of this information is of direct relevance to the development effort of the world's poorer nations. It is, moreover, openly available and could be put to good use by these countries. While acknowledging the right of every nation, institution and individual to privacy and secrecy, Colby nevertheless points out that the evolution of modern communications technology makes it impossible for a country to isolate itself from the rest of the world or even to restrict the outward flow of information and knowledge about itself. In this perspective, the most sensible strategy for developing nations is to achieve the widest possible access to the sources of information and analysis which are available in the industrialised nations.

Important as it is to a nation-state, the intelligence function is also crucial for industrial firms. In his analysis of 'Management Intelligence', Frank T. Pearce brings to light some of the organisational problems of intelligence in a corporation and shows how intelligence can help managers to deal with risk, uncertainty and the unknown. The intelligence function which is only now beginning to be recognised as one of the key instruments of management, might be viewed as the unifying element in a number of corporate activities, from market research to information processing, and from investment analysis to corporate planning.

In his chapter on 'Commercial Intelligence', Michael West discusses the advantages and drawbacks of turning to specialised intelligence firms for information about new market opportunities, new technological trends or the investment risks in a particular country. Commercial intelligence is of direct interest both to government agencies and private corporations. West shows that the critical problem in any intelligence effort is not so much to acquire data or information, but rather to make a correct evaluation of the quality and relevance of this information. He also points to a largely overlooked issue, namely the need for continuity: the essence of good intelligence is not only good research, but the regular monitoring of an issue over a long period of time, and the development of a network of personal relations with contacts and colleagues throughout the world.

In the concluding chapter of this first part, Eric de Grolier ('Governments and the Information Industry') looks at the intelligence function from the standpoint of communications technology and information science. Does our ability to acquire, store and retrieve information not exceed our ability to use it for practical purposes? Are national documentation centres — which might be viewed as the memory of a society — ever likely to become a financially viable undertaking? Should an intelligence and information system by highly centralised, or on the contrary very decentralised? Does our ability to create and operate increasingly large documentation and information services lead to greater transparency, or on the contrary to increasing secrecy?

CHAPTER 2

# The Changing Role of National Intelligence Services

*Wilhelm Agrell*

A number of grave failures of national intelligence — from the Bay of Pigs to the Yom Kippur War — have raised serious questions about the nature and role of intelligence services and have given rise to heated public debate in small and large countries alike. It is not an exaggeration to speak of a crisis in national intelligence as three distinct aspects of their activities are coming in for hard scrutiny.

The first aspect, which has attracted the most publicity, is the need for control. A number of industrialised countries have tried to determine how a traditionally closed and secret organisation should function in a democratic society. The second is the need for productivity, that is, the way in which intelligence works and in which various national and governmental intelligence efforts can be co-ordinated and utilised. The third is the need for relevance, that is, whether or not the present intelligence organisations are working on those questions that are most important for national policy, both for the state and for other national actors.

These problems should be set in the context of an increasingly complex international environment. To survive, governments must be able to see into the near and distant future, and to perceive changes in time to make adjustments. A major difficulty stems from the fact that the intelligence organs of the state still concentrate too exclusively on military security even though intelligence needs are now considerably broader. During the 1970s, for example, the industrialised countries began to fear 'Pearl Harbors' in energy, the economy and technology just as much as military Pearl Harbors. Consequently, the concept of 'security' is evolving from that of a nation-state based on military power to a total security concept embracing all of society.

## The Origins of Modern National Intelligence

A brief historical review of national intelligence activities puts today's problems into sharper perspective. Francis Bacon's definition of national intelligence, formulated in the sixteenth century, is in its simplicity still one of the most accurate: 'Intelligence is the Light of the State'. This means that intelligence is not merely information as such, or information collected through secret, clandestine channels, but the active use of information about various aspects of the environment to guide decision-making in such a way as to forward the goals of the nation.

English intelligence in the late sixteenth century can be looked upon as the first genuine national intelligence organisation. Its aim was to support the long-range goals of the nation. It routinely formulated intelligence needs, pinpointed issues and developed an intelligence doctrine, all basic functions of contemporary intelligence work. The biggest difference between Elizabethan and present-day national intelligence is the nature of its sources: the link between intelligence and espionage, forged at the beginning of human history, was still unbroken and was to remain so for several centuries.

Yet Elizabethan intelligence had begun to take advantage, albeit on a limited scale, of developments in science and technology. Newspapers were a new phenomenon and quickly became a valuable source of intelligence, while the as yet young mail service was put to use for extensive, systematic interception of letters, an early form of signal intelligence. What is most significant is that Elizabethan intelligence was aware of the need to use science and technology and that it was an integral part of a system that understood the link between knowledge and intelligence on the one hand and knowledge and power on the other. In this respect, English national intelligence was undoubtedly ahead of many of its counterparts today.

In the following centuries, military technology brought improvements in warships, firearms and field artillery. This created a need for intelligence on advances made by others. Each time a technological breakthrough occurred, governments had to make sure they did not lag behind. Slowly but surely, nations were swept into a technological arms race and, by the end of the nineteenth century, the first purely military intelligence functions in the modern sense were born.

The twentieth century came to be dominated by the growing awareness of the links between science and technology, warfare and intelligence. As a result, national intelligence became a predominantly military affair, closely tied to armaments and the conduct of military operations. This became abundantly clear in the First World War, when use of advanced technology in warfare went hand-in-hand with such technological innovations in intelligence collection as air reconnaissance and signal intelligence.

Until the outbreak of the Second World War, the most important peacetime sources for intelligence collection continued to be human sources — diplomats, businessmen and commercial agents — as well as such open sources as radio broadcasts and the press. But the boom in science and technology brought about by the Second World War drastically altered the picture. It marked the beginning of a far-reaching change in the nature of warfare and military intelligence and the consequent danger of failing to adapt national intelligence to political, economic and military transformations.

## The Race for Arms Intelligence

Since the Second World War, advances in military technology have made new methods of intelligence collection at once necessary and possible. Concomitantly, the character of military intelligence targets, that is, military structures, has undergone an almost complete transformation. So much so that both political and military decision-makers are demanding ever more rapid, extensive and detailed information on foreign military organisations and scientific and technological developments.

The interaction between these new military technologies and those of intelligence collection is the single most important factor in the transformation of national intelligence. The race for arms intelligence has perhaps been most evident in the attempt to maintain strategic nuclear balance. Nuclear deterrence is based upon the premise that each party has access to very detailed real-time information on the nature, deployment and activity of its adversary's nuclear forces. Among other things, this was a determining factor in the development of reconnaissance satellites.

Satellite intelligence in turn soon became one of the superpowers' most powerful means for intelligence collection, not only on nuclear forces but on almost every aspect of military activity, thereby influencing the nature of warfare. Similarly, military electronics set off a reaction in the intelligence community: electronic intelligence is directed against the signals emitted by various surveillance and fire-guidance systems. Just as missile and space research made satellite intelligence possible, the development of military electronics created a new set of methods for intelligence collection — namely, remote sensing, a broad term that covers various techniques for collecting information from space. With remote sensing, it is now technically possible to survey large areas in detail, even down to tracking down a vehicle or individuals.

**Victims of Technology**

These new technologies for collecting information have brought about a major shift in emphasis: whereas only a few decades ago, intelligence services relied primarily on human sources for information, they now depend almost entirely on technical means. The main advantage is that technical collection methods can supply large quantities of reliable information on the size of foreign military forces and their deployment in record time and at the desired moment. For such purposes, human sources — and particularly, spies and agents — are much less effective.

Obviously, human intelligence continues to play a role in an area where technical collection provides little or no information: the intentions, mood and way of thinking of foreign societies. However, for countries with a developed, accessible knowledge industry, a growing proportion of such information is available or can be deduced from open sources. Paradoxically, the unplanned and largely unpredicted consequence of this shift of emphasis is that intelligence collection is now dictated more by technical possibilities than by actual intelligence needs. To a considerable degree, collection has come to dominate the entire national intelligence process in countries with a high scientific and technological level, and the flood of detailed information pouring in has led to 'information overkill'. The problem is no longer how to use available information in the most efficient way: the amount of information is such that apparently it exceeds men's capacity to use it.

A corollary of intelligence overkill is that the intelligence function runs the risk of becoming a system in which planning, collection and analysis are not geared primarily to the needs of decision-makers. In other words, intelligence is coming to be guided not by what should be done but by what technically can be done.


## Overemphasis on Hardware

The present emphasis on technical collection has made it possible for national intelligence, at least in the developed countries, to obtain an almost complete picture of the strength, deployment and activity of foreign military forces. So detailed a picture was impossible to piece together thirty or forty years ago. The danger is that it might affect the ability of national intelligence services to make correct and relevant estimates of foreign powers, their real military capacity and above all their intentions. It could lead them to believe that they know all there is to know, and that national security can be preserved simply by improving technical methods for continuous, detailed surveillance.

How such an overemphasis on details and on hardware can induce incorrect estimates of both the strength and the intentions of adversaries has been amply illustrated in recent military history. One of the most striking examples was the 1973 October War, when Arab forces succeeded in the seemingly impossible task of launching a surprise attack against Israel, a country renowned for its intelligence service. Even though Israeli intelligence had an extremely good picture of the deployment of the Arab forces in the days preceding the attack, it apparently lacked the ability to draw the proper conclusions from the steady stream of alarming information it was receiving from various sources. Generally speaking, without proper and timely estimates of the intentions of others, intelligence in any field, be it military, economic or political, tends to become blind, inviting policy disasters.

The temptation to collect and compare information about weapons systems and other military objects nevertheless remains strong. Intelligence services tend to concentrate on evaluations and comparisons of military strength based exclusively on numerical factors. This emphasis on number-counting is partly responsible for the inability of military intelligence to moderate the arms race since the Second World War. Instead, the conduct of intelligence has in many instances acted as a catalyst.

## The Intelligence 'Monoculture'

The twentieth century has seen a change not only in the nature of intelligence but also in its role in national policy. In a somewhat simplified fashion, it can be said that the last 100 years have been characterised by huge, often violent confrontations between nation-states with growing economic and military power. In this historical process, war or the threat of war, as postulated by the Prussian theorist Carl von Clausewitz, has become the rational extension of politics by other means and, indeed, a full-blown political instrument.

Because of this, the twentieth-century conception of national security has until now focused almost exclusively on war. Consequently, national intelligence, at least in the Western industrialised countries, has generally been conducted with a very narrow goal — to build up early-warning systems for military purposes. This one-sided approach to intelligence was initiated by an historical process which, according to many signs, is coming to an end. Yet it is perpetuated by organisational and intellectual inertia, just as national security continues to focus on war in the traditional sense, even though the political, economic and social patterns of the industrialised world are rapidly moving in another direction.

## Intelligence and Society

The growing importance of intelligence in a wide variety of fields has raised serious questions about its role in society. The need for control over secret intelligence organisations has been debated in the United States, the Federal Republic of Germany, Sweden, Denmark, the United Kingdom, Italy, Australia and the Netherlands, among others. Parliamentary control has been established or is under way in most of the Western countries. The problem may possibly be even more severe in the Eastern bloc countries. A symptom may be the extreme independence of the KGB in Soviet society and its operations in the Third World, though the closed nature of the political system effectively masks its activities.

The nature of intelligence organisations, and particularly heavy reliance on secrecy, can also affect their performance. With some exceptions, there has been little public debate on the scientific aspects of intelligence work, probably because of the taboos surrounding intelligence activities. Of course, intelligence organisations seldom like this kind of debate, and continue to adhere to increasingly outdated secret methods, even if this leaves them open to the most severe type of malfunction — self-deception. Excessive secrecy and overcentralised organisation tend to limit the possibilities of applying scientific methods to intelligence problems, which demand open debate, criticism and flexibility.

## The Future of National Intelligence

Parallel to the changing nature of warfare, more far-reaching, revolutionary trends have developed. The structural changes taking place in the industrialised countries have made them more vulnerable to forms of warfare other than traditional military ones. The first oil crisis amply demonstrated this new kind of 'economic Pearl Harbor'. The world is being swept into a process of interaction that makes countries more dependent on their global environment, be it in trade, currency, investments, communications or energy. This applies not only to the superpowers and such economic giants as Japan or the Federal Republic of Germany but to very small nations as well.

Sooner or later, these trends are bound to affect the concept of national security. Emphasis will shift from protection against direct attack to the broader protection of fundamental national goals. This in turn will put pressure on the intelligence 'monoculture' and force national intelligence services to maintain surveillance not only on threatening military and political situations but on the full breadth of a nation's global environment. They will have to extend their coverage to such areas as economic development, trade, industry, science and technology, and changes in social, cultural and demographic patterns. With such a wide spectrum of subjects to cover, intelligence 'overkill' will become all too apparent.

Until recently, national intelligence was synonymous with governmental intelligence, which gave rise to powerful agencies working in deep secrecy. This is hardly surprising since foreign intelligence was primarily the concern of the state. In the major industrialised countries, this situation is changing, as multinational and national corporations work in the intelligence field on the same level as governmental institutions.

Moreover, the growth of the knowledge industry has been such that it is conditioning the entire development of industrialised societies. To be able to function, a modern technological society is compelled to produce and distribute a continuous flow of detailed, accurate information on all aspects of society. The more complex the society becomes, the greater the increase in intelligence needs. In this process, each sector of society becomes more and more transparent, that is, open to observation.

The expansion of the knowledge industry is therefore perhaps the single most important factor making for the transparency of nations. Only by deliberately limiting the uses of knowledge industry products can this process be halted, but then only to a limited extent, and with unavoidable negative consequences for the development of that society.

There is an important distinction, however, between potential transparency, that is, the amount of information theoretically available in a society, and real transparency, which depends upon the resources of the observer. The Federal Republic of Germany, for example, has a fixed potential transparency, but its real transparency will depend upon whether the observer is a big multinational corporation or a small African state.

## The Impact of Transparency

The knowledge industry revolution is far from ended. According to some estimates, a tenfold increase in the output of information can be expected within a decade or two. Technological innovations like data banks or earth-resource satellites will be increasingly important in the acquisition and distribution of this mass of information.

As we have seen, this revolution has already deeply affected military intelligence, but as the knowledge industry develops, the same will hold true for other forms of intelligence. The historical link between intelligence and espionage has definitely been broken.

One of the most far-reaching consequences of the knowledge-industry revolution is the widening of the gap between industrialised and non-industrialised countries. Though it will increase potential transparency in the world, it will not necessarily increase real transparency. Because of the industrial world's quasi-monopoly on advanced information technology — and even though its information output will be more open — it will not necessarily become more transparent to the Third World. On the contrary, it will probably become less transparent, while the Third World will become more transparent to the industrialised countries.

The low information output of many Third World countries is already having a negative effect on their own societies, but if they took steps to decrease their own transparency *vis-à-vis* the industrialised world, this could boomerang and make it all the more difficult for them to bridge the transparency gap. The industrialised countries, thanks to their huge knowledge industry, will be able to use secrecy very selectively, thereby avoiding its harmful effects on their own societies. The non-industrialised countries do not have such an option and therefore run the risk of compromising their own development.

The socialist countries present a slightly different case. In some respects, their knowledge industry matches that of the OECD countries. However, the structure of their societies, together with historical and ideological factors, prevents them from using the knowledge industry effectively. In the future, these countries will probably have to choose between introducing more transparency into their own societies to take full advantage of the knowledge industry or else resigning themselves to fall far behind the Western countries. If they choose economic and social progress, they will automatically have to become more transparent to others as well. There are several indications of changes in this direction, brought about by the process of international integration which is affecting the socialist countries. For instance, greater transparency is a 'spin-off' of stepped up industrial and technological co-operation with the West, integration in transport and communications, international loans, and even events like the Olympic games. They all require a greater distribution and exchange of information.

The boom in the knowledge industry has led to demands for an internationalisation of knowledge for such purposes as disarmament and social development. According to its proponents, a 'world information society' must be created so that the technologies of the superpowers, and notably the United States, can be shared. Only in this way, proponents feel, can the gap in knowledge production and consumption between the industrialised and the non-industrialised world be bridged. But this overlooks the relativity of transparency.

As critics of the American remote-sensing Landsat satellites have pointed out, it is likely that this technology, along with others, will decrease rather than increase national control over natural resources. Only those with sufficient scientific and technological resources will one day be able to make full use of the possibilities offered by multispectral world surveys of the Landsat type, and only those with enough economic power and know-how will be able to take advantage of a detailed mapping of natural resources.

The rules of the international power game are not immutable. Direct methods, like those used from the sixteenth to the nineteenth century by colonial powers and the 'gunboat diplomacy' of the Victorian period, have become less useful. Even the more recent indirect methods like political and economic pressures, often described as 'neo-colonialist', are of more limited use. In the 1970s, the cartel of oil-producing countries, for example, severely curtailed the ability of the oil companies and the largest oil-consuming countries to control oil producers and their policy.

As these direct and indirect methods of domination are becoming less effective, the knowledge industry and the steady development of science and technology are creating a new instrument of power, a kind of 'information imperialism' in which national intelligence will play a central role. Superiority in the knowledge industry will become truly significant when used to achieve specific national goals. It seems clear that, in international relations, national intelligence will become the vital link between knowledge and direct political power.

CHAPTER 3

# Comprehensive Intelligence for Advancement

William E. Colby

Modern intelligence has a major role to play in the process of development. This does not mean that James Bond's glamorous intrigues will modernise the economies of the developing world in heroic fashion or manipulate its leaders and peoples to keep them subservient to the 'imperialist' world. Nor does it mean that intelligence will discover a secret plan to permit developing nations to leap forward to material well-being and social peace. It does mean that the techniques and the fruits of modern intelligence systems can make a major contribution to the transfer of knowledge, practical and theoretical, to areas where it is in short supply and where it can accelerate the process of development.

## The Nature of Modern Intelligence Systems

The nature of modern intelligence must be understood to ensure the best use of its capabilities for these purposes. Today it has become above all the central repository gathering together all the facts needed for wise decisions about the complex problems of the world. The centres of information and analysis have become its key elements, and doctors and masters of high academic attainment far outnumber the James Bonds or George Smileys on the staff of today's intelligence services.

Governments today look to intelligence for more than military weaponry or hostile strategic plans. All governments must comprehend and respond to problems in the disciplines of economics, sociology, cultural relationships, psychology, and many more. Thus, intelligence services have developed expertise not only in

41

military orders of battle, but also in energy resources, agricultural production, industrial technology and demography. Intelligence now includes a broad spectrum of scholars and disciplines directly concerned with the processes of social, economic and political development.

Modern intelligence is equipped with technology far beyond the crude implements of the Renaissance spy. It operates from the heights of space and in the depths of the ocean. It searches areas of the earth from which outsiders are excluded by hostile authorities and by forbidding weather or geography. These tools of electronics, acoustics and photography have vastly increased our understanding of the earth's surface. They give new perspectives to our knowledge of geography, geology, weather, agriculture, industry, trade, economic interrelationships and urban and other human living and working patterns. A hexagon identified by the Landsat satellite in the arid Sahel as fertile demonstrated that a programme of herd rotation through its six barbed-wired sectors would allow crops to flourish even in that region. Computer techniques of storing, indexing and retrieving these specifics of information permit the researcher to assemble, compare, analyse and integrate thousands of facts now available about subjects no spy could have comprehended a few years ago.

Most important of all, the reports which are the fruits of modern intelligence go not only into secret dossiers available solely to monarchs or presidents. Increasingly there is a realisation that many individuals and groups in modern society must know the information and assessments produced by modern intelligence services. The American debate over the Strategic Arms Limitation Talks (SALT II) involved refined public discussion of the details of the megatonnage, throw weights and warheads of Soviet and American nuclear weaponry. These weapons are kept most secret by the nations involved, and the intelligence technology used to learn about them is even more secret. But these facts about the weapons were made available to the American public to permit informed debate about ratification of SALT II. Similarly, Central Intelligence Agency (CIA) analyses of a likely major change of the Soviet Union from an oil exporter to an oil importer were released to permit this fact to be integrated into open policy discussions of the future of the oil trade. Electronic sensors in the Sinai desert replaced Egyptian and Israeli fear and suspicion with confidence that neither army could surprise the other in an attack, demonstrating how knowledge gained by modern intelligence methods can help maintain peace rather than stimulate war and conflict. These examples show that it is feasible to reveal the substance of intelligence reports while continuing to protect their sources, as journalists have done for many years.

Many other items of intelligence information and assessments are made publicly available in the United States through a variety of outlets in the executive and in the Congress. Some are the product of programmes which may once have been secret, but which have been opened to public service, such as the satellite photographs available from the Landsat programme or extensive translations of foreign technical publications. Others may come from secret programmes but are issued by other government departments and are not attributed to intelligence origins. This makes the material public but reduces the tendency to sensationalise it as the product of intelligence, and presents it in its true context as information carefully assembled and analysed.

Another element of the changed status of American intelligence has been the frank recognition of the existence of such services and their subjection to the United States' constitutional system. No longer does the tradition hold that the spy service operates outside normal government controls. In the United States, this resulted in a public sign placed on the highway pointing to the headquarters of CIA and to the establishment of official committees of the Congress to supervise American intelligence. In other nations, more discreet but equally clear moves have been made to ensure that intelligence is brought under the constitutional system.

## Intelligence as Part of the Knowledge Industry

These changes brought intelligence out of its traditional shadows and point towards its full membership in the knowledge industry. The process of development over the centuries in Western Europe brought the information scattered in medieval monasteries and universities first into libraries and laboratories and then to the modern world of press and publications. So the growth of intelligence into a modern system will move it beyond the traditional acquisition of bits of clandestine information to a vast central repository of factual data and sophisticated centres of analysis.

There will still be parts of the intelligence function and its products which will and must remain secret if they are to produce, but these already have become a small part of the larger intelligence process. Significant as some of these contributions may individually be, it is becoming clear that most of the really important information in democratic societies — even with respect to closed ones — either is publicly available or in a very short time must be released so that it can play its role in the decision-making process. Strategic weaponry (MX and the neutron bomb), economic targets (OECD energy conservation and official development assistance commitments) and alliance strains (for example, recognition of the Palestine Liberation Organisation) all are open in democratic societies to public discussion.

The intelligence process developed within government channels thus has become too important to be left to governments. We are seeing the development of private centres to serve the numerous demands in modern life for economic, political and social analysis. These benefit from the collection of information by government and the private sector alike, but add specialised expertise and analysis focused on the interests and concerns of particular clients. The disciplines of collection, analysis and assessment have become applicable to many fields and are no longer solely or even primarily represented by government intelligence services.

This larger view of the intelligence process as an element of the knowledge industry makes it clear that it should be intimately involved with the process of development in the less-developed world. Plainly the transfer of information and technological competence are inherent in the process of development. As modern intelligence services have become major participants in the management and transmission of knowledge, so they have a major contribution to make to the process of development.

It is clear that information collected by the intelligence services of industrialised countries, such as photography from satellites, electronic sensing, acoustical identification of variations in geology, the techniques of handling and interrelating masses of information and analysing their significance and the availability of a central source for vast quantities of interrelated information could all be of major assistance to a developing nation. It could help it to plan agricultural and industrial development, adjust trading patterns rapidly to market changes and assist the training of local development cadres and leaders.

At the same time, the richness of these sources could be thought to give undue advantage to the developed nation over the developing society. Access to a wide scope of information in the most intimate detail certainly is advantageous to those close to it or favoured by its managers. The specialised technology of intelligence could give advantage to those groups and individuals familiar with its use. The ability of the developed centre to employ swarms of specialists on every aspect of the problems facing developing countries, overwhelming the few experts available to the developing nation, could obviously favour the representatives of a developed state in a contest with a less developed one. And the old traditions of total secrecy about intelligence have not been changed to eliminate all secrets, so that those which remain do give the possessor power and advantage.

## Information Protection as Information Promotion

A number of political leaders have concluded for these reasons that the inevitable advantage of highly developed over less-developed knowledge industries calls for controls on the transmission of information and its analysis when the interests of developing nations are affected. Some nations are beginning to insist on control of the export of information about their nation, in the same way that centres of archaeology insist on control of the export of artefacts from their history. Some theorists have gone further and insist that a new information order must be generated by which less-advantaged nations share in, if not fully control, the information about themselves, wherever and however this information is generated. In international councils, coalitions of the less developed countries to achieve such equalising authority are becoming important.

This effort is counter-productive. Attempts to develop protectionist walls around information about a nation are apt to be reciprocated by similar walls elsewhere. While the intent may not be to isolate the nation as in pre-Meiji Japan or China at the time of the Cultural Revolution, the effect can be the same. Knowledge and experience of value to developing nations lie not only in the developed nation's centres but in the experience and experiments of fellow developing nations, and attempts to block the flow of information will have their most immediate impact upon fellow developing nations. Indeed, with modern technology, industrialised nations are apt to continue to secure the information they want about developing nations. Limitations on the flow of business information may well restrict the operations of multinational enterprises, but will also limit national enterprises from stepping up their involvement in world trade, which is increasingly conducted in a global market. The temptation to call for a balanced flow of information, or to control the flow, is thus short-sighted compared to the value of a free flow in both directions.

The true interest of the developing nations is to accelerate the contribution of the world's knowledge industry to their own process of development. They should seek maximum access to the centres of information and analysis which can assist their process of development, whether these be in the United Nations and its specialised agencies, in academic centres and think-tanks, or in commercial services. They should vigorously advocate and support public release by all governments of as much information and analysis as is possible, and should call upon the industrialised nations to devote more of their knowledge industry resources, and intelligence services effort, to problems important to developing nations, such as tropical agriculture and diseases and the political impacts of modernisation.

Developing nations should also insist upon vigorous programmes to accelerate knowledge technology transfer through government assistance programmes or through private services for reasonable returns. Training of information industry cadres, establishment of communication circuits and the development of software specifically applicable to development problems and needs should have high priority. Intelligence guides and advisers should be the bridge between the urgent need of these nations for knowledge and the time needed to develop their own industry and talent in these fields. The objective would be to leapfrog the development process in the same fashion that a satellite communications system can avoid the lengthy and costly process of installing land cables and wires throughout a developing country. In the same way, the computer can replace legions of clerks in assembling, sorting and accumulating millions of facts, allowing the human talents of the clerks instead to seek higher education and more productive lives.

The policies available to the knowledge industry and its relationship to the process of development can be compared with the economic philosophies which have characterised trade and industry over the centuries. The earliest economic concept was one of conquest, seizing wealth from the weak and carrying it to the centre of a powerful empire. The analogy in the information field is the old intelligence tradition of secretly acquiring information and guarding it from release.

With the development of communications and transportation, the mercantile economic theory arose. This meant the exchange, not merely the acquisition, of goods so that a net advantage in each exchange was gained by the stronger bargainer. This produced centres of wealth, surrounded by colonies and spheres of influence providing primary products and acting as markets for the products of the wealthy centres.

A third stage in economic theory was that of free trade, in which both sides could benefit from a fair exchange. Sometimes the balance of power, and of benefits, between the two sides was not equal, and the theory merely provided a cover for the continuation of an essentially unbalanced relationship. This situation has been criticised as economic imperialism, the rule of the multinationals, and so forth.

A variety of controls were then established to eliminate these abuses of the free trade system. Rules of behaviour, majority local ownership of joint ventures and other restraints on exploitation have worked well in many cases. In others, the remedies have proved almost worse than the illness.

A fourth technique, more pragmatic than theoretical, has been applied and proved effective. It is the articulation of specific rules of behaviour in the free trading process, in order to eliminate the abuses which could otherwise creep in, but restraining the operation of the free system as little as possible. The concept of free trade does not have to accept child labour or unfair trade practices. Codes of conduct as well as legislation can bar the development of monopoly power, control the procedures of the market-place so that it will remain open, and punish bribery and improper procedures. The key to this pragmatic approach, however, is that each such restriction must be related to a very specific abuse, so that the guiding philosophy is one of open trade and competition, limited only by those situations in which there is evidence that restrictions are needed.

This is the approach taken with respect to tariff and non-tariff barriers to trade in the multinational trade negotiations taking place under the aegis of the General Agreement on Tariffs and Trade. It is equally applicable to trade and transfer in the world's knowledge industry, and reasonable rules and procedures can safeguard privacy, maintain proprietorship incentives and encourage national development. There is also a place in the knowledge industry for programmes of stimulation and promotion of local capacity to full competitive status with outsiders. But promotion, not protection, should be the main theme for the developing nations, to accelerate the growth of their knowledge industries.

This, then, is the best model for the growth of the knowledge industry in the developing nations. The open flow of information from foreign and domestic private, governmental and international information centres must be stimulated and encouraged. This is the best fashion through which developing nations can move ahead economically and socially. The result of such a role for the knowledge industry can perhaps lead to a new meaning for the initials CIA — Comprehensive Intelligence for Advancement.

# CHAPTER 4

# Management Intelligence

## Frank T. Pearce

In universities and business schools, the ideal manager is often presented as someone with a calm, highly professional, scientific approach who uses available hardware and software to identify, quantify and choose between various options. But for many managers, this is a Utopian view. Available knowledge, know-how and resources are rarely sufficient to enable them to indulge in complex techniques of choice.

In fact, most executives have precious little time to think or plan, and often find that information-gathering for decision-making can be more difficult and time-consuming than the decision itself. They carry a heavy load, and their work is highly varied and full of interruptions. They often have to face situations marked by risk, uncertainty and ignorance, and luck can play a larger role in decisions than one might think.

Even though they may not rely on formal logic and objective probability calculations, managers are not gamblers at heart. According to an American study, a surprisingly large number felt that the outcome of their decisions was certain. The same attitude was reported by a British consultant. This might seem to be subjective or false reasoning but it is nevertheless real. The only thing managers really wanted from a consultant, it was discovered, was a 'lucid exposition of background and prospects with a statement of maximum downside risk'.[1]

When managers are preparing to take action, they are less concerned with decision theory and analysis than with accurate, validated and processed information. They must believe that (a) assumptions are tenable; (b) deductions are valid; (c) projections lie

1. B.G. Bodroghy, 'Forecasting the Demand for Novel Products', *Journal of the Industrial Marketing Research Association*, vol. 9, no. 1, 1974.

within a reasonable scenario; and (d) should matters go wrong, the crisis can be resolved by a show of energy and ability. In such circumstances, an intelligence unit has high practical relevance because its job is precisely to provide the first three factors for decision-making and to aid in implementation. Just as important, an intelligence unit can be of great help should things go wrong, for another part of its job is to monitor developing situations and to provide early warning signals.

The message is not being lost on managers. More and more of them are stressing the need for some function that can draw together the disparate information showered on them from both internal and external sources. It is for this hard, basic reason that intelligence is becoming ever more essential to decision-making in the managerial world. Intelligence is not a theoretical construct, but a pragmatic, practical function.

## Management Intelligence: Structure and Organisation

The knowledge and know-how internal and external to the system is generated in part by its structure, in part by the environment and in part by bringing information inputs directly into the decision process. By structure, we do not mean organisational forms, but the way in which things are learned and done, and the way in which continuous adaptation to changing conditions is achieved. It includes the way people react to the demands made on them, their attitudes, their habits of thought and action, and their management style. The group of people concerned is what Galbraith calls the 'technostructure', the guiding brain and mind of an institution. It is more than the sum of its human parts, for there is tremendous potential synergy, to which intelligence can make a major contribution.

The knowledge input usually means a flood of data. It has now attained such proportions that many managers feel they are overseeing some vast data and information generator, in which they have difficulty in discerning the essential parts and the interlocking gears. The technostructure and the knowledge input merge together to form a continuum of great complexity; in it, two basic technologies — physical and process — are linked by a third, management technology.

'Organisation' does not mean formal, diagrammatic relationships but autonomous, self-directing and self-adjusting networks or systems to which feedback is critical. New-style team co-operation, rather than the old-style hierarchical co-ordination, is necessary to achieve stated or tacit goals.

Intelligence systems are at once a device to identify broad policy issues, a way to keep some 'model' of the organisation under control and up-to-date, and a form of direct assistance to managers and executives for planning and implementation and the development of information. Such systems are designed to integrate company information flows, to review and evaluate previously identified problem areas, policies and solutions, and to ensure than the data processed and filtered through to management are optimised and relevant. They provide support to the decision process. An intelligence system can be applied right through to the decision process.

## The Politics of Management Intelligence

Communication is integral to intelligence. Problems arise, however, when the hierarchy is inflexible or when the links between responsibility and authority are not made clear. Problems can also crop up if the distinction is not clearly made between 'structural' authority that arises from the job itself and 'sapiential' authority based on special knowledge and know-how.

Most of the time, structural authority is exercised in line management, whereas intelligence informs and advises. Very complex relationships often lie beneath the formal roles of managers, and it is important to understand this. Thus, within an intelligence system, only structural authority is exercised.[2] Externally, its authority is, with a few exceptions, sapiential. Relations between the intelligence manager and those of equal status are based not on structural authority but on the responsibilities each exercises. From time to time, those on more junior levels may come into direct contact with senior structural or sapiential authorities. Their role is to pass on information, and not to advise. The latter role rests with the intelligence manager.

Job functions in an intelligence unit should be spelled out, and the manager should take special care that staff roles are properly under-

2. T.T. Paterson, *Management Theory*, Business Publications Ltd., London, 1966.

stood, both by members of the unit and by the managers with whom they are in contact. Although such relationships may be familiar to those versed in management theory, they are at present far from clear in many organisations. An intelligence system may have the finest techniques and expertise but remain impotent if it regularly crosses the lines of authority or if staff is confused as to the role it should play. The best kind of manager for a formal intelligence system is one whose acceptability is high. He should be a generalist and a diplomat, rather than a specialist and an authoritarian.

A second problem area is the gamut of misconceptions about knowledge inputs. For example, it is often believed that more data will automatically improve decision-making and reduce uncertainty; that decision-makers know what data they need and can use them effectively; and that more data acquisition and dissemination will improve performance. These are simplistic views.

Intelligence should aim less at greater data and information supply than at sensitising management to issues. Among others, it should practise selective dissemination, better interpretation and integration, and better understanding and support of the specific decision process involved. There can be simply too much input from a proliferation of sources and a multiplicity of techniques. Because processing is often difficult and complex, its costs are high. It has been suggested that information should be processed to the extent that the marginal value added equals the marginal processing cost. This cost–benefit approach is conceptually valuable. However, many institutions can afford to finance only so much knowledge and know-how and, in the not uncommon case where costs and benefits are difficult to quantify, a realistic approach may be to strive for cost-effectiveness.

One last illustration will help exemplify these political complications, which are legion. If the intelligence function is systematised to back up decision-making, then it will undoubtedly become a locus of power that may come into conflict with other loci and be subject to veto. It is also possible that a request for additional information may in fact be a cover-up for maintaining the institutional status quo or for sidetracking embarrassing intelligence results. Much will depend on the status of the intelligence unit and its authority. Situations like this are not simple, because the managers' decision process is played out against a backdrop of personal loyalties which can cloud issues.

## The Nature of Uncertainty

'Whatever reduces uncertainty is information' is now a classic definition. Initially, it was used to measure information quantitatively. The definition is certainly correct when applied to a communications system, but is inadequate for something inherently more complex such as a management intelligence system.

Fine distinctions can be made within the term 'uncertainty': they can range from near certainty, partial risk, risk and uncertainty to ignorance and the unknowable. The term suggests future rather than past events, although historians agree that what they deal with is far from certain facts: a fog lies behind as well as ahead. What is more, information has to be communicated to, and be accepted by, individuals and groups; it does not necessarily convey meaning and can increase uncertainty, for example, when a manager discovers a set of problems of which he had not been aware. From the manager's point of view, a further distinction should be made between information that makes for less uncertainty, and information that can be used for effective action.

Thus, information, informatics, information technology, management information and all the other approaches based on electronic systems are necessary but not sufficient. Management intelligence must be related to a much larger, indeterminate area. It is not merely a data-collection, data-crunching process that can be completely automated. Nor is the common belief good enough that knowledge consists of objective facts gathered by unbiased observation. More facts do not necessarily produce more knowledge. Management intelligence consists of selecting and filtering information, processing it insofar as means allow, superimposing experience and judgement, moving it to the decision point, monitoring it for control and continuously replanning its own procedures.

Relating intelligence to this greater indeterminacy suggests another way one can identify what management intelligence is concerned with, namely, to relate it to types of decision, to the state of knowledge about the environment and to other states of certainty, as shown in Table 4.1.

## Strategic, Tactical and Operations Intelligence

Strategic intelligence is the function that most frequently gets atten-

**Table 4.1** Indeterminacy and decision levels

| Indeterminacy | Consequence | Type of decision |
|---|---|---|
| Unknown | Uncontrollable variables | Company mission |
| Partially unknown | Alternatives cannot be foreseen | Objectives |
| | Rules for making decisions | Strategy |
| Uncertainty | Alternatives known, but not the probabilities | Policies (delegated, contingent decisions) |
| | Alternatives and probabilities known | |
| Partial risk | Occurrence certain, but outcome not | Programme (time-based action sequence to guide and co-ordinate) |
| Near certainty | Occurrence certain and repetitive | Standard operating procedure |

tion. Confining our examples to business, strategic intelligence deals with market structure and demand, company identity, resource acquisition and development. It deals with shifts in the environment, as well as technological and social forecasting. It is crucial to long-term deployment and effectiveness. It involves quantitative and qualitative work combined with experience and judgement.

It is at the level of strategic decision that indeterminacy is greatest. There are often no objectives that can be precisely defined and to which a probability of occurrence can be assigned. At times, the number of alternatives may simply be too great to be handled by traditional analysis. The most difficult part of such planning lies in dealing with changes in non-controllable variables. The only way to proceed may be to develop anticipatory alternative scenarios and plans based on the most likely developments. Of course, monitoring can give early warning signals of adverse changes.

The dividing line between tactical and operations intelligence is not always clear-cut, so there tends to be a good deal of overlapping. Generally speaking, tactical intelligence of the kind used in marketing usually has to do with efficiency and risk areas where policies are contingent, that is, where 'if–then' questions abound. It concentrates on the organisation as it exists in the present, on establishing probabilities, quantifying potentials and applying subjective control to automatic forecasting procedures and assumptions. These matters may be less vital for growth or survival but unquestionably are of concern to management.

Operations intelligence is used to back up decisions in which management has to deal with partial certainty or risk, or to answer such questions as: 'Can the economy of operation be improved in relation to the task performed?' Frequently, a mass of information is available within the firm that management has already paid for but which is usually not fully utilised. Whereas strategic and tactical intelligence are more concerned with the effectiveness and efficiency of an organisation and its mission and objectives, operations intelligence is often more concerned with the economy of operation. It provides fast, reliable details either routinely or on tap.

## Ill-structured Decisions

It would be a mistake to believe that one has only to create a set of intelligence objectives to rationalise work. At higher management levels and in complex, ill-structured situations, those with the heaviest responsibility have to obtain, organise and control resources and either adapt to, or adapt, the environment. Ill-structured decision problems multiply, the concepts needed are symbolic or verbal, and the judgements complex. At this level, intelligence touches the biggest management decisions so closely that its essentially advisory character can be confused with decision and implementation roles. Classic examples at the national level are the Bay of Pigs or Iran. Organisational examples are less easy to find, but they exist.

'Ill-structured decision' means that interest is centred on non-numeric variables and their relationship, on criteria of performance and on relevant and useful things to do. The environment is such that no rule-of-thumb method can guarantee the best solutions, which are acceptable rather than optimised; the number of alternatives is so great as to make trial and error impractical.

## Climbing the Intelligence Ladder

So far, an attempt has been made to outline the day-to-day life of

*The Evolution of the Intelligence Function*

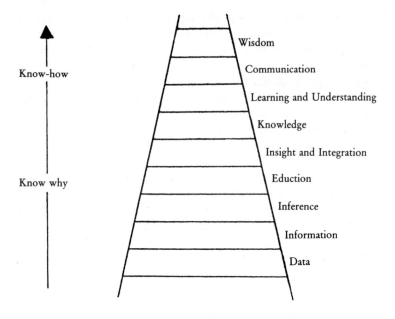

**Figure 4.1.** The intelligence ladder

the manager and the indeterminate world through which he travels. We shall now turn to the world of management intelligence as it applies to everyday reality. Management intelligence adapts and evolves, building on existing information and information support, rather than instituting radical changes in function.

To distinguish between a certain number of concepts that might be confused, let us use the analogy of an intelligence 'ladder' that narrows as one climbs to the top (see Figure 4.1). On the first rung, one finds data, preferably regarded as elements of information that can be reshuffled, repackaged and recombined. Next comes information, that is, organised, processed and structured data. Moving up the ladder, there is inference, which deduces the implications of soft and hard data. Here, classical statistical inference can lead to generalisations, forecasts, estimates and sample techniques. Interpretation is the process of deriving meaning; to a certain extent, it resembles what a language interpreter does. This is the area of numeracy, literacy and creativity, far beyond the simple collection, collation and retrieval level of data handling.

Next comes eduction, not to be misread as education. To educe is

56

to bring out or evolve from some latent or potential existence. It means information development. Integration and insight is a key rung, where the whole is often more than its parts. Here, there is a possibility of fulguration — that is, something new may appear in the systemic properties.

A step above is knowledge, followed by learning and understanding, and then by the complex process of communication. Critical information that fails to be transmitted is negated. At the top of the ladder is wisdom, the peak of intellectual attainment, where persons possess both knowledge and know-how.

To scale this ladder, a fully developed management intelligence system must treat the entire data environment — internal and external, quantitative and qualitative, hard and soft, objective and subjective and short and long. Intelligence then becomes more than the utilisation of regularly collected information and merges into one activity all the work, including research, required to back decision-making at all levels.

## The Eight Sequences of Management Intelligence Operation

What does a major management intelligence operation consist of? Activities can be broken down into eight sequences:

(1) **Data and information handling**. This is basic but in itself inadequate;
(2) **Analysis**. Very relevant to the decision process. Any number of techniques can be used — cost–benefit, multiple variate, probability, sensitivity, risk, and so on — in such departments as operations research, market research, economic and statistical analysis, and management accounting;
(3) **Research**. Original, new data and information acquired for specific purposes by investigations, enquiries and programmed surveys. This department may do secondary desk research, which concentrates on published sources, or primary survey and sampling work using classical or modern methods. This type of work is increasingly concerned with relationships;
(4) **Forecasting**. This has been one of the fastest developing areas, and possible procedures are legion. Forecasting has attracted the interest of higher-level educational institutions and commercial organisations because professionals need to keep up

with accelerating developments;

(5) **Monitoring**. This is not usually considered as a distinct intelligence activity, which is a mistake. Its purpose is to discern underlying trends or changes and to categorise material in a more meaningful way. For current management needs, such work is not merely a complement to forecasting; it has a higher level of priority because it bears directly on control;

(6) **Education**. A precise term for what may be loosely called information development. It deals with the continuous improvement or introduction of basic inputs, and their specific application to management needs and more sophisticated uses. It scraps old channels and inputs as necessary;

(7) **Systems**. This branch of management intelligence is collateral to, but distinct from, that of the organisation system. It goes into model-building, simulation, integration and such organisational matters as staff recruitment and training. Processed information is put into focus for persons and functions, to back the main types of decision;

(8) **Communication**. Without it, the intelligence system is stillborn. It has to do with presentation, information pathology, psychology and politics.

At present, these different levels of activity and decision occur without any predetermined sequence: one management group may stop at acquisition and another at research. Intelligence may be confined to one function — marketing is a favourite — or may be applied to one or another decision level — tactical but not strategic, strategic but not operational. All managers are aware of the need for information but relatively few have grasped the potential of an integrated intelligence system.

## Secrecy for Defence and Offence

All managers have organisational secrets, which they put to use either for defence or offence, and which they feel are necessary for survival. To a certain extent, an analogy can be drawn with the concept of biological fitness for survival. In general, an organism's fitness for survival will depend upon its ability correctly to perceive and interpret its environment. It has to distinguish, perhaps by instinct, between predators and allies. The better it does this, the greater are its chances of performing its life-functions and preserving the species.

In the world of organisations, however, to judge whether given information is essential to survival, a distinction should be made between secrecy and privacy. The term 'secrecy' has been used much too broadly in recent years. For the man in the street, secrecy has come to be equated not only with knowledge but power and privilege. Privacy, on the other hand, is legitimate; it can condition what data the organisation can and should make available and under what terms others may make use of its data.

Both secrecy and privacy have some common elements — denial of access to information, reduced observability and opportunity for control. But the concepts diverge when it comes to the public interest and such questions as legitimacy and morality, deceit and disinformation and their effect on outsiders. This has now become a philosophical battleground. Possibly, the two may be seen as part of a continuum: if legitimate privacy is denied, the motivation for secrecy is strengthened. But if we persist in using the two terms synonymously, then we confuse the debate.

In matters of privacy, it is not unusual for those concerned to assure that a greater degree of confidence is required of them than is actually the case. Top, middle and junior management can be remarkably at odds. In the United Kingdom, for example, the Imperial Group asked some of its executives to make an informal guess as to what proportion of the internal paper flow was open, restricted or confidential; the result was 65, 25 and 10 per cent. Confidentiality of internal papers was then more formally assessed, with a result of 98, 1.5 and 0.5 per cent. One suspects that, could the concept of confidentiality be measured, it would be found lowest at senior management level and on the shop floor, and highest at the junior and middle management levels. Indeed, senior managers, with the confidence born of status and the 'old boy' network, have been known to release to direct competitors what their colleagues would have thought to be highly sensitive information.

Management attaches great importance to its observation of others. Sometimes it can be a covert breach of the other's interest, or what is commonly called industrial espionage. The recent Hitachi – IBM scandal showed that someone authorised payment of $500,000 for a competitor's secret. Far more often, however, results are obtained by interpreting open, public information (even the CIA claims that 90 per cent of its work is done this way). This explains why competitor intelligence, company intelligence and data-bank services are being used so heavily by management, especially at the tactical and operational levels.

Work of this kind can be quite overt and extremely effective. In a well-known case, Company X, a battery manufacturer, was being undercut by 40 per cent by its competitor, Company Y. X was determined to know how Y managed to do this. Data were available but had little immediate meaning. So X's investigator carefully studied the battery type, consulted advisors and made extensive contacts. Customers and suppliers were questioned, as were trade and other agencies. It turned out that public information, when properly integrated, was sufficient to draw a sharp picture of what was actually taking place. Everything was overt and legitimate, but concentrated enough to produce the required decision-making information for action.

## The World of Tomorrow

A generation ago it seemed clear that the role of management would increasingly shift towards co-operative problem-solving and decision-making. As one author commented at the time, authority and responsibility may well be the wrong principles of organisation for highly-educated people. Managers will have to learn not a system of command but an information and decision system based on judgement, knowledge and expectations.[3]

Managers still have reservations about such a system, and it could take another ten to twenty years before full-scale management intelligence systems become commonplace, even in those medium and large organisations capable of financing them. Much will depend upon the extent to which managerial intelligence makes its way into higher institutions of learning and retraining programmes.

Meanwhile, market turbulence is having a considerable effect on chief executives' need for information. Though strategic concepts are still vital, they are now set in a very different context from that of the long growth period that followed the Second World War. Many executives are at present less concerned with the long-term future than with short-term survival. This presents a challenge and

3. P.F. Drucker, 'Managing the Educated' in D.H. Fenn (ed.), *Management Missions in a New Society*, McGraw Hill, New York, 1956.

makes the intelligence function more necessary than ever for strategy, tactical checks on changes of direction and for operations. To come up with reliable contingency plans, industry needs more information flexibility and resilience.

What is new is the perception of the importance of underlying systems based on knowledge rather than experience. Knowledge has become the central resource. What is needed is a better-integrated information function that encompasses many areas so that one hard-hitting contribution can be made.

Management intelligence can be compared to a green field: here and there there are denser, faster-growing patches. Those patches are the sub-disciplines of intelligence — operations research, marketing research, accounting and finance, information science, investment analysis, statistics, computer science and others. The full crop is on its way.

# CHAPTER 5

# Commercial Intelligence: A Priceless Commodity

## Michael J. West

The proposition that the developing countries need better commercial intelligence than they have is almost so self-evident as to need little or no justification. The number of state marketing agencies, trade-promotion bodies and the like, which operate in and for so many of the developing countries, has increased rapidly in the last two decades. No longer do a handful of large, mostly expatriate, companies buy the entire crop and do with it what they choose. No longer does the local agency of a trading multinational contract for the entire output of a factory or a dozen factories. No longer is the only sales outlet the company which lent the farmer, or the industrialist, the working capital he needed during the year. Instead — or in addition — there are the marketing agencies established by the state and an entourage of development banks and funds.

Many state trading agencies do many things well. Where weaknesses exist, they tend to be greatest in the areas of strategic and tactical planning and in marketing and selling. These are very much decision areas where intelligence matters. Long- and short-term questions of product suitability for changing markets, of quantities likely to be demanded, of packaging and presentation, of stock size and location may be, and frequently are, much less well addressed than they might be. Decision on quantities to be released on particular markets at particular times can be and are taken on evidence and information which would not be regarded as adequate by, say, a European or a Japanese company.

Selling and marketing decisions tend to be taken in committees which, by definition, cannot meet frequently, and these decisions tend to remain in force for fairly long periods. While total responsibility for shortcomings in performance cannot be laid at the door of

62

inadequate intelligence, some of the less-than-perfect marketing, selling and planning can be so attributed. The fact that some state trading bodies have persisted in producing moribund products, have appeared to ignore what might seem clear indications of changes in the market, have disregarded the activities of their competitors, or have been apparently so unaware of the international economic environment that higher interest rates have totally disrupted development plans, must in some degree be attributable not to failure to act, but to failure to know that action was required. Failure to know that a matter needs to be examined is a failure of intelligence.

## Underrating Intelligence

The kinds of commercial intelligence described later on in this chapter are in many cases available as much to a developing country state trading corporation as to a Western manufacturer. They seem, however, to be but little used by such bodies, and it is over one of the reasons for this relative lack of use that I part company with many other commentators. One of the basic points normally put forward is that the major Western companies, and the multinationals in particular, have complex computer-based systems for their analysts and researchers, while the developing countries do not. This is true, and indeed few developing countries would regard themselves as able to afford such investments. Again it is true that the sheer availability of information — scientific, technical and commercial — in many developing countries is far less than is the case in an average medium-sized town in a developed country. And there may be some truth in the frequent suggestion that the West in general holds some information quite confidential from those who may often be at the opposite side of the negotiating table.

But while all these points, and many others, are true in some degree, they are far from being the basic cause. Huge data-processing systems are not the core of commercial intelligence work. As for the above argument concerning the withholding of information from the developing countries, it is more often the fact that information is rather not ostentatiously proffered on a plate. The openness of information in much or most of the West is remarkable, but it has to be sought out by those who need it and only rarely will it be forced upon anyone's attention. Those who do not look will not find.

The basic problem then is, in my view, that commercial intelligence is little understood in the developing countries and is therefore very lowly rated. Practitioners in the information and analysis field are generally accorded rather low status: there are few career paths arising from such a beginning, and therefore few ambitious and able people enter the field. To a very large degree the concept that effective decision-taking stems from having and using good information and good analysis — intelligence — has no strong foundation in many developing countries. And it cannot be denied that some of the half-truths which are prevalent do not help the serious fostering of the development of effective commercial intelligence.

If an officer of a state trading company in a developing country believes that the Western countries keep secret much or most of the information which would help him, then he may well feel that the commercial intelligence game is not worth the candle. Sadly, he may be encouraged in this belief by the proceedings of some conferences and the publications of some agencies, which might, perhaps, be expected to know better. This, plus a still prevalent if weakening folk-belief, usually implicit rather than explicit, that the developed countries have and use some secret short-cuts to success, helps still further to explain the low level of interest in commercial intelligence in many institutions in the developing countries.

The proposition is, then, that much of the information which, say, a developing country state trading body could use to help it reach better commercial decisions is potentially available to it: most of it is not unreachable.

It is not the purpose of this paper to provide lists of sources and catalogues of research methods. Rather, I would like to describe some of the intelligence services available from the private sector which, incidentally, involves discussion of basic sources and how these are used by companies, and could be used by any institution. I emphasise the services of the Economist Intelligence Unit (EIU), and the philosophy on which these are based since I know these best, but EIU is only one among dozens of such companies.

## The Economist Intelligence Unit: A Commercial Intelligence Supplier

In the earliest days, soon after the end of the war, the world was in a position of overall shortage of goods: if something could be made or grown, it could almost certainly be sold, and sold profitably. The Economist Intelligence Unit's early services could best be described as supply intelligence and supply research: where and from whom could sugar, oilseeds, structural steel or soda-ash be obtained, at what prices and with what degree of continuity? In subsequent years the emphasis changed to the market end as a sellers' market gave way to a buyers' market, and the question was not 'where can I buy?' but 'where and to whom can I sell?'

EIU's underlying philosophy, however, remained the same. Thus, at the one end, it publishes a large number of regular and one-off research/analysis publications which are available on general subscription. The basic service is the *Quarterly Economic Reviews*, of which there are eighty-three separate ones covering over 160 countries. These cover growth prospects, opportunities and problems in a business-orientated analysis. Then there are seven *Quarterly Energy Reviews*, each covering a particular region of the world and discussing developments in this important matter as they affect business.

Six other quarterlies cover particular world industries — among them motors, rubber, paper, tourism — while there are two monthlies on retail trade and markets in the United Kingdom and the European Community. In addition, up to thirty special reports are produced each year, covering current topics relevant to international business. Recent titles have included *Biotechnology: A Guide for Investors; Saudi Arabia: The Investment Dilemma* and *Non-ferrous Fabricating Industries in Southeast Asia*.

These publications provide thorough information and analysis of their subjects for a reader whose business interests relate, or could relate, to the fields covered. What they cannot be, however, is totally exhaustive.

*Multi-client Studies*

The second depth-range which EIU offers is multi-client studies and subscription services. These provide more detailed information on a particular topic than can be put into a publication. Multi-client studies provide comprehensive data and analysis on specialised topics, often in several volumes, produced with a very large input of research time. Recent titles include *Materials Substitution in the West European Commercial Vehicles Industry*; *The Middle East*

*Economies: Their Structure and Outlook* and *The United Kingdom Market for Home Video Products*. The number of subscribers in this case being much smaller than that usual for a publication, content can be highly specific.

## Regular Subscription Services

This also applies to regular subscription services. EIU currently offers two such services on construction, earthmoving, mining and industrial equipment in North America and in Europe, which include market surveys, forecasts and company profiles and enquiry facilities. In addition, EIU provides an international economic appraisal service, a data bank of macro-economic material on sixty developing countries and twenty developed ones, available on-line or in printed form. Two levels of service exist: Level One provides a continually maintained statistical database extending from 1970 to the present, the whole being constructed to provide ready inter-country comparison; Level Two provides a data base of indicators focusing on the countries' payments problems with current year projections and a succinct written appraisal. Finally, an 'early warning' model provides an original graphical representation of each country's credit rating over the recent past.

These services, and others, have been designed and developed to meet the specific needs of companies and institutions, in particular businesses, often with the assistance of these bodies. They are thus highly focused to provide material which closely fits the purposes of the clients. However, even here there cannot be total specificity because of the need to appeal to a number, albeit only a small number, of users.

Only in the third type of service, the custom-built exclusive service, can a totally customer-specific formula be achieved. Here a service, or a one-off research project, can be designed to provide exactly what a customer requires, in exactly the way he needs it in terms of timing, depth and type of coverage. The direct conse-quence is, of course, a higher cost since it cannot be spread over a number of users. The basic rule in the provision of information, analysis and intelligence, as in so many fields, is that the more the product is tailored to meet the precise needs of customers and the more exclusive those customers become, the higher the costs those customers must bear.

## Continuous Monitoring: The Core of Intelligence

On the whole, regular services, with their implication of continuous monitoring of a market, a country or an industry, tend to somewhat less exclusivity than do research projects. Regular services are in fact what intelligence is really about. Commercial, market or product intelligence is, or should be, a continuing process of obtaining information, analysing it and drawing conclusions, not necessarily frequently (some industries change only slowly), but regularly and continually. By such monitoring, the intelligence user keeps in touch with the world in which he has to operate and is provided with the basic external tools for decision-making.

From time to time, this regular flow of intelligence will indicate a need for extra information, for more detail or for a different type of information from that usually required. When this happens, a research project may be needed, and this highlights the essential difference between market intelligence and market research. Market intelligence is a continuing process of monitoring; market research is a tool of that process.

EIU and other companies in the field can and do provide both research, whether continuing or one-off, and the wider intelligence service which is, by definition, continuing. Such services can cover one or a number of locations or they can be highly international. In order to avoid complicating the discussion, in most of what follows the services are assumed to operate in a single country only. In fact, through its network of foreign offices, associated companies and research correspondents, EIU can offer comparable services in most commercially significant countries in the world. But since methods of work are essentially the same, the nature of a service offered in the United Kingdom can stand for one also offered for India, Malaysia or Brazil.

## Market Research and Market Intelligence

A typical market-intelligence service might deal with the development of the glass-packaging industry for a company engaged in this business, for a company producing a competitive packaging medium, or for a major supplier of material to such an industry. The depth and scope of the service can vary widely, from simple desk research to much more elaborate and expensive research procedures, and it is governed by client need: by how much will the benefit exceed the cost? Given that a term of reference has been established, how is the service set up? How is the material collected, interpreted, stored, retrieved and disseminated?

First, collection. The basis of all research in this area, as probably in most others, is thorough examination of data needs. What does the client need to know and therefore what questions are to be covered? The data needs for those preparing the service will obviously be greater than those expressed by the client, since a background wider than the topics to be covered in the reports to the client is essential to the proper preparation of these reports. Although the client may be concerned only with glass packaging, it is essential for the researcher to be at least aware of tangential developments in areas affecting glass packaging and the industries which either do or might use such packaging. Hence the researcher must first develop the questions.

For a full market intelligence service, there are five main broad categories: (a) What is the competition doing or getting ready to do?; (b) What are the consumers doing?; (c) What are suppliers doing?; (d) What is happening to the environment in which the client operates? (By environment, we mean government measures and attitudes, basic economic conditions and trends, finance and foreign exchange and similar factors which make up the conditions of business life under which the client must operate.); (e) What scientific and other research is going on in universities or government bodies which may affect the product or the market?

There are, of course, additional or preliminary questions which need to be established with the client to define the product, such as the materials used; the machines, equipment and processes; product applications — end-use or intermediate applications; the markets served; the competition, and the like.

## Exploiting Published Materials

Having established the questions within the broad categories, or those with which the service is concerned, how is the material collected? There can be no doubt that the primary source of data is commercially published material, and newspapers in particular. Newspapers can either be used directly by staff or a press-cutting agency can be employed. The business, financial and economic pages are obvious sources of the kind of material which is required.

Other pages should not be neglected, particularly the 'situations vacant' for some types of information. Weekly magazines — particularly *The Economist*, the *Investor's Chronicle* and the like — should similarly be examined; there are equivalent papers in most countries. Next, the trade press. This needs to be studied in the greatest depth possible, including, and perhaps particularly emphasising, the advertisements. The trade-press sources utilised should not be confined to those concerning the product itself.

To return to the example of the study of glass packaging, the obvious trade-press sources are those dealing with packaging, food and other products which may be packed in glass. But the trade press dealing with plant and machinery will also repay study, admittedly with a lower frequency of worthwhile material arising, but possibly with greater overall significance when it does arise.

Among the published sources which are available free are company reports, catalogues, service manuals and other materials which all companies make available to their customers, shareholders and the public. They are, of course, equally available to the competition, and it is often surprising what material can be found in these sources. The omissions too are frequently very significant. Stockbrokers' reports are also often excellent sources, even for technical material and particularly for commercial comment on technical developments and for what is often — but not always — a reasonably accurate assessment of the commercial viability of a new development. Stockbrokers' analysts seem often to get better and more detailed information about a company and its plans than do reporters for the press, and these analysts, or at least some of them, are skilled at picking out the essentials.

There are, of course, also government publications. The problem here is knowing what is available, since Her Majesty's Stationery Office in Britain issues 7,000 or more titles a year. To these should be added the journals of the appropriate societies, best located probably in Butterworth's *World List of Scientific Periodicals* and, similarly, the appropriate abstracting services.

Finally, among the printed sources there are what the *US Marketing Information Guide* once called 'way-out' sources. This is a field normally neglected by the researcher and is probably bound to remain so. It comprises such publications as hobby magazines, where enthusiastic amateurs reveal their researches and where out-of-the-way statistics are frequently given. The researcher into, say, railway equipment would be well advised to study the railway enthusiasts' magazines.

It should be noted here that an exceptionally useful source of data is also very often neglected. This may perhaps best be classified as 'exploiting the publisher'. The researcher can check back on the published material by contacting the editor or publisher and asking for explanation, amplification or even the source of the data. Frequently there is more material available than appeared in the publication and at least some of it can be extracted, although it must be added that the method works better with magazines than with newspapers.

The next major group of sources of importance are the materials and data available inside the company — in the EIU's case this, of course, is the client company — and with the company's suppliers and distributors. This material may be already in the right form but going to people or departments who do not or cannot use it. More usually that data will not be in the right form but can often be readily adapted.

## Exploiting Personal Contacts

The third and last group of sources may best be called 'contacts', which may prove the most fruitful of all. The stock in trade of a company like EIU is its experience and knowledge of people who are likely to have requisite information and who will be able to share some of it. There is then a need to establish a wide range of contacts, through trade and industry associations, professional bodies and similar groups, not only in one's own industry but also in other related fields and areas of potential interest.

In this area of data collection there are, however, far more problems than in the others. Ethical difficulties necessarily arise. This question, as well as that of where the more useful material arises, has been studied in some depth in the United States, where the science or art of commercial intelligence is, of course, highly developed. The most striking thing about these studies is that while they tend to agree that in the United States questioning customers, suppliers and distributors of the competitor, exploiting social or professional contacts and hiring away the staff of the competitor are acceptable, while wire-tapping, bribery and misrepresentation are not, the most useful source of data is the reports of the company's salesmen and the second most useful is published data.

Another very useful source is generally found to be personal or professional contact with a counterpart in a competitor company, and a phrase occurs in a study by Professor Albaum of the University of Pittsburgh which is probably significant: 'The camaraderie among professional personnel often exceeds any company loyalty.' It perhaps may be doubted whether this could be applied so confidently in the United Kingdom (and indeed British researchers would also eschew some of the other methods mentioned). Whether it does or not, the basic rule about contacts is that they work on the mutual obligation system, and it is therefore advisable to be sure precisely how important a question one is asking for fear of incurring a similarly large obligation. None the less, the correct use of personal and professional contacts remains a vital source of information.

## Data Interpretation

The next step is interpretation, not as is sometimes suggested, storage. As a general rule, material obtained should, in our view, be interpreted or at least evaluated before being stored. The process of interpretation is one principally of manipulation of pieces, preferably against the background of a pattern. The interpreter needs to be continually seeking to find a pattern and to assure himself of its continuation, since it is primarily when the pattern breaks or alters that a significant development is discovered. This is probably easiest to illustrate by an example.

Assume first of all that part of the regular information flow across the interpreter's desk is an analysis of advertising expenditures on a group of products by the major producers. According to the pattern — which may be kept in a formal or informal way — Company A should be spending an amount $X$: the analysis shows that its expenditure has declined. Some change is clearly indicated, which may be minor and usually is, but which may have substantial significance. It could mean, for example, that the product is going to be replaced. The interpreter's next step is to call for all the related material. Do the trade magazines or the sales force's reports offer any clues? If they do, this is probably a signal to move over from the normal intelligence service to a project approach.

More data is brought together — the last annual report of Company A, the latest broker's report. Contacts and other sources are used to ascertain whether the company has installed a new plant, advertised for additional or different staff or made high-level appointments. What can be ascertained about these appointments? Did one of the men give an interview to the trade press or, sometimes, the company's house magazine? What can be discovered of his background? He is probably listed in one of the directories or may have been written up at some time in the trade press or again in the house magazine. What does he specialise in and what are his strengths? It may be equally interesting to ascertain the composition of the rest of the project team and how this fits with what can be learned about the plant and equipment which may have been ordered or installed, and how the two components relate to any recent advertising.

Usually by these means — a piecing together of small items of material which is essentially what military and all other intelligence requires[1] — one can arrive at a reasonable hypothesis about what Company A plans to do. Normally the broad outline will be clear: a new product or a development of an old one, and the process too may be reasonably apparent. What will not be clear will be the details: (a) the timing, and (b) the economics. At this point there is a need for other kinds of expertise than the researcher and intelligence interpreter may have. Most probably, these must be sought from other parts of the company (or in the EIU's case, from the client). There may be a need for the research and development staff to consider whether the hypothetical process is practicable for Company A's facilities. Similarly the production department may be required to assess whether the hypothesised economics are within the bounds of possibility.

There may, of course, be additional work for the research/intelligence department. On the basis of the hypothesised costs, what will the selling price be? This again depends on a variety of factors, most notably the state of the market and the effect on it of the new product. A similar calculation will be being made by Company A's own staff and it may be possible, by studying their past record, to draw conclusions as to the findings they will be likely to reach and, therefore, to modify the conclusions about price and effect on the market. Subsequently, still further research may be needed concerning, say, the reaction of other suppliers to the

1. This basic activity in all intelligence work is well illustrated in Sydney Pollack's movie *Seven Days of the Condor*, where Robert Redford, as a junior CIA analyst working with open sources of information, suddenly comes across a major 'hotspot', knowledge of which will, in fact, threaten his life.

market and, of course, the effect of the action which your own company will take. For all of these purposes further data is required and interpretation is needed.

## Data Storage and Retrieval

The most important remaining stage in the process is, or should be, storage and retrieval of data. This is a subject on which a great many words have been expanded. A recent check on half a dozen books relating to the subject showed that in all but one they were deep into automated information centres, time-sharing and multi-market model-building within a few pages. This is not to imply that electronic data processing is not of immense value to the researcher, but rather that it overshadows too much of the storage and retrieval process. In a way, this may be an argument against it.

The first, and by far the most important step in the process — assuming that it has been properly determined just what is needed for the information system — is the process of coding and classification. The precise coding used is a matter of choice but the objective must always be to leave a margin for later subdivision into more refined categories. The same applies to indexing, whether this is to be on index cards or itself computerised. Cross-indexing is important, of course, but may be something of a trap. Adopting too full a system will certainly mean that all possibly relevant data will be retrievable, but in such quantities that it may overwhelm the researcher. This again is an argument for interpretation, or at least evaluation before storage: the rule of the system should be that the researcher can obtain sufficient data by referring to the index and classification, but not that he should be supplied with every word on the subject.

The process of classification should clearly include some kind of rating as to the importance and reliability of the material. Even after evaluation, which should eliminate the worthless, there will be shadings of reliability in the material put into storage and these must be noted at the time. Was the material from a trade-press editorial — often a piece of special pleading — a business note or the result of a salesman's call, and how should it be rated for reliability and significance? Here again, incidentally, is something of an argument against all-out computerisation: nothing looks so definite and certain as a computer print-out, whereas a yellowing cutting in a file may precisely suit the quality of the information contained in it.

The next most important step is a built-in provision for examination and updating of material. This may be called a 'self-activating review and updating mechanism', even though it may merely mean that someone periodically throws away the older and superseded press cuttings and other notes.

## Data Dissemination

Dissemination of information is, of course, the final step in the process. For a consultant research organisation, this is not a problem since the destination of its services is established by the client. The results of these services, moreover, tend to be used more often than those provided by in-house information systems, since they are paid for more directly and more obviously.

For the in-house information system, however, there are clearly problems. Dissemination was described by an American expert recently as sending too many overly long, overly regular reports to too many people. There is some truth in this, and probably too many researchers provide too much material. If the monthly report has always been twenty pages long, the chances are that it always will be, whereas it may be that no more than five pages are needed to pass on the message that very little has changed. The *ad hoc* report is greatly to be preferred if the company can be persuaded that the department is not merely reducing its workload.

For *ad hoc* and for regular reporting there are certain rules which have been established — in part for one's own protection. First, the amount of detail should be proportionate both to the importance of the development being reported on and to the position of the man who will receive the report. The executive summary is frequently worth preparing. Second, the report should show trends and exceptions — patterns and breaches in the pattern — and while it assumes that earlier reports have been read, it also repeats their general conclusions. Lastly, it is essential to identify, first, which are the facts, second, which are the probabilities and, third, where the hypotheses and conclusions begin.

This last point is probably particularly important. The commercial intelligence department, or its equivalent, is going to have to make hypotheses and arrive at tentative conclusions based on less than perfect evidence, even if it should in the future have access to a data bank of almost infinite size and a system of almost infinite sophistication. The researcher in this field is in the business of guessing the whole picture from the evidence of a few small pieces and he can rarely sit on the fence — or at least he rarely should. His role is to provide an early warning service and to interpret and expand on the warning as required. In the future, there is no doubt that he will have extensive assistance from the computer. Increasingly, companies are setting up models of the business, its markets, competitors and customers. These models will not merely be able to accept new updating material, but they will be so programmed that they can warn of significant change with a certainty that all factors available have been considered in arriving at this conclusion. But it will continue to be the intelligence department which decides when a development is critical and it will still be the intelligence department which has to get down from the fence.

This, then, is what an intelligence service of a very specific kind can do. How important is intelligence, and is there any evidence which implies any strengthening or weakening of this importance? Certainly the rate of change in world events, as in product development, has speeded up, and the changes that occur are certainly not smaller than in earlier post-war decades. Product life cycles in many areas — not just those of high technology — seem to be shorter, and while the arrival of major new products has recently been no greater and may even be smaller, the adaptation and development of products is more rapid. This must mean that intelligence need is as great and probably greater.

## Risk Intelligence

One area where the need for intelligence is very evident, and where indeed the actual market for intelligence has rapidly increased with the need — which is not always the case — is country credit risk and political risk in particular. While it would be a mistake to accept entirely that the growth in the demand for this kind of intelligence dates back to the aftermath of the Iranian revolution, there is little doubt that this event — which was apparently not foreseen by the CIA — so alarmed many US-based corporations that an urgent need for more and better risk information surfaced. A variety of commercial companies now attempt to meet this need and serve this market. Perhaps the most interesting fact which emerges from an examination of the methods apparently used by the intelligence suppliers is the recourse to panels of experts. While the numbers who are claimed as contributors may range over the hundreds for the larger practitioners and include businessmen, political scientists, diplomats and political journalists, almost all suppliers use this basic approach. On top of this, each supplier has a team of in-house analysts and some have extensive — and no doubt expensive — computer facilities for processing the information received.

In some cases, too, eminent men, such as former prime ministers and heads of international institutions, appear as board members or contributors in other ways and, indeed, such members of the community of 'the great and the good' are increasingly becoming advisers in their own right to multinational corporations. The value of such counsel is difficult to determine. Its critics argue that such eminent figures were usually extremely well-informed when in office, but that the value of their experience declines rapidly when they no longer have the same direct access to the seats of power. An adviser to a multinational will, of course, retain some access, but how much?

One of the weaknesses of American intelligence in Iran, subsequently identified by a House of Representatives subcommittee, was a lack of widespread contact with nationals of the country, and this must mean up-to-date, continuing contact. It may well be that the role of 'men of knowledge' in work of this kind, as indeed in areas of technology, too, might best be found in critically reviewing, in the light of experience, the material produced by teams of current experts and analysts. The combination could prove to be the nearly ideal one for many kinds of intelligence, with the caution of experience applied to the enthusiasm and receptive attitudes of those currently in touch with the relevant facts and opinions.

### Ability to Use Intelligence Properly

It must be emphasised once again that the quality of the intelligence services available, and the no doubt still higher quality of those which will become available, is only a part of the equation. It is pointless to buy or to create commercial, or indeed any, intelligence unless it is to be used properly. For this to happen, the importance of such material must be understood and appreciated throughout management, and the identity and position of the person chiefly responsible for intelligence must be clear. It may not need to be overly high in hierarchical terms; indeed, in many Western corporations it is not high, but it does need to be identified and it does need to be in a position to deliver its contribution to decision-making. It may not be too unfair to say that in many large and powerful developing country agencies and corporations, this is simply not the case.

Those who wish to improve the flow of knowledge to the developing countries — and particularly the availability of commercial information — must recognise that the ability to use such information is at the moment more limited than could be wished. It is limited because its importance is not recognised, and work related to it does not carry much status or, perhaps more important, much of a share of the budget. There is often no significant tradition of information use and, where there is, it may reside among people far removed from state trading bodies. There are a number of myths — or at least huge exaggerations — which may lead to a defeatist attitude being easily adopted in this area.

To change this situation will not be an easy task, nor will it be achieved quickly since there are no short-cuts. Perhaps the best way, if funds can be made available, would be the establishment of a small number of modest pilot projects. A particular developing country state institution, perhaps a product marketing board, might be selected as a subject. With the help of those experienced in commercial, economic and technological intelligence — which could include consultancy companies — intelligence needs could be assessed and an intelligence operation established, which would actually serve the marketing board and provide on-the-job training for its staff. Its main purpose would, of course, be to demonstrate to other bodies that a useful job can be done with a little experience, a few selected brains, a modest amount of data and a great deal of enthusiasm, and without the largest data-gathering and data-processing facilities in the world.

Although it can be argued that commercial intelligence is very client-specific and that, therefore, demonstration projects are more difficult to learn from than, say, a model farm, the fact remains that techniques, methods and attitudes can be taught. Despite the fact that commercial intelligence takes time to achieve its full potential, since patterns over time need to be established, it remains true that some value can often be seen in a year, and more in two or three.

If it can be shown that a handful of suitable people, tapping the right sources and learning to analyse material, can deliver a major contribution to decision-taking, then perhaps this neglected part of the management process can have a significant future in the developing countries. Without it, Third World commercial managers will always have one arm tied behind their backs.

CHAPTER 6

# Government, the Information Industry and Social Intelligence

Eric de Grolier

We are still only at the beginning of what has been called the third industrial revolution of computers, telecommunications and office automation, and its consequences will certainly equal those of its two predecessors.[1] Having already transformed information retrieval, the third industrial revolution is in the process of reshaping scientific publishing itself, with electronic publishing and projects like Adonis, in which five leading European scientific publishers plan to pool scientific and technical publications on optical discs, in co-operation with a number of national information-documentation centres.[2]

It is just as clear that the computer revolution will change, and is indeed already changing, the way in which scientific data are used — including data relating to the social, demographic and other sciences, since these can also be accessed and manipulated on-line.[3]

The technological gap in this field between the United States and the other developed countries is tending to narrow. There is much

1. Jean Bounine and Bruno Lussato, *Télématique ou privatique?*, Editions d'Organisation, Paris, 1980; Pierre Drouin and Eric Rohde (eds.), 'L'Informatique aujourd'hui', *Le Monde*, Dossiers et Documents, Paris, 1982; Koji Kobayashi, 'Computer, Communications and Man: The Integration of Computer and Communications with Man As an Axis', *Computer Networks*, 1981, pp. 237–50; Bruno Lussato, *Le défi informatique*, Pluriel, Paris, 1982; Gerry P. Sweeney, 'Telematics and Development', *Information Society*, vol. 1, 1981, pp. 113–32.
2. Dietrich Götze, *Perspektiven wissenschaftlicher Information und Dokumentation*, Report to the Deutscher Dokumentartag, 1982.
3. IZ (Informationszentrum Sozialwissenschaften, Bonn) and SGCSA (Study Group on Computers in Survey Analysis, London), *Social Science Application Software Catalogue*. 3rd edn., London, 1982; Edouard Labin, *Les banques de données dans les domaines scientifiques et techniques*, La Documentation française, Paris, 1980.

ground to make up, but computers and telecommunications are coming to be used as intensively in Western Europe as in North America. Conversely, the gap between North and South appears to be widening. In those Third World countries equipping themselves to participate in transborder data flows (such as Morocco, linked to the European Space Agency (ESA) data bank), the facilities are still underused and do not go far to remedy the shortage of information, which contrasts with the excess of information in the highly industrialised countries.

## Good Use of Sophisticated Technologies

The developing countries obviously wish to obtain the most sophisticated technologies, in computing as in other fields. But it is one thing to introduce remote computing and office automation into a developing country, and another to get them to contribute to development. In a country where the illiteracy rate averages some 60 per cent (and over 90 per cent for women), with almost no public libraries, and where publication of the national bibliography has been suspended for over a decade and university libraries are meagre, should it have been a top priority to enable a few favoured individuals to consult nuclear energy or aerospace data bases on-line? Being one of the few developing countries linked to any of the developed countries' data banks may be a stimulus and have a ripple effect. But there should be other priorities, based on an analysis of such real needs as the acquisition of the foreign documents needed for national planning, and the establishment of a national, up-to-date data base for all categories of documents produced in the country or relating to it (an extension of the 'Americana', 'Helvetica', and 'Canadiana' concept which guided the achievements of countries at a time when they were still in the process of development).

## Information Processing Methods

It is surprising to see that obsolete information processing methods are still being used, not only in the developing countries, but also in the highly industrialised countries; for instance, data capture via input forms when text processing machines are now within the reach of practically everyone, or thesauri used for document input even though information retrieval on natural language texts is becoming increasingly widespread, thanks to sophisticated programmes which by now are tried and tested. Automatic methods of indexing and condensing texts, on which research is under way, particularly in Germany, will most probably replace conventional manual processes fairly soon. Automatic classification techniques are not expected to replace conventional methods until they make more use of the results of research in artificial intelligence, but they will certainly supplement the conventional methods.

Investigations under way for more than a decade are challenging present document-cataloguing techniques.[4] These are often unnecessarily complicated, replacing the kind of catalogue file we have been using for over a century with microforms. On-line systems should encourage national information and documentation policymakers to simplify current procedures drastically — and not only in the developing countries, whose financial resources are more limited.

Information processing should be conceived in an integrated manner, linking the various stages with one another. In the processing of newspaper information, it is already usual for the journalist to set his article directly on a terminal. After subbing or editing, it can go for photosetting and eventually be included in the data bank holding the overall content of the newspaper. Several countries, as well as the Council of Europe, have a kind of 'endless chain' of information, from the stage at which a draft is laid before the assembly (regional, national or supranational) to the point at which, having become a legal document, it is included in data banks for lawyers, solicitors and barristers. These processes could be applied in the developing countries but have not been introduced on any large scale up to now.

## Co-ordinating Diverse Information Sources

Any fairly complex decision must rely on information from a variety of overlapping sources, which confirm or disprove one another. Traditionally, information sources have been categorised

4. Michel Callon *et al.*, 'From Translation to Problematic Networks: An Introduction to Co-word Analysis', *Social Science Information*, 1983; Eugene Garfield, *ISI Atlas of Science: Biochemistry and Molecular Biology, 1978/1980*, Institute for Scientific Information, Philadelphia, 1982.

and their management entrusted to different types of agencies, not always on any very obvious basis. This compartmentalisation, stemming more from historical circumstances than from logic, has serious disadvantages. The decision-maker, working under pressure and facing very short deadlines, has neither the leisure nor the ability to explore the various libraries (university, public, specialist, administrative), archives, photo libraries, film libraries, and even museums which might provide him with useful or even essential information.

The drawbacks of fragmentation have been countered in two ways. One approach, notably in some multinational corporations, is to set up a department to marshall all the information, whatever form it may take. The other approach is to recruit specialist staff with the task of gathering information from whatever source available. The US Congressional Research Service is probably the most highly developed of this type of service and is the model copied, for example, by the Service de Recherche de la Bibliothèque de la Législature of Quebec.

Over the last ten years, factual data banks have proliferated not only in scientific and technical disciplines, where they were first built up in machine-readable form about a quarter of a century ago, but also in the social sciences: economics, marketing, accounting, demography, politics, law. At first confined to the United States (which still has the largest), they soon developed in Europe, especially in France, following a decision by the Council of Ministers of 9 April 1980. However, it is mainly government organisations and large firms that use these data banks, and very little use is being made of them by small- or medium-sized firms. In agriculture, their access should be facilitated by what in France are called *conseillers médiateurs*.

This brings us to the role of what, following Derek de Solla Price, can be referred to as the problem of the 'invisible colleges'. Price was mainly concerned with the physical and natural sciences, where advances on the research front are so rapid that passing on information by the traditional method of the scientific publication — the article screened by referees (specialists in each field who receive the author's manuscript, assess its value and suggest possible modifications) — is too slow to distribute research results in good time.

This is probably also the point at which mention should be made of think-tanks that provide policy-makers with material from several sources, based on analyses by interdisciplinary teams. The prototype is the well-known Rand Corporation, which has been copied or adapted in various other countries, notably Canada (whose Institute for Research on Public Policy was established in 1972). Several firms were subsequently formed in the United States for the purpose of providing large multinationals with political risk analyses, and these firms have even set up an Association of Political Risk Analysts, with some 300 members.[5]

One of the problems arising out of this diversity of sources of useful information, and the proliferation of information, documentation and research agencies, is how to identify them. The fullest possible inventory needs to be made and, most important, kept constantly up to date, of all available information resources, as the essential prerequisite for co-ordinating documentation resources.[6]

## Analysis, Criticism, Appraisal and Synthesis

The computer manager's maxim, 'garbage in, garbage out', must be the underlying principle here. While a conventional library can to some extent ignore the question of the intrinsic worth of the documents it is accumulating, and leave it up to the user to sort the wheat from the chaff, a data bank cannot. Whether the information is scientific, technical, social, economic, demographic or political, the quality of what is entered into the memory is crucial. Every information service can perhaps be described as a huge machine for sorting, analysing, criticising, evaluating and synthesising, starting with raw data and ending up with high-definition summaries representing the quintessence or, as Rabelais would have said, the very substance of human knowledge. This is the process used by the British intelligence services. Taken to the extreme, it would produce the constantly updated World Encyclopedia that H.G. Wells suggested more than half a century ago.

From this point of view, the development of analysis information centres in the United States following the 1963 Weinberg report is certainly a good example, but we should not overlook much older undertakings, like the *Handbücher* of nineteenth-century Germany. Some of these are still produced, though now in the inter-

5. Nigel Carruthers and Pat Fitzsimmons, 'The Risk Merchants', *The Middle East* 29–30 May 1982.
6. Aubert Dulong, *Guidelines for Establishing and Developing Referral Centres for Users of Information*, WS/PGI/78/19, Unesco, Paris, 1978.

national language of English: this is the case of the *Beilstein Hand-book of Organic Chemistry*, the *Gmelin Handbook of Inorganic Chemistry* (prepared by the institutes of the same names in Frank-furt) and the great Landolt–Börnstein compendium of numerical, scientific and technological data.

## The Limits of Forecasting

In 1963, at an International Social Sciences Council symposium at Yale University, a very interesting report described one of the first experiments in computer simulation by leading specialists of the origins of the First World War. From a combination of selected data including, among other things, analyses of reports by the ambassa-dors of European powers, speeches by heads of government and heads of state, the London gold price and so on, the authors concluded that from a certain date at the end of July 1914 the war could have been predicted as inevitable. 'Very good', this writer told the speaker. 'You have produced a remarkable forecast after the event. But suppose, which God forbid, we were now in a compar-able situation: could you use the same methods to predict World War III beforehand?' 'Oh!' said the speaker, 'that's highly doubtful, I would never dare make a prediction like that'. It is interesting to consider what reasons he might have had for being so cautious. Could it be that much of the information essential for an accurate conclusion is not actually accessible until public archives reveal it thirty or fifty years later? or could there be some deeper imponder-ables, unquantifiable and perhaps just random data, on which the final outcome largely depends in spite of everything? In some instances, historians have been able to describe such situations when they have had access to the right archive material. Barbara Tuch-man, for example, explained why Mao was not invited to Washing-ton before the final campaign that led to the collapse of the Kuomintang armies.[7] Surely the social and political continuum may have processes comparable to turbulence in physics, where corre-lation between the factors observed at a given moment is lost and, as a result, future developments cannot be predicted?

---

7. Barbara W. Tuchman, 'If Mao Had Come to Washington', *Foreign Affairs*, October 1972 (Reproduced in *Practising History*, Ballantine Books, New York, 1982, pp. 188–207).

The history of the social sciences teems with predictions proved false. Witness the demographic forecasts by the most renowned experts shortly before and immediately after the Second World War, the 1950 Soviet predictions that the capitalist economy would shortly collapse, the optimistic reports to the United States government on the foreseeable collapse of North Vietnamese resistance, the optimistic calculations before the energy crisis that post-industrial societies would enjoy uninterrupted growth or, in a more restricted field, extrapolations of trends prompting the authorities throughout the world to build excessively large airports during the 1970s. As regards information itself, there is an excellent example in a study sponsored by the OECD which, from insufficiently tested premises, overestimated the effects of the so-called information explosion.[8]

To err is human. Many authors have tried to find out why errors occur in social intelligence, and D.J. Urquhart has shown very clearly that a rational country information policy must start by studying the shortcomings and failures of existing information systems.[9] A set of detailed case studies could usefully be compiled for the most interesting specimens of forecasting error. This would doubtless imbue governments and industrial managers with a wholesome measure of humility.

## Problems of an Information Policy

It is ultimately up to central governments to organise social intelligence on as rational a basis as possible — or at least on the least irrational basis. Central government is the ideal locus where information and documentation policy can be most easily formulated and implemented, as can mass communications policy (the frontier between the two fields is becoming easier to cross).

An overall comparative transcultural study of these policies remains to be carried out. It could draw upon methods developed in comparative political sociology. Here I shall touch on just a few special aspects, taking a set of five alternatives.

8. Georges Anderla, *Information in 1983*, OECD, Paris, 1973.
9. D.J. Urquhart, *National Information Policy*, COM.76/NATIS/X6, Unesco, Paris, 1976.

## Nationalisation versus Privatisation

This dimension of the information problem might be thought meaningless in the socialist countries with centralised, collectivised economies. In fact it is only transposed, in so far as their enterprises, universities, press agencies, scientific and technical research centres and academies still have some degree of autonomy. The level of government intervention in the information or knowledge industry is in fact difficult to measure. The United States is conventionally regarded as the prototype of the private-enterprise system, but in fact all the largest private developments in the knowledge industry depend for their growth on massive injections of federal funding, especially in defence-related projects.

The Federal Republic of Germany has little inclination to socialise its economy, yet a document from the Federal Ministry for Research and Technology shows that the central government underwrites between 72 per cent and 94 per cent of the operating costs not covered by earnings in ten of the thirteen specialised information services established since 1974.[10] Sales of information and documentation cover only between 0.3 and 18 per cent of costs (1980 figures), except for two of the systems, chemistry and technology, whose sales cover 65 per cent and 35 per cent respectively.

In France, the lion's share of the budgets for the main scientific, technological and economic documentation agencies (the Centre National de la Recherche Scientifique, the Commissariat à l'Energie Atomique, the Institut National de la Propriété Industrielle and the Institut National de la Statistique et des Études Économiques) is provided by the state or by para-fiscal levies, and it was the government that financed a national organisation to operate conversational-mode data bases and data banks.

## Centralisation versus Regionalisation

In most countries, one of the critical issues is that of balance between centralised and decentralised information services. A typical instance is France, where an excessive degree of centralism, inherited from several centuries of royal power and, perfected by the iron grip of Napoleon, has until recently impeded the develop-

10. BMFT (Bundesministerium für Forschung und Technologie), *Stand und Entwicklung der Fachinformationssysteme (FIS)*, (Referat 216), Bonn, 1981.

ment of effective regional information networks. It was only in the mid-1970s that regional agencies (branches of the Institut National de la Propriété Industrielle, regional scientific and technical agencies, economic branches of the Institut National de la Statistique et des Etudes Economiques) were tentatively introduced, and only in 1983 that the Decentralisation Act provided a more suitable framework for regional data banks and computer networks. In the United States, the WESTAT report, commissioned in 1974 by the National Commission on Libraries and Information Science, recommended a multi-tiered organisation with an 'inter-state' level covering ten large regions.[11] In Canada, the distribution of information tasks between the federal government and provincial authorities constitutes one of the key problems in developing a national 'network of networks' for information and documentation. In all three of the countries a new balance is emerging, not without hesitation and retreat, between centralisation and decentralisation, via a transfer of powers from centre to periphery.

Conversely, in the Federal Republic of Germany, greater co-ordination seems to be emerging between the *Länder* and the central authority, but not without difficulty. The federal government and the *Länder* have not been able to agree on the joint financing of an information system specialising in the social sciences. However, in 1977, the Gesellschaft für Information und Dokumentation was established jointly by the central and *Länder* governments, which finance 65 per cent and 35 per cent respectively of its budget.

## Nationalism versus Internationalism

At a different level, a dilemma arises between nationalism and internationalism. How far can a country, however powerful, make itself completely self-sufficient in bibliographic data bases and factual data banks? The answer is clearly that no country can, not even the United States which perhaps comes closest to this ideal, but depends on external sources in certain areas (American chemists, like all others, use the Gmelin and Beilstein handbooks produced in Germany). Even the Soviet Union depends very largely on outside

---

11. WESTAT Inc., *Resources and Bibliographic Support for a Nationwide Library Program: Final Report to the National Commission for Libraries and Information Science*, Government Printing Office, Washington, 1974.

sources (Russian chemists use not only Gmelin and Beilstein but also the US Chemical Abstracts Service). In France, the Centre National de la Recherche Scientifique (CNRS) has been working since 1939 on a national technical and scientific bibliographical data base. This encyclopedic, world-scale data base has been computerised over the past ten years, but this does not prevent French firms and laboratories from making very heavy use of American data, probably for over two-thirds of their requirements. The American economic data banks are also consulted more often than the French equivalents by large French companies. In Canada, some studies have shown the marked dependence on the United States and the relative inferiority of French to English language sources.

A document prepared for the International Congress on the availability of publications, organised by Unesco and the International Federation of Library Associations and Institutions in May 1982, shows that over half of the approximately 1 million international requests to document-supplying centres in 1979 were received by just one centre, the British Library Lending Division in the United Kingdom. Next in order were France's CNRS, which received 6 per cent, and the National Library of Medicine in the United States which received 2.5 per cent of the requests.

## Specialisation versus an Interdisciplinary Approach

In the German language *Fachinformation* (professional, specialist information) is contrasted with *Massenkommunikation* (mass communications, the mass media). In fact, the 1974 federal plan for the development of an information infrastructure in West Germany was based on setting up information systems for sixteen specialist fields, together with four interdisciplinary information centres covering, respectively, the environment, patents, technical specifications and research projects. In practice, dividing up the knowledge industry into segments which correspond more or less to traditional disciplines has proved somewhat inconvenient.

In France, though not as a deliberate policy, the organisation of information and documentation has been based for more than forty years on two strictly scientific documentation centres, one for the mathematical, physical and natural sciences, the other for the social sciences (both within the Centre National de la Recherche Scientifique), and a series of specialised centres for industrial branches of industry in the technical field.

In the United Kingdom, the preference was given to a single documentation centre, the National Lending Library for Science and Technology (later renamed the British Library Lending Division), extending its coverage to the social sciences and then to the human sciences. Document analysis and exploitation, however, remained largely decentralised.

In the United States, the 1963 report of the President's Advisory Committee, chaired by Alvin Weinberg, recommended that a set of specialist information analysis centres be established either by discipline or by mission. Five years later, a list published by the Committee on Scientific and Technical Information showed no fewer than 113 such centres financed by the federal government.[12] During the 1970s, a number of non-specialised services grew up, such as the Institute for Scientific Information (working mainly with the transdisciplinary Science Citation Index which started in 1961), the Social Sciences Citation Index (1969), and the Arts and Humanities Citation Index (1977), together with digests reproducing the contents pages from a selection of periodicals (*Current Contents*). The large conversational data-base and data-bank operators enable customers to use a single access point to retrieve from a whole series of very wide-ranging data bases and data banks. The largest, Lockheed Information Service, was hooked into 182 data bases and data banks in 1982. The second largest, DSC Search Service of System Development Corporation (SDC), purchased by Burroughs in August 1980, offers access to one-third fewer; the third, Bibliographical Retrieval Services (BRS) is distinctly smaller. In comparison, there are some forty European operators (twenty-eight of whom belong to the European Host Operators' Group) linked to the Euronet–Diane network, offering a total of 363 data bases and data banks, of which a considerable number are also available via operators in the United States.

The wide-ranging coverage of the data-bank operators and of such transdisciplinary services offer great advantages to the user, at a time when frontiers between specialised fields are tending to become blurred and innovations, both scientific and technological, are increasingly occurring at the point where disciplines converge. The risk is that the user may be literally submerged by the excessive flow of information, and that he may not be able to interpret the

12. A. Weinberg, *Science, Government, and Information* (President's Advisory Committee's Report), Government Printing Office, Washington, 1963.

information provided to him. Another risk, which is not so serious in the United States where Lockheed and SDC, among others, have developed systems for automatically ordering documents mentioned by terminal, but which is very serious in the developing countries, is that the user may have no effective way of obtaining the documents containing the information of most interest to him. Hence the continuing debate on whether the final user should himself manipulate the terminal and find his own way through the flood of information or whether it is better to bring in an intermediary — called a mediator, a transmitter, counsellor or information scientist — to retrieve on his behalf, then sift and, so to speak, 'predigest' the document obtained.

## Secrecy versus Transparency

Most of the world's states are faithful to Francis Bacon's recommendation that rulers should know all about the ruled but that the ruled should know as little as possible about their rulers. In other words, if the transparency of a system is measured by the percentage of information about the system and its problems that an intelligent observer can obtain from freely accessible sources, the transparency of the state *vis-à-vis* the citizens should be minimal, and that of the citizen *vis-à-vis* the state should be maximal.

A considerable volume of literature has accumulated over recent years on the problem of administrative secrecy and it cannot appropriately be summarised in this brief report. I therefore confine myself to just a few points.[13]

Fundamentally, the role of state secrecy is the same as has been suggested for politics, the art of preventing people from interfering in what concerns them. The idea is to eliminate as far as possible the 'visibility' of 'disagreeable' aspects (to use a euphemism) of the real situation, and notably those which appear to be against the interests of the majority of the population, or at least of those population groups or classes which do not support the government in place and which are not favoured by its policies. However childish these practices may appear to an outside observer — for example, when a

---

13. Itzhak Galnoor (ed.), *Government Secrecy in Democracies*, Harper and Row, New York, 1977; James Michael, *The Politics of Secrecy*, Penguin, Harmondsworth, 1982; Donald G. Rowat (ed.) *Administrative Secrecy in Developed Countries*, Macmillan, London, 1979 (English translation, updated to the end of 1977, of *Le secret administratif dans les pays développés*, Editions Cujas, Paris, 1977).

government makes a secret of its foreign trade figures, which can easily be compiled from third-country statistics — they nevertheless do have the effect, as El Kholy points out elsewhere in this volume for Egypt, of keeping the majority of the population ignorant of the unpalatable information.

The taste of the developing countries for secrecy often seems anachronistic. One example is the high secrecy surrounding the plans for the capital of a Middle-Eastern country which I visited as a consultant, even though spy satellites can identify everything that is being built. In many cases, information withheld from the population can easily be compiled by making intelligent use of a publicly available sources and contacts with authorised spokesmen. A moderately diligent expert will not find it too difficult on a one-month mission to establish reasonably accurate statistics on the percentage of the population in the armed forces and police, the growth of per capita income, illiteracy rates by region and by sex or even the breakdown of land ownership and incomes. All these data may be 'secret', and the country's nationals are then astonished to see that the foreigner has obtained fairly easily the data about their own country which they themselves need.

The absence of published data may sometimes point to the existence of 'hot spots'. In one Arab country which I have studied, there are no population statistics by mother tongue, and the government budget simply shows *pro memoria* the contribution it receives from a certain national company. No great deductive powers are needed to infer that the country has a serious minority language problem (in fact probably the majority language) and that the firm in question is a sort of state within the state.

It is also clear that the degree of secrecy (or, conversely, of transparency) can vary greatly not only between countries but also throughout time. The general trend seems to be that the proportion of what is secret drops more or less in parallel with the growth of income per capita, though there are considerable differences attributable to historical and cultural factors. However, it could be laid down as a principle that no state is completely transparent, and that the very function of the state, as an instrument of organised social violence, requires a certain degree of secrecy, all the higher if the state is more militaristic and less democratic.

What about transparency with regard to firms, political parties, churches, and other social institutions? Here again it is very difficult to generalise. The broad trend, however, seems to be for industrial and commercial firms to become more transparent. The June 1982 Hitachi–Mitsubishi industrial espionage affair showed how much importance IBM attaches to retaining its manufacturing secrets, but lifted only the corner of the veil as regards the real non-transparency policy of the multinationals, concealed by their 'apparent transparency'. The Communist parties are, not without reason, easily suspected of an undue taste for secrecy, but the degree of secrecy appears appreciably higher for the French Communist Party than for its Italian counterpart. The Catholic Church certainly has a thousand-year tradition of secrecy management, especially in connection with its finances.

Science is indeed based on public knowledge. However, in reality, scientific laboratories are by no means as transparent as they should theoretically be. In one particular case, that of the TEA (Transversely Excited Atmospheric Pressure $CO_2$ Laser), Collins showed that research workers used subtle means to conceal vital aspects of their know-how and, at all events, to exchange information only with those laboratories having something to give in return.[14]

Lastly, I can only mention the problem, with a reference to George Orwell's *Nineteen Eighty-Four*, of the transparency not of the state in relation to its citizens, but of the citizens in relation to the state.[15] The development of factual data banks in the fields of the social sciences, health, education and criminology has prompted a growing and reasonable anxiety in all democratic countries. Some people rightly or wrongly regard the present legal guarantees for the protection of privacy as derisory. Obviously, social science researchers rightly consider that combined data banks would considerably facilitate their studies, but their interest here conflicts with those of the 'guinea-pigs' under observation. However democratic a state may be, the temptation to misuse the personal data accumulated could prove too strong. Surely there is ultimately an ethical problem in this field fairly similar to the ethical problems arising in so many others, for example, in biotechnology and genetic manipulation, as a result of scientific progress.

14. H.M. Collins, 'The TEA Set: Tacit Knowledge and Scientific Networks', *Science Studies* 4, 1982, pp. 165–86.
15. Edward H. Hanis *et. al.*, *Privacy and Access to Government Data for Research: An International Bibliography*, Mansell, London, 1979.

PART II

# Five Case-Studies of the Uses of Intelligence

Recognising the importance of information in the process of economic development is one thing. Mobilising this information to further a country's national goals is quite another matter, and the five case-studies presented here try to shed some light on this issue. The first three cases focus on national experiences: Egypt's difficult transition from a closed society to an open society; Jamaica's negotiations with foreign bauxite and aluminium firms; and the contrasting approaches followed by Malaysia and Sweden in building up their information economy. The fourth case-study looks at one of the most secretive groups of enterprises in the world, namely the big grain-trading corporations. And the fifth case-study looks at one of the main technologies in the intelligence business, namely remote sensing from outer space.

O.A. El Kholy's chapter ('How Egypt's Information Policy Affected Development') shows that the obsession with secrecy is ultimately self-defeating. It cannot prevent a country from concealing information about itself, and while it may render the acquisition of information by foreign firms or by the country's enemies somewhat more costly, it entails enormous economic penalties for the country which is trying to protect itself in a veil of secrecy. Excessive secrecy also means that the top decision-makers cannot find out what is really going on in their own country, unless they develop their own private sources of knowledge. Such islands of transparency in an ocean of secrecy are vitally important and played a key role in Egypt's technology acquisition process and in its negotiations with foreign firms.

In his analysis of intelligence in the negotiating process, Arnaldo K. Ventura ('Jamaica's Bauxite Battle') points to the fact the developing countries often know very little about themselves and suggests that the first important step is to bridge the gap between 'ignoring one's ignorance' and 'knowing one's ignorance'. His story of the ways in which Jamaica gradually built up its knowledge about aluminium and bauxite and used this knowledge as an instrument of negotiation with foreign bauxite firms brings to light a number of other important points. First is the critical role of the intelligence entrepreneur — in this case the Commissioner of Mines who initiated this intelligence effort as a self-appointed, one man 'think-tank' and then gradually built up a small cadre of graduate students to serve in effect as Jamaica's bauxite intelligence agency. Second is the importance of close links between the intelligence team and the decision-makers in the country. Third is the low cost of such an intelligence effort and its enormous economic benefits: the additional revenues which accrued to Jamaica as a result of its successful negotiations with the foreign bauxite firms vastly exceeded the cost of this intelligence work. This points to the fact that investments in intelligence can be analysed from the same cost–benefit standpoint as any other development project or programme.

Björn Tell's analysis of two small countries ('Scientifc and Technical Information: Sweden versus Malaysia') suggests that a country's information infrastructure, with its social networks, its people and its information-processing and -transmission equipment, forms in effect the brain of a society. With its long-standing scientific tradition, its very open attitude towards information and its sophisticated information hardware and information software, Sweden is a typical example of a country with a well-developed 'social brain'. Tell suggests that with the help of modern computer and communications technology, it is possible for a developing country to follow the same path, and he illustrates this point by looking at the development of Malaysia's scientific and technical information networks. What emerges from this comparison is that Malaysia has done many of the right things, notably in the field of physical infrastructures, but still has a number of basic weaknesses in the field of software (transparency, value systems, attitudes towards knowledge and authority, and so on). In other words, it has yet to reach the critical threshold which would allow its 'social brain' to reach its full maturity.

The chapter by Gérard Blanc on the intelligence activities of the big grain trading firms ('The Grain Traders: Masters of the Intelligence Game') can be read on two different levels: first, as an illustration of the ways in which a group of corporations in the foreign trade sector collect, use and withhold information in order to achieve their commercial objectives; and second, as a means of exploring some of the less well-known facets of the knowledge industry and the intelligence system. This 'second reading' of Blanc's chapter suggests that knowledge and information about agricultural crops, price trends or commercial contracts are not merely an input, or production factor, in the daily activities of these firms, but the very basis of their existence. Technically speaking, the grain traders belong to the service sector of the world economy, but they should more rightly be considered as actors in the knowledge industry. Blanc indirectly suggests that the power and effectiveness of these firms rest to some extent upon the fact that their intelligence capability is more comprehensive, more effective and faster to react than that of their partners, be they grain-exporting countries, national ministries of agriculture or state trading boards. When these partners are as good at the intelligence game as the grain traders — as is, for example, the Soviet grain importing corporation — they can be highly effective. The grain trading firms could in fact be considered as a model for the intelligence activities of developing countries in the wider field of commodities and natural resources.

Remote sensing from outer space is a major instrument for acquiring information about a country's natural resources, its agricultural crops or its environmental problems. This incidentally explains why the big grain trading firms are the largest customers of the private US-based photo-interpretation firms. But as J.M.M. van der Broek and J.J. Nossin show in their chapter ('Remote Sensing as an Intelligence Instrument') we are only just beginning to exploit the full potential of remote sensing. New information can be gathered extremely rapidly, at a fraction of the cost of conventional methods, and it can be continually updated. The problem facing developing nations, however, is not so much that of acquiring the necessary information as that of interpreting and using it. This intelligence problem can be solved by training interpretation specialists. One of the main centres in this respect is the International Institute for Aerial Surveys and Earth Sciences (ITC) in the Netherlands, which has trained hundreds of specialists from the developing nations. In this perspective, the ITC might be viewed as one of the important if little-known training institutions in the world intelligence system; it is also a key instrument in the building up of intelligence resources for development.

CHAPTER 7

# How Egypt's Information Policy Affected Development

## O.A. El Kholy

This chapter is the first attempt to review and analyse the 'development–knowledge' nexus in Egypt over the past thirty years which has led to a drastic change in attitude concerning information, knowledge and development.[1]

At the end of the 1950s, a movement got under way in Egypt to combine the well-established state statistical organs with the 'mobilisation committees' formed after the 1956 Suez War. By 1964 this culminated in a presidential decree establishing a Central Agency for Public Mobilisation and Statistics (CAPMAS), and the appointment of an army general at its head. The following activities became punishable offences: the publication of any statistical data not based on CAPMAS outputs; the use, hire, or purchase of statistical machinery, ranging from desk calculators to computers, without authorisation from CAPMAS; the implementation of market surveys or public opinion polls without its approval, and the use or release of the results without clearance. These restrictive measures covered an ostensibly open-ended gamut of activities, ranging from university research by students and staff in the physical sciences to national reports prepared for United Nations agencies and even the activities of commercial consulting firms. One manager of a national consulting firm was arrested for failing to seek permission to collect data on imports of tomato-paste canning machines which, it was claimed, could lead to fairly accurate estimates of the strength of the armed forces. The fact that this information was available abroad did not seem to be relevant.

---

1. For a detailed discussion see the El Kholy and MacAlister paper presented at the Seminar on 'Technology Policies in Arab States', organised by the Economic Commission for Western Asia (ECWA), Unesco, Paris, 1982.

Fifteen years later, under a bilateral aid agreement, the Academy of Scientific Research and Technology embarked on an ambitious project to establish a national scientific-technological information network. Its principal goal is 'to ensure maximum availability and optimum utilisation of accumulated knowledge in science, technology, and ultimately social sciences in pursuit of national development objectives'. Phase 1 of the project consisted of the first nationwide survey of existing information resources and their utilisation, as well as of current information needs, revealed by an elaborate, multi-tiered effort including exhaustive field work. The survey served as the basis for the design of the national information network. Clearly, then, Egypt has seen a major shift in outlook on information. Though this review was originally conceived to cover technological development only, it soon became apparent that it would have to venture into more complex, abstract fields, raising questions on such things as the decision-making process, policy and social organisation in a developing country.

None of these issues, of course, is particular to developing countries. In fact, the literature on intelligence in developed countries gives the impression of *déjà vu*. But the social context, the special complexion of these problems in a developing country and, hence, the possible remedies are, it would seem, radically different. And though the social and political systems as well as the historical antecedents and stages of development vary considerably within the Arab world, Egyptian experience in the last few decades seems to relate strongly to the situations prevailing in other Arab states.

## 1952–67: A National Embargo on Information

The 1952 Revolution in Egypt is still considered to be the beginning of a remarkable development effort marking a clear, if not clean, break from an undesirable past. It soon became clear that its two main thrusts were a land-reform programme and industrialisation. It should not be forgotten that this was a journey into the unknown; there was little, if any, previous experience of a country of this size and background to draw upon. Egypt's leaders were a small group of dedicated army officers, headed by a staff college instructor, who had no professional experience of socio-economic problems and who relied mainly on the expertise of indigenous bureaucrats, businessmen and academics, on the one hand, and foreign technical assistance and expertise from such as Point Four and A.D. Little, on the other.

Within a few years, the concept of national planning emerged. It led to the realisation that there was a real need for systematic data-gathering and analysis. The nucleus of an indigenous capability in the systematic compilation of national statistics based on carefully formulated classifications and in the theory and practice of sectoral and national planning was established and has been the seed from which all later achievements have grown.

Several influences shaped the national attitude towards knowledge. The conscious desire to break away from the past led to a distrust of past expertise. It was believed, quite logically, that reliance on the old guard could only hamper the realisation of desirable, drastic changes. Reliance was instead placed on mobilising the public in the effort to realise great achievements. If public morale was to be maintained, information would have to be controlled. This attitude was only strengthened by foreign military intervention.

Gradually a situation developed in which decisions were taken as much by revolutionary intuition as by careful analysis. Remarkable successes, achieved in a number of cases against all odds, reinforced this trend. Most notable was the success in operating the Suez Canal after its nationalisation in 1956. Though the country's technocrats accepted that canal pilots had to have almost super-human qualities and needed very long, elaborate training to do the job, the leadership refused to believe this, and indeed very young naval officers performed the job without a hitch, almost overnight.

All this took place within an authoritarian, monolithic power structure with no established procedures for monitoring change. Considerable damage could take place before the need for corrective action was recognised. Even so, it is not surprising that knowledge was not held in high esteem by the leaders of change, at least in the early revolutionary stages.

## The Technocrats' Debate

For various reasons — interesting in themselves but not relevant to our discussion here — achievements fell short of expectations, and the leadership was soon pressing for a national development plan. Specialists split into two factions. One group insisted that drafting such a plan was no mean task and that, if the plan were not to boomerang and cause yet more disappointment, it would take considerable time and effort. The other group dismissed this attitude as pedantic and actually produced the first industrialisation plan within a few weeks. Their logic was simple: needs were so obvious that no one could go wrong at this stage. The debate was essentially among technocrats, for by now leaders of the business community had dropped out of the race and the majority could not move from the micro (project) scale to the macro (national) level. The public at large was not involved or even informed. The subsequent result was that technocrats, suffered a general loss of credibility, as people became disillusioned with their 'magic' powers.

## Whom Do Political Leaders Follow When Specialists Disagree?

The Suez War, known in Egypt as the Tripartite Aggression, created an entirely new situation. Military intervention stared Egypt in the face only a few months after seventy-four years of British military occupation had come to an end. Egypt was forced to mobilise for the first time in its modern history, and it became painfully clear that there was no reliable information on the resources to be mobilised. I myself was commissioned to take over an establishment, only to find out that it had been liquidated several years earlier.

The sequestration of British, French and Belgian property, mainly in banking, insurance, trade and some industries, led almost accidentally to the creation of a public sector. This was Egypt's first experience in state management of such relatively large-scale enterprises. Also for the first time there was not a clearly defined enemy from without, who had known ties with allies within. The distinction between the 'trustworthy' and presumably ill-informed and the 'knowledgeable' and presumably untrustworthy was sharpened by this new threat and became the subject of a public debate which raged on in the mass media for several years. It was something akin to the conflict in Mao's China between 'Reds' and 'experts'.

## Secrecy: For Whom and For What?

A number of factors combined to underscore the need for more careful handling and suppression of information, till then freely available within the government system and essential for the proper drafting of plans for national action and the monitoring of the national effort. First, the full extent of the build-up of armed forces and their ambitious modernisation programme had to be kept quiet. By that time, Egypt was also committed to the active support of national liberation movements in a number of Third World countries. More relevant was the growing realisation of the need to bolster public morale in what came to be commonly known as the development battle. Success stories and national achievements had to be emphasised and perhaps slightly blown up, while failures had to be glossed over or even refuted. Washing dirty linen in public was — and still is — socially condemned; it is considered destructive and defeatist. The need for secrecy was exaggerated beyond reasonable limits and even extended to information on foreign inputs, which was freely available abroad. The absurdity of the situation was dramatically demonstrated to the country's leaders on many occasions, but the fact remained that the majority of the population, if not the outside world, was kept unaware of protected or unpalatable information.

Meanwhile, even though there was a growing realisation that information in the skilful hands of the enemy could become knowledge dangerous to national security, no systematic effort other than in the field of military intelligence was undertaken to create a national intelligence capability in the service of development.

## Who Determines How Secret a Developing Country's 'Secrets' Are?

As more and more of the 'trustworthy', particularly ex-army officers, took over the proliferating government departments and public enterprises, the practice of doctoring information became the norm. In particular, it served to hide mistakes and to play down difficulties and, hence, to belittle the knowledgeable but suspect elements in overcoming them. There were some remarkable exceptions; a number of individuals had both access to the leadership and the courage to warn it of impending disaster. Generally, however, a silent, intimidated minority came into being, who were well informed and highly critical of what was happening. What is most interesting was the attitude of the leadership, which was not unaware of this dangerous trend. Generally each leader, be he the head of state or a cabinet minister, had his own intelligence advisers behind the scenes, collecting data, analysing it and making forecasts. Even so, this was an unhealthy situation. Conflicts were not entirely objective, nor were they resolved within an open framework of confrontation and discussion. In fact, there was a tendency to compile confidential files on individuals and organisations, rather than to make a deliberate and conscious effort to remedy faults. The situation was aggravated by the absence of political parties, which might have performed the role of critics within a recognised and open power structure.

During this period, momentous decisions — such as union with Syria or military intervention in Yemen — were taken almost on the spur of the moment. In neither of these cases was there a detailed analysis of the full implications of the decision, nor the ability to cope effectively with its logical and foreseeable consequences. In all fairness, there was not much time to ponder over the issues involved before taking a decision. When Syria broke away from union a short while later, the decision to intervene by force to restore the union was reportedly rescinded after one military adviser expounded the full geopolitical implications of that decision.

## Protecting the Leaders Against Their Own Propaganda

The day of reckoning came in the mid-1960s when cheap imports of wheat — a cornerstone in the development plan — were abruptly halted. In 1965 the new cabinet admitted for the first time that all was not well and that a process of national stock-taking was called for. Two years later, Egypt experienced the trauma of the Six Day War. The national ego was brutally deflated, and heads rolled.

A new phase had started, which culminated six years later in the 1973 October War. During this period, in spite of even more pressing security needs and almost continuous military harassment causing substantial destruction, it was possible to maintain a viable economic system and continue the development effort. Simultaneously the country rebuilt an efficient, modern war machine and mobilised in almost total secrecy for what is generally regarded as an original military operation, in which new and indigenous technology made it possible to overcome what most foreign experts considered an insurmountable barrier.

## Intelligence and Technological Development in Egypt

Technological development became the major field of application of
the new intelligence and information policy of the country. During
this period, technological development was almost synonymous
with the building of a national industrial base, the framework of
which was a strategy of import substitution mainly for consumer
goods, later expanded to basic heavy industry. The term 'technology transfer' is generally used to describe such a situation, despite
the fact that technology transfer, in the proper sense of the term, is a
natural, two-way process when it occurs between industrialised
countries; imported knowledge is effectively and quickly transformed into an economic advantage exceeding the cost of transfer.

The issues involved in a developing country are considerably
more complex. In fact, a developing country is actually doing
several different things at once. It is creating a national production
base, which includes plant, equipment, raw materials, semi-finished
products, processes, management systems, qualified and trained
personnel, mainly through massive imports from abroad. This has
to be integrated in the existing body economic, and reasonably
smooth working relations with older institutions have to be established. More often than not, this proves to be a painful and dis-
orderly process. It is very difficult to turn the acquired know-how for
the physical facilities purchased into a product or service that
achieves an economic advantage. More often than not, the resulting
product or service has to be adapted to the local physical and social
environment. The technology supplier is not always willing or
capable of fulfilling this task, nor can the embryonic indigenous
expertise be expected to do so.

## Transactional Expertise or Technological Capability?

It is obvious that the first two tasks — creating a national production base and integrating it into the economy — are basically
different. What in fact was being transferred to Egypt was not
technology (know-how), but rather the products of technology
(plant and equipment). The distinction is crucial to a discussion of
intelligence in technological transactions. For example, such transactions by definition ruled out consideration of the role of intelligence in technological innovation — at least in the initial phases of

the exercise. It tended to focus attention on intelligence in the negotiating process. Even here, Egyptian experience seems to indicate that emphasis was placed on economic rather than technological intelligence, that is, on inside information and on the reputation of the supplier rather than on the technology itself.

Within a decade, Egypt had a team of fairly well-informed and skilful negotiators of commercial terms in technological transactions. The centralised structure established in 1957, which came to be called the General Organisation for Industrialisation, permitted fairly rapid accumulation of knowledge and skills. There is no doubt that a high price was paid for this learning, in the form of inappropriate choices, unfair contracts and wrong procedures. None the less, a learning process generally took place.

A systematic analysis of this experience has yet to be made, though perfunctory enquiries have yielded some impressions. In transactions with Western free-market enterprises, one of the common strategies seems to have been playing one competitor off against the other as a means of gleaning intelligence. At a later stage, when dealings with the socialist bloc became more prominent, Egyptian negotiators armed themselves with alternative offers from the West and drove remarkably hard bargains. With time, unpackaging increased, and local resources and capabilities became more involved in project implementation. Established procedures were formulated for international competitive bidding, and the analysis and evaluation of tenders. However, not enough attention was paid to the acquisition and exploitation of know-how rather than its products, or to mobilising human and material resources specifically for this purpose. One cannot help feeling that this was encouraged by most technocrats, who concentrated on managing their enterprises and on their relations with the foreign sources of know-how rather than tackling the more challenging task of national involvement in design and development of plant and equipment.

## The Concentration on Military Technology

In almost complete contrast to this was the conscious, deliberate policy adopted simultaneously in the field of military technology. In spite of many setbacks and the obvious fact that this could not possibly have a significant impact on the balance of military power in the battlefield, there was a sustained interest in the design and development of weapons systems, including military aircraft, jet engines, missiles and even submarines. A whole generation of Egyptian engineers was involved, with a reasonable degree of success, in extensive design exercises in these projects. Considerable interest was shown in technological intelligence. Brochures, periodicals, personal contacts, exhibitions and visits came to be recognised as valuable sources of technological information. Some technological spying was carried out. The software and hardware acquired was carefully studied with a degree of effectiveness. One of the more remarkable achievements at the time was the copying and batch production of a small jet engine of unconventional design.

Concentration on the war effort in the late 1960s and early 1970s meant that efforts in national infrastructure sank to a dangerously low level. The country failed to keep up with, and to introduce, developments in many fields of technology. After the October War, it was natural that an attempt be made to reorientate the national effort. This ushered in the era of the so-called open-door policy. Particular importance was attached to the role of foreign capital in revitalising the economy and, it was felt, in introducing new technologies. The joint-venture company became the magic formula for catching up. Egypt witnessed an unprecedented influx of foreign consultants who paved the way for foreign investment and new aid programmes, mainly from the West.

The opening up eventually involved information on Egypt itself, which foreign consultants had to have access to. As it turned out, they came armed with considerable information already and could ferret out more within the country with relative ease. Calling in foreign consultants became the order of the day, even in fields where national expertise had till then been considered competent. It looked, at least to leaders in many walks of life, as if a synthesis of the 'trustworthy' and the 'knowledgeable' had at last been achieved in the person of the foreign expert. Entrenched attitudes on the sanctity of information began to change, and what only a few years earlier had been considered as sensitive information now circulated more freely.

The ease with which foreign investors produced intelligence on Egyptian activities came as a mild shock to many Egyptians. Negotiators were surprised to find that their Western counterparts across the table were remarkably well informed on the economic situation of the country, had at their disposal up-to-date information on the organisational structure of the government, on the performance of

107

specific sectors and enterprises, and even on the past experience of the Egyptian negotiators themselves.

Gradually Egyptians came to realise that this was the outcome of systematic collection and analysis of published, freely-circulated information which they themselves had failed to recognise as valuable. The old belief that foreign elements in the country could use seemingly innocuous information to their advantage was now encountered in business transactions. This striking evidence of the value of raw information as a resource for producing knowledge, along with the new atmosphere of freedom in dealing with foreigners in private business transactions, set a new trend. Information centres and data banks proliferated and are now becoming the hallmark of modernity. However, there is little evidence that the newly-established information units have as yet the know-how and competence for them to play a significant role in decision-making or that this will happen in the near future.

This is borne out by interviews with top personnel working on thirty major projects in the new Five-Year Plan. It would seem that decisions are taken without insisting on the provision and analysis of information as a prerequisite for sound decisions. There is no clear comprehension of the role that an organised information system is expected to play in decision-making. There is a general feeling that the needed information is in existence somewhere within the system, but that it is not accessible, even though it is realised that outsiders succeed in obtaining it. Nor could a gate-keeper be identified in many cases. There is a strange misconception as to who should seek and use information in joint-venture companies. In many cases, it was felt that this was the responsibility of the foreign partner. Lastly, there is a willingness to invest in information systems, mainly as showpieces and particularly in up-to-date hardware. Very little attention is paid to developing the capability to assess information, analyse it and turn it into knowledge.

## The Future of Egypt's Information Policy

It is now clear that taboos and restrictions on information are slowly disappearing. Recent studies seem to indicate that the information sector in the Egyptian economy is far from insignificant. The figures compiled by the author suggest that, at the end of the 1970s, just under 16 per cent of the labour force was working in the information sector. These information workers contributed just over 28 per cent of gross domestic product. It is also perhaps true to say that there are considerable flows of information from abroad, and enough information in existence somewhere within the system. It is reasonable to expect in the light of the above that fairly adequate information systems will eventually come into existence.

One major issue, however, still remains. What use will be made of these facilities? Will there be a conscious effort to acquire the ability to turn information into knowledge in the service of development, that is, into development intelligence? In my opinion, the national business community will most probably be the first to achieve this breakthrough. A reaction is slowly building up against the swamping of the economy by foreign investments. These investments have for the most part been short-term, non-productive and of the hit-and-run type, enticed by the remarkably generous concessions offered by the open-door policy. A new class of Egyptian entrepreneur, who served his apprenticeship in the public sector and who is knowledgeable and sophisticated, is emerging; with the private sector expanding rapidly he is ready to play an active role. He appreciates the role of information and intelligence in exposing current abuses of the open-door policy, and in the careful planning and execution of its new actitivities. There should be no great difficulty in fostering the skills needed for this task. There is reason to believe that this group will exploit its social relations and prestige in redressing the balance in favour of the local entrepreneur and that life will become increasingly difficult for ephemeral foreign investment. There have already been two scandals involving investments of this type, and in both cases effective intelligence has forced the government to take drastic action, leading to the cancellation of at least one major concession.

Yet the decisive role in fostering an intelligence capability in the service of development can be played only by an aware, enlightened, courageous, dedicated and incorruptible leadership. Such leadership cannot emerge from a backward, illiterate and suppressed society. Social intelligence involves, if not a whole society, then at least substantial sectors of its elite — bureaucrats, technocrats, academics and businessmen.

CHAPTER 8

# Jamaica's Bauxite Battle

## Arnaldo K. Ventura

What characterises many developing countries is their astonishing lack of knowledge about themselves, their friends, their enemies and their technological, social, economic and ecological environment. Although a good number of these states have invested substantial amounts in acquiring data, and indeed may have reams of information at their disposal, this information often lies dormant and never seems to be processed into relevant usable knowledge. There may be libraries, documentation centres and similar institutions furnished with computers and other paraphernalia for information storage, retrieval and dissemination, but these institutions are usually not organised into a dynamic intelligence system which constantly illuminates important national problems and missions. They seem merely to adorn national prestige.

Some countries handle their information so badly that even though they undertake various surveys and feasibility studies and collect scores of reports from visiting experts of all kinds and abilities, these congeries of information lie buried in a mass of confusion only vaguely remembered when the next study or survey is contemplated. Often, it is easier to proceed with a new investigation from scratch than try to retrieve existing information.

The ability to undertake intelligence work can be rudimentary, and the level of social intelligence itself so low that recognition of the very fact that social awareness is stagnant is not clearly comprehended and accepted. So functionaries at leadership levels can remain in a sort of parochial trance about their common sense and political skill, which may have limited local usefulness but which is of little value in the broad front of development. This self-indulgent attitude obscures the fact that a surfeit of applicable non-proprietary information exists in accessible places such as ordinary libraries, but simple investments in time and effort to digest them are very seldom made. While this valuable reservoir remains untapped, dependency and sycophantic behaviour can generate an ever-increasing rhetoric about the lack of free access to knowledge. This is not to say that unwarranted secrecy and over-possessiveness regarding information by the industrialised countries does not exist, but this should not prevent the creative use of accessible information. The following example can illustrate this point. An information officer of a central organisation in Jamaica is known to have written to a European agency for information regarding pharmaceutical patents in Jamaica. The officer was duly informed that no records on Jamaican patents were available outside Jamaica, and indeed that the information could be found in the Jamaican Registrar of Companies.

In the active democratic environment of some developing countries, a good deal of intelligence gathering takes place primarily to gain local political advantage. Political tussle takes all forms, from legitimate criticisms of policies, programmes and implementation schemes to sabotage, mendacity, blackmail and subterfuge. Usually, an endless rumour campaign is sustained by a series of innuendoes, misrepresentations, hearsays and downright fabrications. As the rumours spread, confusion reigns in the land, and no longer can fact be separated from fiction, as the local media become perpetrators themselves in return for political patronage and privileges. Emotion takes over from logic and reason, and the hapless population is maintained in ignorance.

This type of local ambience militates against any decent form of social intelligence. Secrecy is impossible within the government. Each side seeks to gain advantage or score political points by disclosing the most intimate of government secrets.

Although developing countries are still rather weak in social intelligence, isolated cases of successful application of intelligence for development have been observed in these countries. One such case is the bauxite negotiations which took place in Jamaica during 1974. The relevance of an intelligence approach was amply demonstrated in the preparations for these negotiations to seek more revenues from the foreign-owned bauxite and alumina companies operating on the island. Jamaica is the third largest producer of bauxite, and this industry is the main foreign-exchange earner for the island. Also, the bauxite and alumina industry was regarded at the time as the most important economic concern in the Caribbean. The sequence of events during these negotiations highlights the

111

Five Case-Studies of the Uses of Intelligence

importance of social intelligence in a small developing country.


## Building a National Bauxite Intelligence

Two years after the coming to power of a young, innovative Third World-orientated Government in Jamaica in 1972, the six North American bauxite and alumina companies on the island were summoned to negotiations to secure more equitable returns from this diminishing resource. Eight weeks later, in mid-May 1974, these deliberations were terminated with Jamaica unilaterally imposing on these companies a production levy and a new rate of royalty and subsequently acquiring greater shares of the bauxite and alumina operations.

This occasioned a substantial increase of revenue for the island, as reflected in the fact that earnings for 1973 were J$26.8 million, while for the fifteen-month period from January 1974 to March 1975, earnings rose to J$132 million. The total cost of the negotiations was estimated at less than J$500,000 by the present director of the Jamaica Bauxite Institute, who was intimately associated with them. An analysis of the genesis, evolution, conclusions and follow-up actions to these negotiations provides a concrete example of the need for strengthening the knowledge base in poor countries and of the material gains which can accrue from small investments in intelligence.

Although it was felt among an enlightened few that the financial returns to Jamaica from the mining of bauxite were too small and that this valuable resource was not being managed in the best interest of the people of the island, hard facts to substantiate these opinions were scarce. Fortunately, a Jamaican student of mineralogy, Dr V.G. Hill, who began his career as a technician in one of the bauxite companies in 1943, took a strong interest in supplying this type of data. He later became Commissioner of Mines and continued this task by assembling a team in 1969 to review the distribution, mineralogy, chemistry and other techno-economic aspects of this important mineral. In essence, he became a self-appointed intelligencer on the Jamaican bauxite and alumina industry. He explained how his first years with the bauxite companies gave him insight into their operations and emphasised the value of the mineral to Jamaica. The respect and friendship he was able to foster were indispensable in obtaining information during the early

112

investigations.[1]

The cardinal step in this intelligence exercise was the recognition of the state of ignorance which prevailed on the island concerning the bauxite industry. Once this cognitive gap was bridged, the other intelligence functions could flow naturally.

Perusal of the old contracts between the bauxite companies and Jamaica led to the discovery that these companies had agreed to provide the Jamaican government with bauxite samples for analysis. This important find prevented scarce resources from being committed to independent drilling for samples, which were necessary to estimate the resource potential and the distribution of the mineral throughout the island. At the time, the companies regarded the Jamaican efforts to learn more about their operations as useful because additional knowledge of their plants could improve their national profile and certainly assist with their safety programmes. The local intelligence operations were therefore made easier by the shallow view the companies had of the government's intentions.

The training of bauxite specialists was well advanced by 1971, and by 1972 a mineralogy laboratory was established. By then, the fact that the economic parameters of this industry were intimately linked with technological possibilities was fully appreciated. A seminar was consequently held to exchange information between all the bauxite companies, on the one hand, and the newly emerging national intelligence group, on the other, to highlight the need for Jamaica to gain technical knowledge about the bauxite industry. During this seminar, the enlightened professionalism displayed by the Jamaicans forced frank and open exchanges, so much so that sensitive problems such as the environmental hazard of red mud[2] were scrutinised without reservation. Prior to that, such a controversial topic would not even have been mentioned. There was relatively free flow of information. This flow was facilitated by the Commissioner of Mines, who, as we have seen, had worked for many years in the industry.

From activities such as these, together with serious study and search for technological information, certain myths about the industry were exploded. The oft-repeated threat by the companies to

1. See also V.G. Hill, 'Bauxite and the Alumina Industry — Reserves and Technological Alternatives', *Minerals and Society*, vol. 1, 1977, pp. 135–47.
2. Red mud is the iron oxide-rich residue obtained in extracting alumina from bauxite. It is highly alkaline and has a tendency to seep through limestone rock formations into ground-water. It is a serious environmental hazard in Jamaica.

obtain their aluminium from other raw materials proved to be an overstatement. From technological and logistical information, it was determined that the use of clays and other rocks did not present a reasonable alternative to bauxite in the short or medium term. Likewise, the extent of the Jamaican bauxite resources had been grossly misrepresented. Instead of the reserves lasting for only twenty-five to thirty years at projected rates of mining, the deposits were estimated to be at least 100 years. Information such as this was vital to the outcome of the negotiations. However, although the team had gained some competence in manipulating technological information, their capabilities were still immature and did not allow sophisticated forecasting. Consequently, there was on their part an incomplete appreciation of the possibilities relating to the technology for the blending of various bauxites with Jamaican ore, which eventually led to a higher rate of substitution of Jamaican bauxite than was anticipated.

Meanwhile, a new, more innovative government with clearer national goals had been elected. It immediately began to take keen interest in the economics of the industry and promptly set up a national bauxite commission. This commission was an advisory body to a newly created Ministry of Mining and Natural Resources. Its functions were to review the conditions in Jamaica's bauxite and alumina industry, and to advise on the better utilisation of this resource for national development. The composition of the commission reflected the serious intent of the group, which was headed by a highly-skilled negotiator. Also included in this group were technicians, lawyers, an international diplomat of high stature, ministry officials and a high-level member of the ruling party.

To support the commission and to set the stage for more self-acquired information, students were sent abroad to gain additional experience in mineral research management and mineral economics. These initiatives were assisted by the fact that the social science department of the local university began to focus on the regional bauxite industries and their impact on Caribbean development. An important adjunct to these activities was the efforts by the Jamaican government to launch the International Bauxite Association (IBA). This eventually took place in July 1974 and its headquarters were located in Jamaica. The manoeuvres to gain support for this association were important in setting the international stage for the Jamaican negotiations.

Quietly, the commission began to accumulate detailed information on all aspects of the national and international components of the bauxite industry. So secretive was their work that the most widely read daily newspaper criticised the commission for being asleep. Since secrecy was regarded as essential, a conscious effort was made to exclude multilateral organisations like the United Nations, as well as experts from industrialised countries, from this mission.

## The Benefits of Intelligence Efforts

After just over a year's work, the commission confronted the bauxite companies for increased returns from mining and exporting the mineral. Although these developments were not a complete surprise, what shocked the companies as the bilateral discussions progressed was the substantial quality of intelligence possessed by the commission and the skill with which they were able to negotiate with each company in turn. They were thoroughly armed with the most intimate facts about the technological operations of each company and fully acquainted with their international activities. As the picture unfolded, it became clear that the bauxite and alumina companies were not simply voracious capitalists but that they were taking advantage of the country's ignorance. They were in fact basing the financial returns to the Jamaican people on the cost of operation at the local level, instead of fixing these returns on the value of the resource on the international market.

The negotiations nevertheless dragged on, until Jamaica decided unilaterally to impose a levy on the export of bauxite by the companies. Although disgruntled by this manoeuvre, the companies were forced to act judiciously because the commission had skilfully gained the support of the government of Canada and the Black Caucus in the United States, as well as other bauxite-producing countries such as Haiti, the Dominican Republic, Australia, Surinam and Guinea, which were to become members of the IBA. The clincher came when Jamaica indicated that she was contemplating hosting an international seminar to discuss bauxite management. The companies thought that such a move might prompt other countries to undertake similar intelligence actions, and reluctantly went along with Jamaica's demands.

The unprecedented success which Jamaica had in these negotiations was significantly aided by certain social and political factors. Firstly, against the background of growing global inflation, which was being further aggravated by the steep rise in the price of fossil fuels engineered by the Organisation of Petroleum-Exporting Countries (OPEC), the psychological state of the entire nation was uncompromising about better returns for the nation's most valuable mineral resource. Essentially there was no significant opposition to the principle of deriving more from the foreign bauxite companies. The former government had been discontented with the bauxite companies, and had been seriously considering reviewing the existing contracts. Accordingly, the opposition gave full support to the government when the announcement of the negotiations with the bauxite and alumina companies was made.

The most striking aspects of these negotiations were the level of professionalism on the part of the Jamaican team, the climate they created for the negotiation, and the adroit timing of the negotiations. The fact that OPEC price increases had precipitated a dire climate on the island at a time when aluminium market conditions were most favourable — aluminium prices doubled between 1972 and 1973 — and that it was coupled with an inauspicious attitude of the American government made local and foreign sympathy for these negotiations high.

The outcome of the bauxite negotiations was a major triumph for Jamaica, not only because it succeeded in extracting a more equitable return for a valuable natural resource, but also because the nation had become infinitely more knowledgeable about a business which was at the centre of its economy. Seeing the necessity to continue the intelligence functions after the negotiations, the Jamaican government removed the mineralogy laboratory and the mineral economics section of the Ministry of Mining and Natural Resources from the Civil Service and fused them into a statutory body, the Jamaica Bauxite Institute (JBI). The main purpose of this institute was to monitor the development of the bauxite industry in Jamaica.

Unfortunately, the negotiating team did not formulate adequate strategies to deal with the obvious disgruntlement of the bauxite companies and did not sufficiently anticipate their retaliation.

One of the major criticisms of the Jamaican negotiations from the local standpoint was that the national commission focused exhaustively on bauxite and not enough on the aluminium industry as a whole. Their intelligence operation was still conditioned to a certain extent by a dependence syndrome. Since the companies were mining

116

bauxite, and some alumina was processed locally, this apparently dictated the maximum horizon of the Jamaican effort.

The fact that this highly sophisticated industry could not be managed for optimum local benefit by simply maximising proceeds from the export of bauxite was not fully realised. Also, the concept of making maximum use of aluminium, the end product of the whole process, was still to gain full acceptance in national planning. Unappreciated was the fact that since Jamaica was a significant producer of aluminium, this metal should be substituted where possible for traditional but foreign metals and materials in the island's development.

An illustration of this lack of appreciation was the fact that while the preparations for the acquisition of greater knowledge of this industry were proceeding, the government of the day was installing a galvanised iron plant to use non-indigenous raw materials. This plant was set up even though operations to fashion aluminium products were small and technologically unsophisticated.

Another concept which did not receive sufficient attention was the fact that the high energy demands of aluminium production warranted linkages with friendly countries possessing cheap energy in the form of hydro-electric power or significant reserves of fossil fuels. This could allow the island to be more intimately involved in the highest stage of the beneficiating process. In other words, a partner with sufficient, cheap energy to produce aluminium from Jamaican bauxite or alumina would do so, and afterwards, quantities of the metal would be returned to the island for manufacturing aluminium products. Recent attempts to forge such links with Trinidad, Venezuela and Mexico ran into what appear to be political difficulties.

## Obstacles to Social Intelligence in Developing Countries

From the foregoing, it is clear that a number of factors militate against the development and deployment of meaningful intelligence functions in poor countries. These obstacles are enmeshed in international constraints, in culture, language, politics and illiteracy, among others. Many of these impediments have become chronic and seem to be welded into the fabric of society.

The most important action in initiating social intelligence systems is to assemble individuals to launch the systems. Although most developing countries possess individuals with the calibre to form the initial core and substance of such a system, it is not easy to identify them. Even if they exist in sufficient numbers, they are usually reluctant to come forward because of hostility and scepticism towards social intelligence. In most situations, however, the psychological and physical conditions are such that the combination of calibre, stamina, intellect, political savvy and national commitment necessary for active intelligence work is rare. It must be remembered that little educational opportunity exists for the vast majority in poor countries. Even if ample educational opportunities were provided, the small size of some of these societies make it unlikely, for purely statistical reasons, that these attributes will be found in many citizens. Also the level of poverty predisposes many to pre- and post-natal malnutrition, increased disease susceptibility, insufficient health care, and attendant reduction in mental capacities, which further reduce the possible number of 'intelligencers'.

## Cultural Incompatibility

Social intelligence can be retarded by cultural patterns and linguistic barriers to modern concepts. Patterns of fatalism, strong traditions and suspicion of modernity can act as deterrents to the acquisition of new knowledge. In cultures where religion is strong and directs daily life, the quest for new knowledge is made subservient to religious dogma. Furthermore, the knowledge explosion in the Western world has dictated that languages such as English and French are absolutely essential for convenient interaction with international knowledge sources. In many countries where these dominant languages are not widely used, only a few individuals will find easy access to recent information. This leads to privileged minorities and slow progress towards an informed public. Certain languages, because of their original roots, cannot easily accommodate new technological concepts, making communication and diffusion of these bits of knowledge difficult on a mass basis.

## Insularity

Ignorance of the effect of global influences on national development allows for a host of political and economic mistakes and misrepresentations. Behind ruses like global inflation and transportation problems, exorbitant price rises are introduced, shortages contrived and hoarding tolerated. Restrictive industrial regulations are imposed, and commercial guises become convenient tools for bribery and graft. Democracy in these instances often means the privilege to gain undue advantages. Political patronage and corruption run rife and the general level of national self-respect remains low. Great admiration for little understood foreign systems and achievements is vaunted as good reasons for mimicry, migration and dependency, while most local endeavours and standards are unceremoniously criticised and often ridiculed. Workers who labour to achieve national excellence often give up in disgust and join the brain-drain, either abroad or to less demanding but more lucrative professions at home. Lessening of national pride makes it difficult to achieve a strong social intelligence system, as lack of confidence in the present and the future derides the type of national commitment demanded for intelligence functions. Furthermore, progressive changes in the system are stoutly resisted by those in privileged positions, such as those under the umbrella of the Civil Service and those nestled in politically protected corners.

## Indifference Regarding Science and Technology

Heightened social intelligence depends on meaningful interactions between science, technology and society. The understanding by the public of these types of interconnections is relatively low in developing countries. Science and technology are therefore regarded as academic exercises unworthy of serious social attention and support. Consequently, scientific reasoning and approaches remain foreign to such societies.

The lack of a scientific tradition, and consequent pedestrian social intelligence, also hampers poor countries in their quest for foreign technologies. Not only is the selection of technologies from various options imprecise, but bargaining for them is weak. Without strong social intelligence in various departments within the public and private industrial sector, successful technological bargaining is impossible. This is a critical failing because, in the short and medium term, transfer of foreign technologies will be the most important factor in determining socio-economic improvement in poor countries.

## Change in Attitude towards the Acquisition of Knowledge and Self-Perception

Once intelligence functions are officially recognised as important tools for national development and a cadre of exceptionally gifted individuals is assembled for this purpose, installation of an intelligence system has begun. The mere realisation of the need for social intelligence is a major step in establishing such a system, because this usually requires a change in attitude towards oneself and the world community.

Countries such as Jamaica, which presumably have suffered the ill effects of covert intelligence from foreign countries and which are politically highly polarised, may react unfavourably to the news of an intelligence unit. The national character of this group therefore must be clearly understood from the outset and its creation must not be kept secret. Secrecy in a gossiping society is impossible, and it will only lead to misunderstandings of the unit's intentions. Support from all political parties and pressure groups must be sought in the nation's interest. It may be naive to believe that unanimous support will be obtained at the beginning and that the ruling party will not gain advantages which will spark jealousy. Nevertheless, it is prudent to have the widest approval of the operations of this intelligence unit. This is not to say that the activities and recommendations of this group must be given widespread publicity. What is advocated is a broad-based national sanction which will increase the unit's effectiveness.

Political and economic matters are usually emphasised in poor countries while technological, psychological, emotional, recreational and general cultural concerns attract little attention. Some information pertinent to these interests is gathered, but often without a clear national purpose and hence without the required specificity or detail. In general there must be some underlying philosophy and reason why information is being collected and catalogued. Information which is just stacked away in neat corners without continual analysis and interpretation is virtually useless. The versatility and willingness to use the system rest on the manner in which the raw data is moulded for practical use. The tendency to use exclusivity of access as a measure of importance must be curtailed. Such has been the case with scientific data, which are hammered out in public-sector institutions after great effort and expense, yet more often than not are regarded as confidential. So confidential can this information become that eventually no one has access to it as it remains classified forever, with no rules or regulations to declassify it.

A vital function of local information networks is the ability to follow unpublished data and to monitor ongoing research. This aspect of information-gathering is extremely weak in poor countries because of the fragmentary and rudimentary state of their technological infrastructures. Tradition dictates that up-to-date information is to be sought in prestigious journals from rich countries. Very seldom is it realised that data found in these publications are often several years out of date and mostly incomplete. Further, it is not unusual to find there is some familiarity with recent foreign work while that which goes on down the hall is not known. Information from countries with similar problems is not solicited with any degree of seriousness, while proposals to invest large sums in automatic data bases concerned mainly with problems of rich countries are constantly being forwarded. It ought to be pointed out that each time information is sought outside, the status of the inside is betrayed.

As stated earlier, recognition and subsequent change in attitude towards knowledge as a *sine qua non* of national development are crucial to the establishment of a social intelligence network. This incisive change in perception has to take place at the highest political level for the intelligence thrust to have maximum effect and gain full support. Politicians in poor countries are often so engrossed in urgent social problems that they are prone not to think of medium-range solutions, and simply ignore long-range planning. They are, therefore, forced to plan from positions of deep insecurity. This is especially true of the tottering democracies in the Third World where political life is short. Politicians operating in thankless societies are often totally preoccupied with their own political careers, so they are indisposed to work from knowledge and logic with national ideals in mind, but rather jump from one vote-catching gimmick to another.

## Selection and Encouragement of Intelligence Workers

Essentially, what is required for social intelligence is an enlightened head of state who is not afraid of what the 'light of knowledge' will reveal. If the head of the nation is convinced that the country cannot

121

survive as a sovereign state without exercising unfettered intelligence functions and proceeds to appoint an intelligence adviser, then a national social intelligence system will be born. The first job of the chief intelligence adviser would be to institute intelligence functions within the government bureaucracy. It must be noted, however, that a good number of government heads have various confidants and a host of advisers of all sorts and descriptions — from family favourites and in-laws to blackmailers and strong-arm-men. Facts, knowledge, honesty and logic are mortal enemies; consequently the first step of intelligence advisers will be to remove this circle of backwardness. This action will immediately remove the deluge of conflicting information and advice that is dictated by selfishness, ignorance and spite, and which now confounds national leaders. They are then more capable of making firm decisions dealing with social intelligence.

During the early stages of instituting intelligence functions, the intelligence group will be mainly concerned with strengthening local information networks, determining domestic intelligence needs and setting national intelligence targets. These tasks cannot be undertaken satisfactorily without recourse to current international knowledge. Flows of information from abroad can conveniently be augmented by foreign emissaries and diplomatic bodies. These national institutions will have to play a far greater role in information. They will have to become the eyes and ears of the national social intelligence system.

The employees of embassies, consulates, trade missions and tourist boards have to be selected on a basis other than that currently prevailing in many poor countries. No longer should the local trouble-maker, the political outcast or retiree, those with relatives in the respective countries or with a penchant for foreign tastes, or those who wish to migrate, be selected for employment in these overseas bodies. Commitment to country, aptitude for intelligence work, and strength of character have now to be considered desirable traits. Too often nationals with failing patriotism become more useful to host countries than their own land. It is no secret that before many of these individuals settle in their jobs, they are courted by the host countries. While on the job, they are showered with expensive presents and special privileges. This type of psychological barrage weakens the faint of heart and heightens the tendencies towards non-patriotism.

The intelligence advisers to top government officials will surely become the target of transnational corporations, other commercial interests and external intelligence operations in the area. These counter-intelligence operations surely will find the local intelligence system an attractive source for sensitive national information, and 'intelligencers' must be fully aware of this reality.

## Equipment

There is no doubt that human resources are the most important component of any system dealing with knowledge and development. However, it is worthwhile to point out that in the modern world, human resources alone are not enough to install a functional intelligence system. Modern equipment such as micro-computers, together with associated software and hardware to store and collate information, are also indispensable in dealing with current advancements. Furthermore, to establish priorities and allocate resources, a thorough understanding of the domestic environment is necessary so that correct questions can be posed in pursuit of development goals. Therefore, one of the first tasks of developing countries in setting up a proper intelligence system is to increase the knowledge about their local environment. This usually requires sophisticated remote sensing devices such as now operate from satellites, as well as other current diagnostic hardware and detection machinery. Without this type of basic information, the local intelligence system will be ineffective.

## Democracy

Before a social intelligence system can be realised, it is obvious that a high level of democracy must prevail. Likewise, national development must be assiduously sought by the leadership. If knowledge is to be used primarily to maintain authoritative power, then it is obvious that much information will have to be suppressed or modified. Misrepresentations of social realities lead to wasteful or damaging actions, with subsequent failure, bitterness and abuse of power.

For the intelligence advisers to install their information networks and discharge their intelligence functions efficiently, they must be given a free and unrestricted hand to conduct their duties. It is important to realise that the persons selected need not necessarily be in unison with the philosophy of the head of state or engrossed with

123

his ideological stance. In some ways, it is better that differences of opinion exist to prevent a slide into fawning relationships. However, of overriding importance is that each adviser should be fully dedicated to the policies laid down by the custodians of society.

## Promulgation of Relevant Information Policies

What has been stated so far about the minimum requirements for establishing a national intelligence unit makes it clear that the promulgation of a national information policy is paramount. This policy must be a dynamic instrument embracing all types of information and with enough resilience to deal with trends and projections at the local and international levels. The main purpose of this policy is to promote socio-economic and technological forecasting. The most effective information policy is one that gains recognition and support from every citizen and which is able to engender the feeling that each is an integral part of the nation's information network. If it is too idealistic to expect that each citizen will become an intelligence officer for his country, then at least each should become aware of the potential of knowledge. The mass media should work towards this end. For this to happen, structural and managerial changes in the local media may be necessary to ensure that the information being fed to the public from overseas does not represent the contrived impressions emanating from a few international wire services. Freedom of the press in poor countries must be seen in this context, as the media are one of the most influential means of raising the social intelligence level of a nation.

Before meaningful information policies can be promulgated, certain facts will have to be appreciated. It is useful to remember that a loose intelligence system may already be in operation. The participants in these activities may not even be aware of their role, or of the results of their actions. Since many political or financial leaders and managers in developing countries are trained abroad, there is a tendency for them not only to retain the attitudes, values and characteristics of these foreign countries, but also to defend and adhere to their objectives even if these objectives run contrary to domestic policies. It appears then that developing countries need to become more knowledgeable of the detailed workings of bilateral and multilateral agencies which ostensibly are in place to serve them.

This type of attempt to gain detailed, legitimate and vital information on the intricate functioning of international bodies, or any other entity for that matter, which can affect national development, must not be confused with spying and fifth-column work. This is mentioned because the representatives of developing countries in multilateral agencies tend to retain archaic concepts and values as vestiges of colonialism, which dictate stronger allegiance to the mystic power of foreigners and which therefore might instil reticence in dealing with them.

An important inclusion in any national intelligence system is the security forces, especially the army. The army in developing countries wields great national influence, yet it is quite vulnerable to the doctrines and dictates of external forces, mainly due to the military's dependence on software and hardware. It is important, therefore, for the local militia to take a keen interest in the socio-political life of their respective countries and become an element of the national intelligence system. This type of integration will allow for better understanding on both sides of the security fence.

Another aspect of social intelligence which requires careful thought is the intelligence functions dealing with the poor, especially the rural poor, in developing countries. Although poverty is scorned and rebuked by all, the factors which contribute to this human blight are scarcely known and those which are appreciated are improperly understood. A testimony of this is the fact that many national and international programmes to eradicate poverty have been dismal failures. Instead of reducing the number of poor people, many more each day seem to fall into this situation. The intelligence functions of any nation faced with the spectre of poverty must begin with the understanding of the dimensions and causes of this bane.

Since most poor nations depend heavily on agriculture as the basis for their economies, the rural poor must occupy a special place in the intelligence activities in these countries. Ways have to be found to redistribute land and energy so that more can participate in national development. The importance of improving traditional technologies and of introducing more appropriate agro-industrial methods must enter the intelligence equation if social intelligence is to have a clear meaning to the citizens of developing nations.

## Collective Self-Reliance

Intelligence is equally important to co-operation and trade among poor countries. These countries must be able to relate easily with one another on an intimate basis. The situation which prevails today dictates that information about poor countries is acquired by consulting the rich states. Direct connections between the developing states are often weak or non-existent. Machinery for the easy flow of up-to-date information is lacking, and misconceptions abound. This often frustrates the best intentions for co-operation.

An example of this recently occurred in the Caribbean, where one island with large deposits of limestone sought and obtained a market for this indigenous resource in another island. A contract was then signed for the supply of the material. Although it was known that the limestone was to be used as a building aggregate, the precise specification for its application was not determined, primarily because the customer was unaware of his detailed requirements. Unfortunately, the aggregate supplied did not meet the specifications of the job. This caused deep disappointment and occasioned a spate of suspicion regarding technical co-operation among developing countries. With hindsight, it was clear that if more intelligence work had been done, this mistake would have been avoided. In this case, it should have been clearly understood that the technical competence of the customer was such that he was unable to determine accurately what he required and therefore technical assistance should have been part of the contract. If this type of work had preceded the delivery, a good market could have been established for limestone, and the technical competence of both countries would have been enhanced.

## The Growth of Social Intelligence

Social intelligence, of necessity, will improve in most countries which set out seriously to attain higher levels of development. However, the way in which this improvement takes place will undoubtedly vary according to the situation in each country. It would appear from the Jamaican experience that the concept of intelligence functions will evolve slowly, starting in discrete sectors or as circumscribed necessities. The recently formed Trade Union Research Centre is such an example. This important step in social

126

intelligence was taken in Jamaica recently when, for the first time in the Caribbean, the most powerful trade unions on an island, representing six different political affiliations and ideologies, got together to establish a Trade Union Research Centre. The primary objective of this research centre will be to collect a wide range of statistics related to the national economy. The centre will collect and keep up-to-date information on wages, allowances, working conditions, company profits, employment statistics, price movements, labour legislation, as well as all the International Labour Organisation's conventions and recommendations. The basic function will be one of advice and information to enable individual unions to act from a basis of reliable information in keeping with national aspirations. The notion that intelligence functions are central to responsible labour relations has been learnt by the island's trade-union movement.

Another fact which points to the growth of social intelligence in Jamaica is that the island's decision-makers are slowly coming to realise that scientific and technological knowledge is as important as economic and political erudition in matters of development. This will not only minimise the number of faulty technological decisions, but it will open up a range of alternatives which would not be otherwise considered.

Growth of social intelligence will be determined by the number of receptive minds in a population. Therefore, an education system which offers a sound education to all citizens, starting with all children, is indispensable. This education must include all the intricacies of the technological age. The present primary school population should be viewed as an emerging new generation of enlightenment.

Success with initiatives such as these will eventually lead to similar methods being applied in other areas and the nation will come to be run on an intelligent basis.

CHAPTER 9

# Scientific and Technical Information: Sweden and Malaysia

*Björn Tell*

Few of the developing countries have realised that the opportunities held out by scientific and technical information (STI), backed up by an intelligence system, require planning and action. The activities of all those involved in the generation, collection, storage, retrieval and dissemination of information have to be integrated. Collection-building and the deployment of documentary sources — in short, library work — must be given the highest priority because knowledge in a communicable form is a prime factor for development. A comparison of what has been done in two small countries — Sweden and Malaysia — highlights the type of governmental action that can be taken to forge an STI-cum-intelligence policy.

## Information and Intelligence Systems in Enterprises

There are a certain number of analogies between intelligence systems in companies and a system to be drawn up for an entire nation. At present major firms in the industrialised countries are actively involved in setting up communications systems for the benefit of their intelligence analysts. In Sweden, firms like Volvo or L.M. Ericsson have established various elements of modern information systems, single or in combination. Information retrieval from foreign data bases, for example, is now commonly practised: in 1984 Sweden accounted for over 30,000 terminal hours on foreign data bases containing STI. Some perform daily searches of European and American data bases to keep abreast of the latest developments but also for such factual data as molecular structures or the prices of commodities. Hundreds of companies have applied for passwords to Sweden's public data network that was recently set up. Many Swedish company headquarters keep in touch with their affiliates or subsidiaries through tele-conferencing, or by what is known as 'informatic performance'. Conferencing by television links is carried out between major cities and can save a good deal of time compared with meetings to which colleagues must travel long distances. Now and then, of course, Swedish multinationals like Atlas Copco deem it necessary to call the representatives of their international network to seminars or workshops at headquarters. These are occasions for an exchange of views in which field intelligence can be confronted with the policies and performance of the parent company. At such meetings, a whole gamut of problems, from research and development (R&D) practices to financial and marketing prospects up to the year 2000, are tackled.

STI is now available to the public, but in order to tap data bases, intermediary information officers who know the system's mechanics — passwords, command language and the like — are still in short supply. Unfortunately few people care to learn them. Management intelligence also collects information from intermediaries outside the company, to which it adds internal information. It then digests and analyses the information and elaborates a synthesis of alternative actions for decision-makers. This task calls for an intermediary of a higher calibre than an information officer, namely a gate-keeper or middleman, to borrow the term used by Alvin Weinberg in his 1963 report on information to the President of the United States. It is the gate-keeper who synthesises information for policy and action. In some Swedish firms, such middlemen have the rank of directors so they can channel intelligence directly to members of the board.

## Government Action to Promote the Knowledge Industry

Small industrialised countries like Sweden are characterised by a large number of small and medium companies which, unlike multinationals, cannot afford the luxury of having their own comprehensive information systems. To improve the country's overall procurement of STI, the government must implement a policy designed for industrial enterprises as well as for universities and other public and private bodies engaged in R&D. For the moment, Sweden is one of the few countries to have taken action.

To set the Swedish government's information policy in context, it is useful briefly to review the infrastructure of its knowledge industry. Over the centuries, Sweden built up a network of libraries, archives and census bureaux, among other institutions, that serves both the government and decision-makers at all levels as well as the average citizen. The Royal Library dates back to 1611, followed a few years later by the National Archives. The first general census was taken in 1794. The libraries at the University of Lund and the University of Uppsala were set up in the Middle Ages; in the seventeenth century, they were given the right, along with the National Library, to receive copies of every Swedish publication, a grant that was later extended to all university libraries.

This progressive development of libraries and archives created a pattern of information supply disseminated in various centres. Over the years co-operative ventures were launched, resulting in country-wide loans of publications and, more recently, of photocopies between public and private libraries. Joint library catalogues, first drawn up in the nineteenth century, have since become a key to knowledge held in physically dispersed collections.

On the regional level, the Scandinavian countries, although separated by different languages and traditions, have learned to work together. They collaborated on the setting up of a document procurement centre, SCANDOC, in Washington, DC, that has enhanced their opportunities to exploit STI generated in the United States.

Sweden's infrastructure also facilitated the establishment of a national computerised system, LIBRIS, which offers a unified catalogue of books and periodicals. Earlier investments in telephone lines paid off handsomely when the Nordic packet-switched network SCANNET was introduced; in this way, information retrieval on-line can continue to grow.

Sweden's long tradition in information collection certainly presented advantages. However, when it comes to introducing new technology, this is not necessarily an advantage, for there may be entrenched resistance to change. The fact that Malaysia only recently entered the knowledge industry is therefore not necessarily a drawback.

## Malaysia: A Young Information Network

At the turn of the century, Malaysia was still a book-poor society. Most of its historical documents were to be found primarily in

Portuguese, Dutch and British archives. The British had established the Raffles Institute in Singapore in 1823, followed by King Edward VII College of Medicine in 1905 and Raffles College in 1929; these institutions were merged to form the University of Malaya in 1949. Even so, when the country gained independence in 1957, the number of books in the entire country was less than that of a single large library in Sweden.

The new government, through the national plan, took action to increase the number of institutions of higher learning and libraries: the Cabinet established Sains University in 1969, the National University in 1970, the University of Agriculture in 1971 and the Institute of Technology in 1972. The universities were all given funds to build up what are today impressively comprehensive, up-to-date libraries.

## The Implementation of an STI Policy

If a country wants to become more information-efficient, the government must lay down a policy that will ensure easy access to world sources of STI and to take stock of what is available and what is needed for such a system. In 1965, the Swedish government promoted a bill declaring STI a national resource, comparable to raw materials, capital, energy or labour. It therefore was directly implicated in promoting the acquisition, processing and dissemination of STI. This opened up new possibilities for projects that aimed at efficient transfer and use of STI.

The government's reasoning was quite simple. Sweden depends heavily on a steady influx of new ideas; domestic research accounts for a meagre 1 per cent of the world research output. The rest, generated abroad, is essential if Swedish researchers are to develop the country's science and technology. Moreover, since the 1950s, the public sector had been actively involved in computers and data processing, so that trained personnel and suitable hardware were available to process computer tapes with STI content that were just beginning to appear on the market.

Thanks to government initiatives, computerised retrieval services for medicine, scientific research and industry were started in 1967, following OECD initiatives to promote such tape services. Unlike Malaysia, Sweden had more trained manpower and hardware available for processing STI tapes, but the price of this early start was

131

heavy investment in hardware utilisation and the construction of programme packages for information retrieval.

In those days, the work had to be carried out on large computers, and optimal programming for efficient search evolved slowly on a trial-and-error basis. Since then computers have come down drastically in price and size, so that today any country can afford to buy computer power for STI intelligence purposes. International organisations and private firms now provide powerful software packages. Moreover, the pioneering work done by Sweden to set up a tailor-made network by telecommunications in what is known as a packet-switched mode was far from easy. The technique is now tested and proved, and can be applied to any telephone network.

The starting point of all this development was the Swedish government's awareness of the need to take initiatives. It was the government that commissioned background reports for decision-making and made them public, producing the necessary bills and funding to start up a new kind of STI service.

In Malaysia, such an awareness seems to be slowly emerging. The National Library Act, passed in 1972, contains a promising clause: the library is 'to promote and co-ordinate the development and use of library resources of the nation'. With this in mind, the Chief Librarian called a meeting in 1974 to discuss the feasibility of using magnetic tapes produced by the British Library as a substitute for cataloguing. In conjunction with the Malaysian National Commission for Unesco and its permanent delegation in Paris, he urged Unesco to choose Malaysia as the host country for a pilot project — a research-library network that could serve as a model for all of South-East Asia. As a result, Unesco set aside $45,000, which was more than twice the amount that the Swedish government had allocated to the Royal Institute of Technology in 1967 to set up a computerised STI service.

To date, the Malaysian government has concentrated on collection-building in academic libraries. For a few years, the funding made it possible to add from 20,000 to 30,000 books a year to each library. This is a spectacular figure, compared with the low rate of collection-building in such countries as Indonesia or Greece. As far as policy action for STI was concerned, the government began by setting up a committee for the establishment of a Malaysian Information System. A large computer was installed in a government building with the stated aim of introducing a management information system, which has, however, proved to be less effective than

132

envisaged. Despite these pioneering efforts, it would seem that the government has not yet fully understood the impact it could have in organising an orderly access to STI.

## Managerial Choices of Government Action

What managerial practices can a government adopt to enter the era of information technology? Sweden, for example, got off to a modest start in two institutions, the Royal Institute of Technology and the Karolinska Institute. The government set up a grant-giving body in order to get things going in the right direction. In retrospect, part of Sweden's success can be attributed to the competition that reigned between the two centres. They had to prove their effectiveness in order to attract funding to train additional manpower capable of handling the new technology.

With a show of both ingenuity and know-how, the Karolinska Institute implemented a system called MEDLARS by applying a Honeywell search programme to an IBM system. As for the Royal Institute, it undertook the construction of completely new search systems, such as ABACUS, VIRA and BRIP, which were later run by centres abroad. In 1972 on-line search services were introduced, and since then the interactive, on-line services have grown steadily.

Industry was willing to co-operate in these initiatives, and government funds were deployed for decentralisation. Sweden's participation in the Scandinavian Council for Applied Research resulted in the initiation of the packet-switched network, SCANNET, a precursor of the Swedish public data network, which made it possible to build up to tens of thousands of terminal hours on various host computers in Europe and the United States.

In Malaysia, industry in the Penang area was given access to the content of scientific and technical journals and reports through a manually operated system called MIDAS, run by the University of Sains. In 1980 Unesco and Malaysian universities funded a project to make the changeover to a computerised service. A Canadian software package was installed, and an experimental Selective Dissemination of Information (SDI) was started, using such data bases as Chemical Abstracts, BIOSIS Previews and Food Science and Technology Abstracts.

Unfortunately, the Malaysian government was not forthcoming with funds so that it was not possible to take advantage of an

unexpected opportunity: in Singapore, TYMNET installed a connection point, or node, which could have connected any terminal
user with host computers in the United States. In 1979, it was
demonstrated in Kuala Lumpur that, by means of telex, it was
possible to gain access to the Lockheed and Systems Development
Corporation information systems in California. Today, telex facilities are available in university libraries, but are restricted to inter-
library and inter-university communications. Compared with the
high cost of collection-building in Malaysia, that of new data-
processing and telecommunication technology should not prove to
be a barrier, if it were realised by these means, collections could be
effectively deployed.

Meanwhile, the obstacles to be overcome are of two kinds,
conceptual and financial. University authorities have set aside funds
to continue the experiment with this new technology, in addition to
seed-money from Unesco, which recognises the importance of this
endeavour. However, to obtain government funding, the costs and
benefits of the service have to be demonstrated. The best way to do
this is through a user survey.

Generally speaking, a new service can be appreciated only if its
merits are demonstrably proved. That is why the Swedish SDI
service was run free of charge for more than a year. A similar service
would be more than justified in a developing country. For the
moment there is scant awareness in Malaysia of just how useful an
SDI system could be. The country still has a long way to go before
STI becomes decentralised and available to various socio-pro-
fessional categories.

That operations in Sweden are more advanced and efficient than
in Malaysia seems to be due in part to the lack of clear-cut governmental policy and funding. If new priorities were set, Malaysia
could be just as efficient as Sweden, for it has the manpower and the
know-how.

There is also the question of how these countries perceive their
future. If the development of industry and society is to be effective,
and if investments are to be put to the best use, a detailed plan of
preparedness is necessary. In Sweden, short-term forward planning
and longer-term strategic planning receive substantial commitments. Planning is widespread, and planners try to get information
from a variety of sources.

The prevalence of team organisation, research groups, working
committees and participatory democracy in the management of

public and private enterprises gives many people the chance to air their views, so that a consensus can be reached. Individuals can interact and reinforce one another's creativity and productivity. Sweden is one of the most open societies in the world; there is a free flow of information and exchange among decision-makers both in government and in private firms. Compared with many developing countries, decisions can rapidly be translated into action.

Even if the government of Malaysia is aware of the benefits of an open society, there are too many constraints of a political nature for it to move very fast in this direction. Planning generally takes place through the 'old pro' network, and the layer of decision-makers is thin, concentrated as it is in the upper echelons of the hierarchy. This seems to be the only explanation for the fact that the status quo is so slow to change. Top management continues to adhere to such traditional norms as a strong hierarchical structure, and there seems to be some unwillingness to accept the fact that a certain amount of tension or even conflict is inevitable. In view of Malaysia's history and its relations with other Asian countries with different ideologies, this is quite natural. None the less, it does hamper the exchange of information; newspapers or books with political overtones risk being censored or put on the index.

Sweden is taking advantage of the transparency of other industrialised countries; researchers regularly browse and select what is in their data banks for new technological developments. The importance of such an intelligence function has not yet surfaced in Malaysia, with the exception of inter-office dissemination of knowledge in the rubber-production sector and at the University of Sains.

Several reasons account for this delay. First, information workers in libraries and documentation centres have low social status. Young professional librarians, who have been trained abroad and who could serve the country's intelligence function, are regarded merely as book custodians. Second, a good deal of the work done in libraries is subject to complicated international cataloguing rules, which results in low productivity. Third, a monolithic power structure tends to put faith in shortcuts, by means of appropriate technology. If the present downgrading of expertise continues, it will no doubt prove very difficult for Malaysia to cope with the enormous problems ahead.

Moreover, many people in Malaysia, like those in other developing countries, continue to believe that Western countries are deliberately withholding important STI from them, as was attested by the United Nations Conference on Science and Technology for Development in 1979. When one looks at what has been done in Sweden, this seems to be a misapprehension of the present state of affairs. The fact is that, given the transparency of the industrialised countries, it is quite possible to obtain access to STI.

A case in point is the action Sweden took to solve its information needs on environmental questions. In 1974 the Swedish Council of Environmental Information was established with the aim of building an information centre to serve citizens and public bodies. One of its tasks was to study the relation between job environment, urbanisation and such other external factors as dangerous or toxic substances. It was also to act as an early warning system by notifying scientists or special interest groups about changes in the environment. A third task was to provide back-up information for new legislation or other policy activities.

STI from foreign information systems was to be utilised, along with that of national data bases. From the outset, special support was given to the library, to documentation and records management. The latter was deemed important, for a good deal of information is contained in public records about occupational safety and health.

The environmental analysts had to dig up information, compile new statistics about health hazards and review the relation between certain substances and teratogenic effects. At the international level, the analysts were to screen information which could be contributed to the United Nations Environment Programme, as well as to its information system, INFOTERRA, and to IRPTC, a system identifying potentially toxic substances.

In addition to creating a single, comprehensive data bank for Sweden and ensuring wide access to it, the analysts had to validate the information gathered and compare it with other information sources, such as ENVIROLINE and BIOSIS. The system eventually grew into a number of data bases.

This example of how Sweden went about solving its environmental information problems clearly shows that the new technology offers any country the chance to provide STI more efficiently, more fully and at lower cost than was previously possible.

A number of similar services are now operational in Sweden. There is a system for the preparation and tracking of legislation, a data base of case law accessible on-line to the courts and to the Department of Justice so as to improve its legislative work. A system for a land-utilisation data base, developed at Uppsala University, is now run on an experimental basis at the University of Sains in Malaysia.

Modelling systems for intelligence analysts and decision-makers have also been established. For example, in the energy field, a user can define the values he wants to attach to a number of parameters — say, the desirable ratio between coal, oil, nuclear and hydroelectric power, the expected price structure, the capacity of the generating units and a forecast of future energy consumption. Using the present energy balance as a basis, the system will give the number of heat-generating plants or the number of coal-burning plants needed, for example. In this way, environmentalists can comprehend the magnitude of scale to be taken into account.

At present, systems and data bases are fragmented and accessible only if a user takes the trouble to find out how each one works, that is, if he learns the passwords, the command language and operating procedure. Should a problem come up, he may have to browse through more than one data base.

To overcome such problems, Sweden would have to set up a function whose purpose it would be to organise a gateway to all the available but scattered systems, so that politicians, decision-makers and other interested parties could find the pertinent information about a specific problem area. Users should not have to worry either about the mechanics of getting at information nor about its credibility or exhaustivity. Instead they should be able to spend more time on creative thinking.

What is needed is a function for social intelligence, in which knowledge professionals are legitimated to operate STI systems. Sweden has set up a mechanism on the highest level — the Delegation for Scientific and Technical Information, under the Ministry of Education — to investigate this question.The Delegation also acts as an umbrella organisation for liaison activities with Scandinavian and international bodies.

## Lessons to be Drawn from the Swedish Experience

The establishment of an intelligence function to take advantage of the present information transparency in the industrialised countries is certainly needed in the developing countries. The Swedish experience shows that almost all the information needed for national planning is available from sources open to the public, that is, once a country has taken the necessary steps to acquire it.

There is no reason not to be optimistic about developments both in Sweden and Malaysia. Though a small country, Sweden has made considerable progress towards improving its provision of STI, even if still more has to be done to unify the fragmented system of its data bases. Till now, the government of Malaysia seems to have been so preoccupied with day-to-day operation and collection-building that it has not had time to give its full attention to the new opportunities. When this happens, it will no doubt take initiatives that will lead to change.

What has been said about Sweden and Malaysia can be applied to other countries. The question is, how to set up a structure that suits the developing countries? As the United Nations Conference on Science and Technology for Development showed, this is a matter of international concern. The heavy stress on setting up a single national focal point may be good advice, but it may halt further developments in countries where there is a weak STI infrastructure. It is equally important to stress the need for setting up ministerial networks for a social intelligence function, into which libraries, documentation centres and information analysis centres could be integrated. The need to build up academic libraries and to promote library networks is amply demonstrated by what has already been accomplished in Malaysia.

One possible approach would be to set up a few centres in the developing countries along the lines of the Swedish model. These centres could grow into centres of excellence. One could be located in a country like Malaysia, which could provide the necessary support in terms of equipment, maintenance, supplies, postal services, telecommunications links and the like. If the centre were an international venture, it could attract highly qualified and experienced staff for system analysis and networking. Some of the costs could conceivably be recovered by charging for services. Taking its inspiration from the successful co-operation among the Scandinavian countries, international activities could concentrate on regional development, say, in the South-East Asian region. Progress in one country could then be used as a model to enhance development in other countries, so that the combined resources of the entire region could be put to use.

# CHAPTER 10

# The Grain Traders: Masters of the Intelligence Game

## Gérard Blanc

Very few studies on hunger and food policy have devoted much attention to the key role played by information in the world grain trade. Yet a handful of commercial companies have for over a century recognised, consciously or not, that the production and use of timely, open or secret knowledge is fundamental. These grain companies have developed an excellent intelligence system and have succeeded in turning secrecy into a social intelligence resource. They are often better informed than governments.

The development of their intelligence network, its organisation, daily operations, manpower and strategy offer ideal case studies of corporate and, more generally, commercial intelligence. It shows how modern technologies, in data collection and processing or in other seemingly distant technical fields, are followed — and sometimes anticipated — without neglecting 'softer' intelligence activities on political, economic and socio-cultural factors.

Similar studies could be made for other major agricultural commodities or, with few changes, for minerals. Indeed, the elements contained in the grain intelligence policy presented here are of interest to other countries, which could benefit from the sometimes costly lessons of the grain industry.

## Grain Sources, Demand and Supply

Grain production is determined by climatic and geographical factors that are much less diverse than those of other basic resources. Wheat accounts for about one-quarter of world grain production, and the major producers are located in temperate or cold climates:

the Ukraine and Western Siberia in the Soviet Union, the Great Plains in the United States and Canada, Western Europe, Argentina and Australia.

Thanks to technical advances, total world production nearly doubled between 1950 and 1970, rising from 690 million tons to 1,240 million tons; by 1981 it reached 1,670 million tons. But there are still great discrepancies between industrialised and developing countries.

The world demand for grain has increased not only because of growth, but also because of changing food habits. While direct per capita demand seems to be decreasing in relation to per capita annual income in industrialised countries, it is largely compensated for by indirect demand to produce meat, poultry, dairy products, and the like. By the early 1970s, animals consumed about as much of the annual world grain harvest as humans did; livestock and poultry in the United States and the Soviet Union alone accounted for 20 per cent of the total production. In Africa, Asia, and Latin America, new tastes, and especially the habit of eating Western-style bread, have changed national grain balances. These countries, which are not well suited to wheat cultivation, saw their position shift from net grain surpluses prior to the Second World War to massive shortages a generation later. In 1973 and 1974, these countries imported $6 billion worth of food, most of it grains.

The grain business is very special. Unlike most other commodities, it is not easy to pinpoint who is in control of the world grain economy. The United States accounts for between 40 and 50 per cent of total grain sales, but it is the only major producer that does not have a special agency, authority or marketing board to supervise or handle grain imports and exports, which are left entirely to commercial companies. The offshore operations of these companies make it very difficult to tell who is selling what to whom and above all at what price. In fact, there is no straightforward answer since, at any given time, there can be hundreds of prices for wheat, corn or rice throughout the United States and around the world.

However, some long-term trends are discernible. Until 1971 grain prices declined steadily with no major fluctuations, but the market suddenly reversed, and by 1973–4 prices spurted to their highest level since the Second World War. Local harvest fluctuations, adjusted through commercial channels, have a relatively strong impact on prices, especially in the absence of an international system to stabilise them.[1]

## The Most Discreet Corporations

For nearly a century five giant companies — Cargill and Continental in the United States, Louis Dreyfus in France, André in Switzerland and Bunge in Argentina — have quietly but efficiently operated at the heart of the grain trade. The first book to shed some light on their activities was *Merchants of Grain* by Dan Morgan.[2] Not surprisingly, a Cargill brochure in the early 1970s boasted that 99 per cent of their customers had never heard of them.

Before the huge 1972 American wheat sales to the Soviet Union, most people knew nothing about these companies, which could trade a cool 10 per cent of American wheat in a single, multi-million dollar transaction. According to Dan Morgan, Continental's president-owner Michel Fribourg would 'rather lose a million dollars than get his name in the papers'.

The classic image of a multinational corporation is one of anonymity and hazy, intricate links with other multinationals. But if there is one question about the grain business that is easy to answer, it is 'who owns them?' This is not a secret, for it is the very families that founded the grain companies more than a century ago. Though they now rank among the largest multinational corporations, two of them are still the largest privately held companies in the United States and a third is one of the largest in the world.

This unique structure of private ownership may be accidental or it may reflect the very nature of the grain business. As large amounts of capital were not necessary to start operations, outside shareholding partners were not needed, unlike the oil business or manufacturing. The main assets of these companies — connections and experience — are not material, and so they were able to finance their own growth and remain compact, family-controlled businesses, in spite of the size of their transactions.

The companies soon discovered that this was a distinct advantage: the absence of public stockholders made detailed financial reports unnecessary. This enabled them to move money around easily and gave them a certain degree of immunity from official investigations. Even after a failure or a major loss — which can sometimes happen — they are able to withdraw behind their curtain of privacy.

---

1. For further data see Thomas Grennes, Paul R. Johnson and Marie Thursby, *The Economics of World Grain Trade*, Praeger, New York, 1978.
2. Dan Morgan, *Merchants of Grain*, Viking, New York, 1979.

Transactions affecting world grain supplies are often kept quiet for months, and even if the deals later become public knowledge, the actual prices paid are often known only to the companies themselves. Information about the companies' finances is perhaps even better guarded; Cargill first publicly announced its sales and profits in the *Wall Street Journal* only in 1973. And the announcement itself was as much of a surprise as the figures: net sales of $5.2 billion, net income of $107.8 million and net worth of $352 million for the previous fiscal year!

A bit of intelligence work on the companies themselves gives some idea of their mastery of information management. It shows how they have built up their global corporate intelligence and how they have become experts in the art of risk management and using secrecy as a resource, even managing to outwit the United States government during critical negotiations with the Soviet Union.

## The Companies' Global Intelligence Service

The grain companies have never owned vast plantations or costly physical assets, but this lack of control has not proved to be a drawback. Their assets are intangible and more powerful: speed, mobility, instant world-wide communications and superior information, which is then turned into operating knowledge. They run these intelligence services all over the world like 'private news agencies that never print a word'. It is these qualities that have made them indispensable to governments everywhere.

Cargill headquarters in Minneapolis resembles the central command post of a huge multinational army. The company boasts 140 affiliates or subsidiaries in thirty-six countries. No matter where money is to be made, the decisions are taken there in the Minnesota woods. It operates a network of offices overseas, gathers information, keeps in touch with its emissaries in dozens of countries, channels money to far-off places and assesses the impact of political, financial and economic development on its foreign operations. Cargill has its own private computerised telegraph system that links 250 locations in North America and sixty abroad in thirty-six different countries.

Like all the other companies, Cargill maintains its own steady flow of information, receiving more than 14,000 messages a day (which means a staff of thirty people, if only one minute is needed to process each message!). The men working on the wheat, corn or oats desks in the trading rooms of these big firms are on the look-out for news: almost any event in the world could potentially affect grain prices, with a reaction delay much quicker than in any other commodity, agricultural or industrial. Tradax, Cargill's overseas subsidiary in Geneva, is positioned to take advantage of a myriad of variables affecting the internal price of European Community grain, minute fluctuations in harvests or international exchange rates.

By the size of their global operations, the big grain companies have managed to turn information into a real productive asset. Economies of scale arise in the co-ordination of information from multiple sources and the execution of transactions based on that information. Two special features of these information networks contribute to these benefits. First, fixed costs of acquiring information (in a stock or flow form) can be spread over numerous transactions. Information needs may thus yield increasing returns. Second, in markets with continuous and rapid fluctuations, information is highly perishable, and the trader must act upon it instantly to realise its value. Hence there are economies in the continuity of a trader's activities.

Access to information is only one part of grain intelligence. Equally important, companies have the people and the expertise to interpret the data. Some of their highest-paid employees are likely to be world travellers who at any given moment have a pretty good idea of what the year's crops are like and whether a particular country will be buying grain. Actually, an overall picture of what is really happening in the grain economy on any given day can be gained only by synthetising thousands of data, which only the multinationals are capable of doing.

Working simultaneously in different countries, the grain companies, like many other multinationals, can make money on price and exchange-rate fluctuations. But unlike many other multinationals, price is a permanent question mark. Only the major companies are able to know what is really going on because they are simultaneously buyers and sellers. All the grain companies came to recognise the need for a global strategy, and thanks to their foreign subsidiaries in Panama, Geneva, Seoul or Buenos Aires, they can play the game and operate freely.

*Five Case-Studies of the Uses of Intelligence*

## Building Up Corporate Intelligence

The grain companies began to build up their corporate intelligence more than a century ago. In the 1860s, a Minneapolis trader perpetrated one of the very first acts of industrial espionage in the grain sector by copying and improving on a Hungarian flour-milling technique.

At the end of the nineteenth century, the grain barons prospered from the growth of American business and advances in agricultural technology which helped increase yields considerably. But the rapid spread of new communications and transportation were the key factors in their success. Chicago offices were already flashing prices to the corn belt by wireless in the 1900s. By the 1920s, good timing and logistical expertise determined profits in the grain trade. For New York exporters, good communications, connections and knowledge of the European markets were what counted most.

Another aspect of corporate intelligence was the development of what can be called legal intelligence, or the art of finding loopholes in the law. This is not specific to grain multinationals, but they were pushed faster and further in this direction because of increasing national and international regulations. One company, Louis Dreyfus, has created an entire division to grapple with the complicated financial rules of the European Community. At the national level, American companies, by their determination, their lobbying and superior information, have been able to shape, to a not inconsiderable degree, the laws in their home country.

It is patently clear that grain trading companies have understood that this aspect of corporate intelligence is an ongoing process, constantly requiring new inputs. Though it is very difficult to know exactly what is happening inside such discreet firms, it would seem that an increasing part of their manpower is devoted to this building up of corporate intelligence.

## Risk Management is the Name of the Game

Grain companies are one stage beyond the production process, and they have always tried to offset unpredictable fluctuations. Whether prices are going up or down, they generally succeed in making money, carefully hiding the occasional failure.

Mastery of the two major unknowns of the grain trade —

production and prices — has been achieved by a variety of intelligence techniques. Prices present no great problem: it is easy to know the spot price for the wheat that farmers are selling to grain elevators in the United States. But the closing price at which international transactions are made on any given day is next to impossible to learn, except for a few big importers and government marketing boards. The large trading companies have been able to penetrate the top levels where prices are determined, first by being both sellers and buyers, and next by becoming members of the committees which set them.

The other side of risk management is crop forecasting. In the 1850s, at the height of the Californian wheat trade to Europe, Isaac Friedlander developed one of the very first systems for estimating and forecasting the size of the California crop. His agents and intelligence sources fanned out through California each spring to collect crop estimates. He was thus able to rent the right amount of ships at the best price and keep control over ocean shipping, which was the key to the trade.

Nowadays, the big companies have once again been able to put themselves in the best possible position to predict fluctuations. They all use professional weather services that keep track of daily rainfall everywhere in the world. Reports from private professional crop forecasters receive careful attention and are checked and cross-checked. Computer models and predictions for wheat and corn have proved to be a good investment, for many have turned out to be extraordinarily accurate. Grover Connell, one of the big American rice traders, was one of the first to understand the potential of such intelligence investments. He did not buy processing plants — important in the rice trade, contrary to other grains — mills or grain elevators, but invested rather in computers and hired the most expert merchants he could find. By the end of the 1960s, his company's computer model for predicting crops, food supply and demand was being consulted by government agencies. The grain companies were in fact the first to see the exact benefit they could derive from computer models.

## A Monopoly on Inside Information?

At first glance it would seem that a handful of big grain companies enjoy a monopoly, not on the material goods which they trade but on inside information that no one else can get. Governments rely on them for information about grain transactions taking place all over the world. As an American Assistant Secretary of Agriculture put it in 1976: 'There is a public US interest in supporting the companies. They are the ones who keep us posted as to what is going on all over the world. Their system is ahead of our system.'

The grain trading companies have been criticised for concealing information. This is true to some extent, but a great deal of information is in fact available to the public. Newspapers, commodity news tickers and statistics collected by international agencies all provide the pieces needed to fit together the puzzle of the world food situation. None of the news items cleared by grain analysts around the world is especially confidential. All that is needed to put them to advantage is the expertise and organisation to get them in time, sort them and take the appropriate decisions. With the rise of new techniques like remote sensing and computer models, world grain situations and forecasts could be available at a reasonable cost to anyone. Where, then, does the companies' purported monopoly on information lie?

## Secrecy as a Resource

'Whatever the source of their anxiety, their secrecy was part of their means to alleviate it, part of their knack for survival.'[3] Grain companies understand the power of secrecy. Their executives justify their firms' policy of not publicising their transactions. According to the Vice-President of Cargill: 'What commercial secrecy prevails in the grain export business is not an attempt to conceal from the public facts in which they have a legitimate interest, but rather to protect individual exporters from commercial disadvantage in a highly competitive, narrow-margin business'.

As they have grown and diversified, the companies' code of conduct has been to keep a low profile and to conceal as well as possible their wealth and power. They are reluctant to advertise their strategic importance in the seed distribution system, for example, and they refute the idea of playing a central role in the international economy. This attitude is not unique to private corporations; it seems to be part of the game in the grain trade. The Canadian Wheat

3. Ibid.

Board, a quasi-governmental monopoly, is often as secretive as they are, never revealing the price it gets for Canadian wheat and justifying its secrecy as 'protecting the interests of the prairie wheat farmers'. Purchasing agents of the socialist countries and the Soviet Exportkhleb agency are not exceptions to the rule. There is a consensus at almost all levels. The principal grain trade magazine, *Milling and Baking News*, never reveals the identity of the companies involved in the transactions it reports.

The companies' determination to keep their activities secret goes a long way. In 1963 the major trading companies met in Ottawa to try to determine a common attitude *vis-à-vis* offers. But wariness and suspicion prevailed; the grain cartel never got off the ground, for it might have disclosed too much secret information.

## The Realities of Food Politics

Socrates said: 'No man qualifies as a statesman who is entirely ignorant of the problems of wheat'. The story of the Soviet Union's massive grain purchases in the 1960s and 1970s and the way the companies outwitted the United States government illustrates how effectively grain intelligence can be used. Although the Soviet Union is the largest wheat producer in the world, the size of its harvests fluctuates considerably from one year to the next, and the country sometimes has to resort to massive imports, which put heavy pressure on the world wheat market. In 1963, Canada sold the Soviet Union 6.8 million tons of wheat for about $500 million. It was the first time that the Soviet Union relied on foreign imports to offset a grain shortage. The companies understood the importance of this policy shift and realised that it would be the unknown factor in world grain markets. They therefore began to monitor the Soviet crop situation. In 1972, the Soviet Union was facing a shortage of corn for livestock. In one of the biggest grain transactions in history, Continental offered a bargain which took the American government completely by surprise.[4] In 1975, the Soviets negotiated even more secretly and were able to buy over 12 million tons of North American grain, despite the Ford administration's firm intention to get some political advantage from the grain.

4. The 1972 grain deal is described in detail in James Trager, *The Great Grain Robbery*, Ballantine, New York, 1975.

While the Soviets have long understood the realities of food politics, the American government was slow to realise the inefficiency of Soviet agriculture and underestimated the Soviet Union's grain needs on the world market.[5] The trading companies are in a better position to know what the Soviets will do than the Central Intelligence Agency, the US Department of Agriculture, the Economic Policy Board or other American agencies, which are perhaps too numerous and badly co-ordinated. The grain traders can provide the services the Soviets need: access to grain all over the world, as well as secrecy.

The Soviets therefore went to the companies, and not to the American government, to negotiate with the best-informed people, at the highest level and without any risk of disclosure. Besides, they found themselves dealing with an organisation which was much more familiar to them than the American agencies. The way in which the grain companies operate strongly resembles that of Exportkhleb, the Soviet agency in charge of the grain trade, with its discretion, secrecy and hierarchical structure. Or perhaps is not the contrary true? The Soviets have given their agency a degree of freedom far greater than that of their other bureaucracies, because this might well be the most efficient way to operate.

## Modern Tools for Grain Intelligence

One reason for the success of the grain companies has been their constant ability to maintain a balance between 'hard' and 'soft' information investments. During the first half of the twentieth century, telecommunications were the single greatest intelligence tool for their operations. Since the 1960s and 1970s new weapons have been added, three of them of technological significance. The first two — space technologies and computers — are already integrated in the grain companies' daily operations. The third, control of grain seeds and genetic resources, shows that, once again, the companies quickly take advantage of new opportunities, this time those offered by biotechnologies.

---

5. For a detailed examination of this issue, see Lester R. Brown, 'U.S. and Soviet Agriculture: The Shifting Balance of Power' in Lester R. Brown, *Worldwatch Paper no. 51*, Washington, 1982.

*Satellites and Remote Sensing in Agriculture*

Observing the Earth from above — that is, remote sensing techniques which combine the use of satellites, multispectral sensors and data processing — has become one of the most important recent innovations in grain intelligence. Most applications of data from the American Landsat and other survey satellites, however, are still more or less experimental, especially in developing countries. But they are already giving useful information on crop acreage (with an accuracy of 75–95 per cent, depending on land-use patterns), soil survey and yield forecasting. Unfortunately, relatively few areas in the world are structured as simply as wheat fields in the United States. In complex environments, present images are not precise enough for correct crop identification. Short- or medium-term technical innovations may soon provide better delineations of soil boundaries and better crop forecasting. In the long term, they should reduce the margin of error in estimates.

Remote sensing equipment is not cheap. In the early 1980s, a Landsat ground receiving station cost about $8 million, with annual operating costs ranging between $750,000 and $1.7 million.[6] For countries with no such station, data can be received directly through an antenna for an annual fee of $250,000. The investment in digital processing equipment may range anywhere from $300,000 to over $1 million, depending on the computers and peripheral display and colour recording devices used.

Of course, these sizeable investments are wasted if the trained manpower is not there to turn this information into intelligence. For the moment, such a shortage exists in this area in the developing countries. The US National Academy of Sciences has published a rough estimate of the aggregate needs of some 100 developing countries in the 1980s.[7] The number of people who should receive non-degree-level training in visual interpretation is estimated at between 1,800 and 2,400 persons a year and, for degree-level training, at between 2,000 and 5,000 persons per year.[8] For computer

6. *New Scientist*, 17 April 1980.
7. National Academy of Sciences, *Resource Sensing from Space: Prospects for Developing Countries*, Washington, 1977.
8. Non-degree-level training involves supplementary or specialised instruction in the applications of specific remote sensing techniques (duration: three to twelve months); degree-level involves university courses and research, which includes in-depth instruction and experience in the application of remote sensing technology (duration: one to four years).

analysis, between 9,000 and 15,000 persons should be trained at non-degree level, and between 1,000 and 4,000 persons at degree level.

A one-month course for the advanced training of foreign participants in the United States cost around $4,500 in 1979. Agriculture and crop forecasts would require about half this manpower. A rough calculation gives an average of around $200,000 per country to turn university graduates into satellite data interpreters and analysts for the evaluation and prediction of agricultural crops. All things considered, it is a very cheap and worthwhile investment.

Some 65 per cent of all data requests come from within the United States, while only one-third of the data is generated there. Medium-sized consulting firms and the federal government are the two biggest customers, accounting for 34 per cent and 38 per cent respectively of Landsat imagery. Japan, Australia and France are the largest foreign customers. Major resource companies, including the grain giants, purchase Landsat scene enlargements and computer tapes.

In developing countries, the situation is quite different. Requests for data are made not by large firms but by individual research scientists. They complain that they may sometimes have to wait as long as two months before receiving data about their own country.

This question of access to sensitive information has been a long-standing item on the agenda of the United Nations' Committee on the Peaceful Uses of Outer Space and was also discussed at the 1982 Unispace Conference at Vienna. The question of a country's right to prior consent before data from satellites about its own territory are given to a third country has been unsuccessfully debated for more than a decade. United States policy favours an open-skies approach, where everyone can have access to the data. Third World countries, on the other hand, feel that since these data concern their own natural resources and national security, they should have control over who has access to them. The distinction between access to rough data and access to information derived from the data is of the utmost importance here. The American attitude gives a clear advantage to the institutions, companies or countries that have the expertise to transform data into usable information.

The problem of the commercialisation of satellite remote sensing data will most likely come to a head in the coming years. The United States intends to proceed with a complete transfer of the operation and management of satellite data to private industry, which will then set prices. On the other hand, France, which is likely to be its only competitor (with its SPOT system) plans to set up a special marketing and support organisation, in which the government and semi-governmental institutions will have a controlling interest. But, in both cases, will the price of data be established in accordance with the real financial possibilities of developing countries?

## Computer Models

Crop production and econometric forecasting — which involve complex interrelationships, a large number of data that change periodically, well-identified input variables, and the like — are exactly the kinds of problem that computer and data-processing techniques handle very well. These computer models have become one of the most powerful tools for grain intelligence ever available.

The AgServe programme developed by Control Data Corporation (CDC), a leading manufacturer of large computers that offers data services, is presented as 'a new concept in predicting large area crop production' and 'a unique commodity information service to be used in risk management for profitable decision-making'. It is certainly the most sophisticated grain model available at present.

It combines a sophisticated agricultural data base, together with physiological crop modelling techniques, a weather data base, statistical tools and connections with demand assumption models established by Wharton Econometric Forecasting Associates (EFA). A key point in grain intelligence is expressed in the AgServe presentation brochure: 'Since this data [used by the programme] is public, it is easy to gather, sort, interpret and present. We will concede it is available, but not easily combined into a useful form. Our strategy is to use public data when there is a high degree of confidence in their accuracy.'

AgServe provides large-area crop-production reports for American corn, soybeans and wheat, Canadian and Soviet wheat and Brazilian soybeans, and monthly price forecasts. It allows users to determine the impact of weather and other environmental factors on crop yields or to run alternative scenarios. The results have been quite impressive and justify CDC's advertisement that it is the 'state of the art in crop forecasting'.

Who has benefited from this tool up to now? In the United

151

States, customers include the big grain companies, of course, but also co-operatives, mills and smaller agrobusiness firms. In Europe, the only users are found in France and, faithful to the grain business tradition, they wish to remain anonymous.

Models like AgServe, with a single-crop approach, do not attempt to integrate the interrelationships between different agricultural commodities and other sectors of the national or world economy. A world agricultural model like the one proposed by Wharton EFA[9] disaggregates world agriculture, first by commodity and then by country and region. Cocoa, coffee, corn, dairy products, meat rice, rubber, soybeans and soybean products, sugar, tobacco, wheat, wine, wool and vegetable oil sources are broken down by production, demand, prices, consumption, inventories and world trade sub-models.

Linked with the Wharton models of American agriculture and its planned world macro-economic model, it could offer a complete coverage of world agricultural trade. Basically orientated towards the United States, the model will naturally focus on American agriculture, which suits the needs of the major grain traders, who can play at the global level with such commodities as grains, meat and soybeans, of which the United States is a major exporter.

It might not be as accurate and valuable for day-to-day operations as AgServe, since it will not provide detailed production forecasts for different crops in a given country. Its role will be for medium- or long-term planning and strategic decisions taken at the highest levels of private companies or in governments. In this sense, it could be vital for developing countries whose economies are often heavily dependent on exports of a particular agricultural commodity like sugar, coffee or cocoa. For the moment, none of these countries has developed a single-crop model.

However, no computer programme can take over decision-making. Identifying crops and measuring acreage are only one step in the process of forecasting crop production,[10] and cannot in themselves replace grain intelligence overnight.

### Genetic Intelligence

The world's farmers need the commercial companies to sell their

9. Wharton Econometric Forecasting Associates, *A Research Proposal for a Model of World Agriculture*, Philadelphia, 1977.

10. 'Remote Sensing in Development', *Science*, 5 October 1981.

grain: the US Department of Agriculture estimates that 70 per cent of American farm co-operatives' export-bound grain is sold directly to the major companies; the same situation pertains in France. But farmers also rely on the big companies to procure seeds.

Virtually all the corn planted in the United States, as well as most of that in Argentina, Brazil, South Africa and France comes from hybrid seeds, which have the biological particularity of not giving similar seeds for the next harvest. From a commercial point of view, the key fact is that farmers have to buy new supplies each year, which come from a handful of companies, among them the grain trading companies that dominate the business. Similar research is being conducted on wheat and could lead to a comparable situation within a few years. Farmers also depend on the grain companies on the second level of grain use. For example, chicken hybrid lines sold by a Cargill subsidiary in the Philippines — and fed with grain sold by Cargill to the Filipino farmers — are good for only one generation because chickens raised from their eggs lose their distinctive qualities. The next generation again has to be bought from Cargill.

Many of the grain merchants have bought up, or taken majority participations in, seed companies. It can be asked whether this is not a take-over of the ultimate source of grain intelligence: the genetic information which centuries of natural and human selection have incorporated so that cultivated cereals fit a specific environment with the best possible yield. This issue is of prime importance for developing countries that are trying to devise their own grain intelligence policies.[11] It has begun to be debated but its solution will ultimately depend upon international discussions and agreements.

## Towards a Grain Intelligence Policy for Developing Countries

The dependence of developing countries on cheap grain imports or food aid will continue in the foreseeable future, even if these countries are determined to improve agricultural policy or are offered more favourable prices. Companies like Cargill, Continental or Bunge will continue to affect future markets by the mere fact that they decide to stay in or out. Most of the poorer countries will

11. See, for instance, Pat R. Mooney, *Seeds of the Earth: A Private or Public Resource?*, ICDA, London, 1979; Jean Robert, 'Graines de vie, graines de mort', *CoEvolution*, no. 2, Paris, Autumn 1980; and *Wild Genetic Resources*, Earthscan document no. 33, London, 1982.

therefore have to try to secure supplies for import requirements on the best possible terms.

In many developing countries food imports, rather than improved agricultural production and distribution, have seemed to be an easy way out. The grain intelligence approach shows the contrary; as long as large-scale food imports are necessary, they must be managed with the best intelligence available in the country.

A comprehensive grain intelligence policy that integrates material and technical investments as well as economic, organisational and social decisions is the most important step towards greater autonomy in food.

Grain intelligence begins at the ground level, with the knowledge of agricultural resources. Traditionally, resource information has been acquired from various sources, gathered by a variety of means, and is often scattered in separate agencies. A few countries have begun to recognise the value of an integrated approach to resource inventories and management, and have regrouped data-collecting units into centralised resource-data collection, analysis and planning services. In this respect, remote sensing, as part of a fully integrated system of modelling, accounting, budgeting and forecasting crop production, could be revolutionary in many ways.

Software — or organisational — investments should also be made at governmental level. Agrarian conditions and distribution policy are bound to become primary factors in grain supply. In countries that export agricultural commodities, it is easier to begin by controlling local production factors, rather than trying to control the international companies which will trade the produce. In a period of heavy speculation of soybeans, for instance, Brazil managed to impose stiff export taxes so as to keep its production off world markets and maintain pressure on prices. For countries that import large quantities of grain, the Soviet agency Exportkhleb is an excellent example of an efficient organisation, which has sometimes succeeded in fooling the grain giants themselves. It is in constant telephone and telex contact with the Western European offices of the big companies. Its operating methods are almost unique in Soviet bureaucracy: 'The people who work for it are unusually privileged . . . . They have authority to make quick decisions based on conditions in the marketplace. In short, Exportkhleb operates like a Western grain company in many respects'.[12]

12. Morgan, *Merchants of Grain.*

It is neither necessary nor advisable for a developing country to begin by building up a giant company; a team of specialists who could strengthen its expertise in the grain trade is a much better investment. Some countries already have such units, which have proved to be quite successful, but their overall planning is in need of a more integrated use of this intelligence.

## Basic Inputs for a Grain Intelligence Unit

The model developed by Cargill or Louis Dreyfus is certainly the best one a developing country could try to copy to build up a basic grain intelligence unit. It requires few people, a handful of university professors from such disciplines as agriculture, plant genetics, economics, meteorology, information sciences and political science, and above all a group of trained specialists who know the crop they are in charge of, know their country's needs or export possibilities, and are able to assess the impact of world events on this particular commodity trade.

It may be useful to distinguish between daily operations and the more strategic duties of such a unit. India's State Trading Corporation, one of the largest importers of edible oils in the world, offers a good example of the day-to-day activities of such a unit.[13] It has carefully assessed its information needs and has developed a highly efficient market information system, thanks to a good telecommunications and information network. Information and intelligence are not seen as ends in themselves; to serve their purpose, they must be promptly and efficiently disseminated to decision-makers. Daily market reports are distributed to those involved in making purchasing decisions. Weekly and monthly reports are also prepared for higher executives and operating managers.

Strategic or long-term duties involve three kinds of tasks. The first is to know the country's agricultural production, yields, weather forecasts, population trends, import needs, financial resources and the like, by integrating all the data available. Unit members should not be afraid of announcing unpleasant facts like forecasts of poor agricultural results, persistent bad weather or risks of grain shortages to the decision-makers. Equally important, they must monitor the devel-

13. 'STC's Market Intelligence System', *International Trade Forum*, Geneva, April–June 1981.

oped countries' grain trade. This may sometimes seem like a waste of time but it is indispensable. Exporting countries' policies determine the amount that developing countries will be able to dispose of, when and where. Decisions in North America or in the European Community can affect the entire world grain trade, as, for instance, when the Canadian government decided to regulate grain transport tariffs at home. If the decision to reduce exports is taken, the poorest countries are the first to suffer. They are much more vulnerable to a loss of imports than exporting countries are to a drop in exports.

The third strategic task assigned to any grain intelligence unit is to try to co-operate with grain multinationals and with other developing countries. At present, there are great disparities between multinationals and developing countries in exploiting remote sensing data. If the developing countries could acquire the equipment and trained personnel to carry out their own surveys and the legal experience necessary to bargain, relationships with multinationals could improve substantially. Resource surveys could become a co-operative effort, with both sides gaining from equal availability of information.

On the international level, co-ordination of national wheat policies is probably impossible, apart from a central statistical service and consultations. But developing countries could pool their grain knowledge, and even if it were for only a few countries, a grain intelligence unit might be more feasible. Each participating country could benefit without forsaking its own capacity for decision-making.

Resource sensing from space, organised and managed as an international co-operative enterprise, could bring into sharper focus both the complex challenges facing the world community and the necessary interdependent answers required to deal with them. World inventories of renewable resources like grain, quickly made and frequently updated, could be a powerful new tool for a more rational management of the world's agricultural resources.

A promising example of such a co-operation scheme is the Agrhymet programme in Africa south of the Sahara, which uses a satellite and a network of ground stations to provide weather and agricultural information to farmers and agricultural planners.[14] It focuses mainly on practical information, like data on the start of the

14. *Afrique-Agriculture*, no. 70, June 1981.

rainy season, but it could easily be extended to crop forecasts on a regional basis. Agrhymet is already able to predict a harvest shortage, for example, if weather conditions are not favourable at flowering time.

All these steps are only part of the whole process of building up national — and international — grain intelligence. Only by their combination and their interactions can they become truly valuable. Each alone is almost worthless. Indeed, even a grain intelligence policy is worthless if it is not part of a larger national intelligence policy. Then, and only then, can the process of building social intelligence become the answer to the challenges set by world hunger.

# CHAPTER 11

# Remote Sensing as an Intelligence Instrument

## J.M.M. van der Broek and J.J. Nossin

In recent years the capacity to generate and collect data through remote sensing techniques has grown to such an extent that developing countries now have at their disposal a major tool for planning. For the moment, the full implications of remote sensing — for resource exploration and management, for crop development and for rural land uses, among others — have not been fully realised, let alone fully utilised by those involved. However, remote sensing, like other information-generating activities, is only a tool. Without the capacity to apply the information gathered to decision-making, it will remain an underutilised resource.

Remote sensing is a general term applied to collection of data relating to objects on the earth's surface from a mobile platform some distance above the earth. Aerial photography can therefore be properly included in remote sensing. Most recently the term has also come to mean non-photographic techniques of data collection, notably electro-optical sensing of electromagnetic radiation on a spectral range broader than the optical wavelengths used in photography.

The various systems, including some that are not mentioned here, provide data that are largely complementary, though some gaps in the total picture still exist. By using a combination of systems, however, the potential of each is enhanced. For example, a synoptic overview taken from a Landsat satellite can identify areas of study and then be used in conjunction with aerial photography studies that provide larger-scale views of important areas. Gaps in the picture, caused by cloudy areas, can then be filled in by using airborne radar.

## Landsat

The best known system so far is the American Landsat satellites. Since 1972 these experimental satellites have transmitted over a million scenes to earth. Once every eighteen days, or sometimes every nine days, they sweep over the same area. Each scene covers 180 square kilometres. The advanced version, Landsat 4, was launched in July 1982. Its spatial resolution — that is, the smallest element discernible — was improved, from about eighty metres square in previous satellites, to thirty metres square. The digital data format permits computer-assisted interpretation, while visual interpretation techniques can be applied to images generated from the digital data.

The Landsat system operates in or near the visible part of the spectrum and captures reflected sunlight. It therefore operates only in daylight and cannot penetrate cloud cover.

While Landsat data can be applied to many of the same fields as airphoto interpretation, the system has opened up new ones thanks to its repetitive coverage and to the broad synoptic overviews of very large areas that cannot be obtained by aerial photography. Landsat data, when combined with meteorological satellite data, have given rise to experiments in crop monitoring and harvest forecasting. They have also led to the discovery of large, hitherto unknown, geological structures. An important fringe benefit is that Landsats are supplying data for areas for which no maps are yet in existence.

The system, operated by the National Aeronautics and Space Administration (NASA) and being transferred to the National Oceanic and Atmospheric Administration (NOAA), makes all its data available to anyone anywhere in the world. What is more, the unit cost of such data is extremely low, for over 32,000 square kilometres are covered in each frame. Charges may vary from one data centre to the next, but imagery works out to only a fraction of one US cent per square kilometre. Digital data on tape is slightly more expensive, but in 1982 it still cost less than one US cent. Imagery can be examined directly; all the user needs is qualified manpower and rather simple equipment.

## Radar: Data Collection Round the Clock

A powerful and very promising system of data collection by remote sensing is the use of imaging radar from aeroplanes and satellites. It is an active system, which means that it beams energy to the earth's surface and records the reflected signal. It is therefore capable of operating by day or night; the nature of the radiation is such that it also passes through clouds, making the system weather-independent. Operational and economic requirements make airborne radar applicable in those areas where a permanent high degree of cloudiness hampers or impedes aerial photography: the humid tropics as well as some high-latitude areas.

So far, the largest application of radar has been for topographic mapping of the entire Amazon basin, parts of Central America and Nigeria. It is also being used for resource surveys of areas that are difficult to reach and for which no aerial photography exists.

Satellite-borne radar is still in the experimental stage. One radar-carrying satellite — Seasat — functioned in 1978, and other experiments have been carried out on board the Space Shuttle.

## Aerial Photography: A Conventional Source of Data

Though aerial photography is a very common technique for collecting data about the earth — for topographic mapping, for the assessment of natural resources, the study of settlements and infrastructures — not all countries are fully mapped in this way, nor do all maps offer the same reliability. A normal topographical map obtained by this method packs a great deal of information for geographers and earth scientists but it is often inadequate for planners and decision-makers, who need a tool better adapted to their specific purposes.

Another drawback of maps under the present production system is that they rapidly become out of date. The time lapse between a survey and the production of printed maps is on the order of two to three years in many countries. Updating of existing maps occurs every ten years or so. Map-makers are working hard to devise faster methods of representation and updating, which may give rise to products other than the very expensive and elaborate maps that have traditionally been in use. The purpose of maps is undergoing a conceptual change, from a presentation of what exists to the identification of a future situation.

Air-photo interpretation consists of extracting information about the earth's surface from aerial photographs by stereoscopic observation. It can be applied to all those fields of science that deal with the spatial distribution of features on the earth's surface or those that reflect conditions beneath the surface, under water or in the atmosphere. The human sciences still tend to underuse this tool; it has great potential for urban survey, rural land-use and settlement studies.

## Future Developments of Remote Sensing from Space

More sophisticated remote sensing systems than the ones used during the past decade are now being introduced, and more are on the way. Operational earth observation systems are being considered by the United States and France, as well as by the European Space Agency (ESA). Other countries, and particularly Japan, may also enter this field.

Apart from the advanced version of the American Landsat, a system was developed by France called SPOT (Système Probatoire d'Observation de la Terre). Launched in 1986, it provides black and white imagery with a resolution of ten metres and multi-spectral images with a twenty-metre resolution.

Further developments will undoubtedly take place in photography from manned satellites. Presently, the Soviet Soyuz-Salyut system supplies photographic data from space, though distribution of the data is limited. The American Space Shuttle and the ESA Spacelab are also opening up new possibilities.

As for radar from satellites, experiments are being conducted mainly on board the Space Shuttle. The ESA is presently developing a radar-carrying satellite for ocean monitoring and coastal area studies, which it hopes to launch in 1987.

In general, satellite data, apart from improving capacities for mapping and related activities, will greatly increase the capacity for detecting and monitoring change.

However, the improved resolution of these new systems may reactivate the debate on the consent of those countries under a satellite's flight path. Some countries are questioning the right to have data of their own territory taken and made available to users elsewhere. The problem is compounded by improvements in delivery time, that is, the time it takes to make the information available after sensing from the satellite. The Tracking and Data Relay Satellite System will make it possible to obtain real-time information from Landsat at a single receiving station.

This combination of high spatial resolution, high temporal resolution and real-time data collection will create a system which could raise strong security objections on the part of many of the countries overpassed. Of course, it is extremely likely that such systems exist already, in the form of military intelligence satellites.

## Monitoring

The repeated coverage at regular intervals of the same swath of the earth's surface by satellites can be considered as the most powerful new element in this sector of the knowledge industry. This monitoring capacity is also the least developed of the satellites' information-collection possibilities. Traditionally, mapping dealt with stable situations, whereas monitoring involves the tracking of change over time. Till now, weather satellites have afforded the best opportunity to learn about monitoring.

Earth scientists have by and large neglected to adapt their way of thinking from a static to a dynamic outlook. Changes in the earth's surface are due both to natural processes and to human activity. Monitoring natural processes — coastal changes, floods, snow melt and the like — as well as man-induced processes like crop development or factors governing the quality of the environment is now a distinct possibility. To do all this, however, real-time or near real-time data must be available. Technologically, there are no insurmountable problems; indeed, some have already been partially solved. The biggest obstacles lie in the fact that considerable investments in hardware are necessary, backed up by a substantial reservoir of knowledge — two major drawbacks for developing countries.

## Data Collection for Development Planning

It is generally agreed that the development of remote sensing technology is years ahead of the capability to use it fully for domestic purposes. Originally, of course, many systems were developed for military purposes and, once declassified, were modified for civilian use. Then, too, most systems have been experimental, with manufacturers continuously making improvements, which has made potential users hesitant to invest in the new technology.

None the less, remote sensing has made significant contributions to the state of knowledge about resources and the spatial distribution of features on the earth's surface. Knowledge could grow even faster if users were better equipped to specify their requirements. Indeed, from the viewpoint of data collectors, users make up an ill-defined group, and are sometimes not even identifiable. Moreover, it is not enough to know that the users of integrated survey data are, say, government planners, if it is not known what they are planning, at what level and for what time period.

Even so, much data is routinely collected for surveying, a good deal of which can be used for mapping and updating and for geo-information and statistical data. Once the information is collected, users are found for maps, atlases and the like. This is not necessarily the wrong approach, but too often such maps present the user with superfluous information while some really vital information may be lacking. Manifestly, users' needs may not have conditioned technological advances in data collection; on the other hand, users may well be unaware of technological developments and may consequently formulate their requirements on the basis of outdated technology.

Starting from the premise that geo-information is being used, and that users therefore exist, more concentrated efforts have recently been made to identify user-groups for various types of information and to promote interaction between those who collect data and those who will use it.


## The Interaction between Technology and Decision-Making

Economically advanced countries have set up research programmes to study the possible applications of satellite technology for their national economies. This will give them a lead over developing countries, which have less facilities for such research. To date, research and development has concentrated on communications as well as earth observations, in such fields as geology or agriculture, and more specifically the survey aspects of these fields. In both cases, however, the intrinsic components are information and information transfer, and the persons or groups with access to the information and the power to use it.

This raises the question of the applications of the new forms of information to planning and policy-making for socio-economic development. Adapting the decision-making structure to new technologies is more difficult and consequently less advanced in these fields than in communication and the technical sciences. Developing countries are handicapped here as well, because their public administrations are far less prepared to make the necessary adjustments than those in the industrialised countries. They are in fact caught up in a vicious circle. Better decisions would be possible if there were better information. The technologies exist to obtain better information, but they are applicable only if the capabilities of the administrative infrastructure change, which in turn depends on decisions based on better information.

Gradual evolution is in most cases not possible. Countries are forced into a series of choices; if certain choices are not made, these countries will find that they lag even further behind. The utilisation of remote sensing for development planning, for example, is barely in the initial phase. Its application to the decision-making process is not merely a technological matter, but a political choice.

## Need and Demand

Development planning is an ongoing activity that constantly requires fresh information. New information can lead planners to alter previous decisions, starting up the decision-making process afresh. In development planning and administration, the term 'information needs' covers two distinct aspects: the need and the demand for information. Need, of course, refers to information required by users in a decision-making process, while demand is the request formulated by information-users and addressed to information-suppliers. Obviously, the basic components — data, information, knowledge, intelligence, need and demand — are interrelated. However, various inconsistencies crop up between the user and the supplier of information, due to a lack of communication between the two; between need and demand, due to inadequate problem identification; between data and information, due to insufficient understanding of the decision-making process; and between information and intelligence, due to illogical deductions or inexplicable factors.

In the case of aerial survey and remote sensing especially, there are a series of constraints accounting for such inconsistencies: national security; the political concept of progress and development; a lack of technical knowledge and skills; a dislike of modern, complicated technology; an insufficient infrastructure for large-scale data handling; a lack of dialogue between various parts of the administrative structure; unawareness of the information capabilities of these systems at the planning and decision level; and traditional views on the importance of secrecy.

Before the user's information requirements can be determined, the users themselves have to be indentified. The user community can range from public research units and industrial firms to national, regional and sectoral authorities. They must all identify their function either as users or as suppliers of data, information or knowledge.

## Formulating Information Requirements

Data-gathering on exploitable resources and on natural or socio-economic processes has become a high-priority activity in many countries. International organisations as well as bilateral assistance programmes have been instrumental in building up and reinforcing the data-collection and data-management capabilities of a number of developing countries. Consultants, both private and governmental, in numerous assistance programmes have helped establish data bases in these countries for development planning and decision-making. Over the past three decades, there has been a cascade of investigations and surveys whose purpose was to promote development. The fact remains that much of the collected information did not contribute to the envisaged development process.

One can then ask what benefits could accrue from remote sensing inventories, which would merely enlarge the already considerable volume of information but would not contribute directly to the effectiveness of planning and decision-making. This criticism is not directed at modern technology as such, but to the way in which modern technology is sometimes applied to processes involving human societies. This holds not only for Third World countries, but for some of the industrialised countries as well. The point is how and to what extent modern technology, and remote sensing in particular, can support and reinforce the development process.

It seems clear that, in order to draw up development plans, the first step is to establish a balance sheet of resources. Planners must ask themselves the following questions: What and where are the resources? What is their potential? What are the conditions for their exploitation? What are the side effects of their exploitation?

Remote sensing is, of course, the ideal instrument for answering some of these questions; it provides information on the resource situation of the country and monitors change. Mathematical modelling can then give insight into the effects of resource exploitation, constraints, administrative infrastructure and the consequences of development interventions.

The fact that the technological possibilities for information supply are available but not yet adequately utilised points to the lack of co-ordination between the decision-making process and the planning process, and between the planning process and the data-supply process (survey and investigations).

As we have seen, the positive impact of remote sensing techniques will depend upon the creation of a reservoir of human skills and knowledge, both in understanding the information requirements for planning and decision-making and in transforming and interpreting remote sensing data into usable information. To this end, the International Institute for Aerial Surveys and Earth Sciences (ITC) in the Netherlands is trying to sensitise planners and policy-makers from developing countries to the potential of remote sensing data.[1] An international university, ITC offers postgraduate courses for participants from developing countries in the use and applications of modern survey techniques, including remote sensing (aerial photography, radar and satellite imagery), manual and digital data processing, cartographic presentation techniques, as well as the establishment and operation of geo-information systems.

Developing nations in particular should become more aware of the fact that remote sensing systems are readily available. The major investment lies in training men capable of handling the data and in creating a reservoir of knowledge on the subsequent use of this information for planning. Training of this kind is not getting the priority it might, as was stressed at the Second United Nations Conference on the Exploration and Peaceful Uses of Outer Space

1. Two offshoots of ITC — the Centro Inter-Americano de Fotointerpretación in Colombia and the Indian Institute of Remote Sensing — are now independent institutions. They pursue the same types of activities. The first serves Latin America, and the second serves the Indian subcontinent.

(Unispace 82). If this situation is allowed to continue, technological developments in data collection will still be years ahead of these countries' capability to use them.

PART III

# Towards an Intelligence Policy for Development

The chapters in this third part take a closer look at the organisational, political and cultural issues facing the designers of a development-orientated intelligence policy. One of the general themes
brought up by the authors is that the development of a country's
intelligence capability depends not only on tools and money, or
equipment and people, but on a state of mind and a set of attitudes.
This is well illustrated by Francisco Sagasti in his analysis of 'The
Role of Techno-Economic Intelligence', which stresses the importance of a country's information environment. One of the big
problems of the developing nations, according to Sagasti, is their
cognitive dependence on highly industrialised countries. Two of the
author's practical observations deserve to be stressed here. The first
is the need to recognise that the information overload which characterises the information age has brought about a radical qualitative
change in the nature of intelligence systems and information networks. The dramatic increase in the density and number of interconnections in informations systems means that it is much easier to
acquire information and knowledge. Since the channels of access are
so much more numerous, the management of secrecy is becoming
less important, and all countries have to compete in an increasingly
transparent information environment. It should be observed here
that the richness in neural interconnections in the human brain is
one major factor accounting for the intelligence — in the psychological sense — of an individual. Sagasti's second important observation concerns the need in any national intelligence effort for what
he calls the 'synthetist' or 'pattern recogniser' — a profession which
was first described by science fiction writers.

In his chapter on 'Intelligence in a Science and Technological
Policy', Pierre Piganiol suggests that national science and technology policies, in addition to their obvious function in the promotion of scientific and technological innovation, also have a central
role to play in a country's 'intelligence' (the term being taken here
both in its narrow psychological sense, and in its broader definition
used elsewhere in this book). This leads him to map out a number of
new policy directions. One of these is the possibility — indeed the
necessity — for the developing nations to exploit in a much more

171

effective way the 'intelligence' or understanding of specific development problems embodied in the brains of a small number of local
science and technology specialists. Another is his suggestion that in
the scientific and technological system, there are certain types of
activities or institutions (for instance testing laboratories) that are
largely neglected by policy-makers but which are in fact crucial
intelligence centres. Piganiol's third proposition is that a much more
substantial intelligence effort should be devoted to the 'traditional'
technologies still widely used in the developing countries. His
fourth proposition relates to the need for 'intelligence about choices'
and intelligence about the future, which are essential to industrialisation and development.

A country's intelligence effort can also be approached from a
systems-analysis perspective. In his chapter ('An Intelligence Model
for Managers'), Thomas Lindberg presents an interesting model drawn
from his experience as a senior industrial manager. One of the
important points he raises is the need to distinguish between 'hard'
and 'soft' information, and to acknowledge the fact that information
about the future is always 'soft'. According to the author, a country
or a corporation's intelligence efforts are most likely to succeed if
they concentrate on the intelligence 'window', that is, the point in
time which lies at the frontier between the predetermined future and
the 'malleable' future. A major difficulty in designing, or running,
an effective intelligence system is that of communicating intelligence
results within an organisation. In his concluding remarks, Lindberg
suggests that developing countries, which have not yet turned
themselves into production organisations, have yet to become learning
organisations.

In 'An Open Letter to Top Decision-Makers', Yehezkel Dror
addresses himself to the very concrete problems of forging an
effective national intelligence tool for development. This is done in
the form of advice to national rulers, followed by an annotated
bibliography for intelligence beginners. Dror begins his lesson by
pointing out some of the pitfalls in decision-making. One of these is
national leaders' tendency to base decisions on facts and predictions
of facts, without realising that facts are only distorted images of
reality. Another is the danger, faced by many heads of state, of
being misled by the half-truths, myths and disinformation supplied
by their entourage. The author's advice could be summarised in the
form of do's and don'ts that are easy to state but probably more
difficult to implement: (a) insist on high-quality intelligence products; (b) develop mechanisms for reducing intelligence failures; (c) avoid
monopolies on intelligence; (d) respect the needs of good intelligence; (e)
start from scratch . . . and read the books recommended by Dror.

CHAPTER 12

# Techno-Economic Intelligence for Development

Francisco R. Sagasti

Acquiring, processing and using economic and technological information for the purpose of policy and decision-making in developing countries is no mean problem. Rather than describing what exists or has been done in practice — very little indeed! — these notes offer some speculations on the changing information environment and its implications for future techno-economic intelligence activities in developing countries.

## The Information Environment of Developing Countries

A techno-economic intelligence group in a developing country usually has to operate in an unfavourable setting characterised by a general lack of resources of all types. The level of understanding and acceptance of these activities by policy-makers is generally low. Rivalries are heightened because of the small size of the technical and political elite, and because access to bureaucratic power is a limited and highly-priced good. The international context is changing rapidly: political realignments, military alliances, and economic activities appear to be in a constant state of turmoil. Last but not least, the prevalent conceptual frameworks, values and perspectives that are given to the developing countries from abroad are generally alien to their thought processes and modes of behaviour, and are imposed to a large extent through the pervasive influence of international mass media.

## Cognitive Dependence

With this in mind, it seems that a techno-economic intelligence group in a developing country probably needs something akin to a split personality. It should pay attention to local reality, the local culture, the values and outlook of the population at large and of the country's elites, the nature and evolution of local power struggles, and the degree of understanding and acceptance of techno-economic intelligence activities by policy-makers. At the same time, it should follow closely the international scene, the frontiers of knowledge in areas of critical importance to its own country, the evolution of spheres of influence and power in international relations and the possibilities of exploiting to the maximum the limited room for manoeuvre available for autonomous development. This requires some sort of institutionalised schizophrenia, in which the international and local components of a techno-economic intelligence group would evolve independently from one another in organisational terms, although they would be integrated in an organic fashion in the minds and actions of the leaders of the group.

The great expansion of knowledge-generating activities in the highly industrialised nations, the growing degree of concentration of resources in scientific research, the increasing extent to which modern technologies are based on scientific discoveries, and the widespread use of those science-based techniques in the productive system characterise the evolution of the highly industrialised nations that belong to what has been called the 'First Civilisation'. In contrast, the developing countries of the 'Second Civilisation' have not managed to acquire a research base of their own to generate scientific knowledge in a systematic, large-scale and continuous fashion, to transform this knowledge into production techniques, and to incorporate these new science-based techniques into production. In these countries, science, technology and production have grown in an imitative, fragmented and disjointed way, each being almost totally dependent on the evolution of their counterparts in the highly industrialised countries of the First Civilisation. The contradictions and conflicts between the two and the process of searching for a 'Third Civilisation' are likely to be the dominant features of international relations during the next half-century.[1]

1. F. Sagasti, 'The Two Civilisations and the Process of Development', *Prospects*, vol. 10, no. 2, pp. 123–9.

The importance of a techno-economic intelligence group in a developing country can be appreciated only in the face of the huge differences in the capacities to generate, select, absorb and use knowledge. A techno-economic intelligence group deeply involved in the process of development would have to undertake the seemingly improbable task of acting as the main focus for the gathering, transfer and processing of critical information for the process of development. This difficult task appears more tractable when the concept of critical information for development is given a restricted meaning: a techno-intelligence group will have to adopt a selective approach, limiting the scope of its information gathering and processing activities, and organising them sequentially in accordance with the priorities of the developing country.

## Intelligence and National Security

Even though the military aspects of intelligence are of prime importance for developing countries involved in actual or potential conflict zones, they are less important to most developing countries. Furthermore, there appears to be a general shift away from the purely military aspects of conflict towards economic, social, scientific, technological and even cultural battlegrounds. The new arsenal includes economic sanctions, the food weapon, barring access to technological resources, the use of mass media to conduct sophisticated cultural battles of concepts and ideologies, recourse to international fora to engage in battles of words in international negotiations, and a variety of more subtle forms of warfare that go well beyond classical military confrontations. From this perspective, the issue of national defence and security has been transformed: from a strictly military programme, it has become a broad multi-dimensional problem of national intelligence in all spheres of a country interacting with the world environment.

Indeed, as early as the mid-1950s, the Peruvian Centre for Higher Military Studies, for instance, was already advancing the concept of an integral security doctrine, in which national defence and security were closely tied to socio-economic development. For example, it claimed that a country could not be defended adequately from a foreign aggressor unless it had a well-developed economic system to back up its defence. To a large extent, this doctrine justified the social transformations introduced in Peru during the first years of the Revolutionary Government of the Armed Forces that took power in 1968.

## The Evolution of a 'Social Brain'

The enormous flow of data that has been put at the disposal of managers, government officers, executives, policy-makers, researchers, and in general anyone who is interested in gathering information for decision-making purposes is threatening to swamp those in the developed countries. But for the developing countries, it is more like a tidal wave that suddenly and massively engulfs policy- and decision-makers, threatening to drown them in a flood of data, most of which is likely to be irrelevant. A quick review of the origins of this situation would be useful to explore the ways in which a techno-economic intelligence group in a developing country might react to such a mass of suddenly available information and learn to operate effectively in a heavily overloaded information environment.

The last eighty years have seen three stages in the process of change in the information environment. From a first stage in which information sources were rather easy to identify and gain access to, there was a period of transition (especially after the Second World War), during which time the amount of technical, economic, scientific, political, social and cultural information grew at a rapid pace, and special efforts were required to follow the evolution and characteristics of information sources. We are now entering a third stage, in which the information overload is so great and sources have multiplied to such a degree that, paradoxically, it is once again possible to identify easily a potential source of information and even to gain access to it without much difficulty.

### First Era: Easy Information

In the first stage, the sources of information were scattered, relatively easy to identify, and had few interconnections among them. An information-gathering and processing organisation could operate as what cyberneticist R. Ashby called an iterated system, in which the various interactions between the system and its environment can be dealt with independently. Reaction time to disturbances is short, adaptation responses are fast, and the changes do not pose serious threats to the existence of the system. At this stage, the structure of the web of information sources corresponds to what Emery and Trist call 'the placid-clustered' environment of an organisation, in which it is possible to ignore the interconnections within the environment of a system. Therefore the organisation's capacity to process and use information probably exceeds the capacity of the environment to generate information. Using a literary analogy, the typical image of a techno-economic intelligence officer in such an environment would be Somerset Maugham's Ashenden, a British secret agent in the 1920s, who has adequate personal connections with information sources, who does not use technical gadgets, who is mostly interested in human nature, and who employs his personal judgement to assess the validity and relevance of information. Ashenden's main ability is a capacity to anticipate reactions and to search for interconnections between facts, personalities and possible future events.

## Second Era: Managed Information

During the second stage, there is a substantial increase in the generation of information, a multiplication of data sources, and a rapid growth in the amount of information provided to policy-makers, planners and decision-makers. The performance of an organisation is governed to a large extent by the advantages gained through its access to privileged information and by its capacity to acquire and process reliable information from specialised services. In this information-sensitive environment, the management of secrecy (selective withholding of data, protection of information sources, dissemination of erroneous information, and so on) becomes a crucial aspect of competitive strategies. The increased speed of information transmission makes it necessary for an organisation to develop short reaction times, which in turn means that it must make use of computer processing, mathematical models and telecommunications facilities, and set up specialised information-processing units.

At this stage, information processing and decision-making take place simultaneously. This is the era of management information systems, of computer data networks, of teleprocessing facilities, and of the 'information on information' schools of thought. In cybernetic terms, the new information environment corresponds to what Ashby has called the 'poorly joined system', in which many interconnections exist among the components of the environment and the system. To react adequately to changes in the environment, the organisation needs vastly increased information-processing capabilities. The new information environment also corresponds to what Emery and Trist call the 'disturbed-reactive' environment in which not only the interactions between the organisation and its environment must be taken into account, but also the changes that take place within the environment itself. In literature, the typical image of a techno-economic intelligence officer during this period would be Ian Fleming's James Bond, a man who can react quickly to unforeseen situations, who is helped by an array of technical gadgets and who has access to information that allows him to take advantage of the most unusual situations.

## Third Era: Information Overload

At present we are entering into a new stage in the evolution of the information environment, that of an information avalanche. Many sources exist for each unit of information and there is a large amount of redundancy and interconnection in the networks and channels. There is no need to devise sophisticated strategies for gaining access to data and for preserving secrecy.

With such overload and richly interconnected information networks, it is not necessary to obtain access to a specific individual source or to worry about accuracy. There are ample opportunities to compare different sources of information, checking them against one another. The management of secrecy becomes less and less important, and strategies have to be devised to compete in a transparent information environment. In cybernetic terms, this new environment corresponds to what Ashby calls 'the richly-joined system', in which every change in a component of the system or its environment affects all the other components, even though, because there are so many interconnections, the effects of a change are attenuated and dampened by a series of reactions and counterreactions. In a sense, the system acquires a certain immunity to environmental disturbances. In organisational theory terms, this new situation corresponds to what Emery and Trist call 'the turbulent environment', in which the main task of a system is to maintain an unstable equilibrium and to develop organisational response capabilities.

Using a literary analogy, there is a return to the traditional concept of the intelligence officer and a reinstatement of old ways of handling information. The image of a techno-economic intelligence officer now corresponds to John Le Carré's George Smiley, a man who knows how to survive in a bureaucratic jungle, who is capable of judging values and motives, who can assess the importance of data, and who has the ability to offer interpretations while facing an information overload.

In a certain sense, the excess of data, the multiplication of channels and sources and the generalised availability of information create a situation similar to that prevailing during the first stage, when there was relatively little information, and sources were easy to identify and gain access to.

## New Strategies for Information Gathering and Processing

This newly emerging information environment raises several interesting issues. For example, the fact that it is possible to put two randomly selected persons in contact through a limited number of intermediaries — around five[2] — shows that it is rather easy to identify the individuals who generate information on a specific subject. In turn this makes it necessary to alter information-gathering and -processing strategies. At one point, for all practical purposes, information will become a free good or at least a relatively cheap commodity. At that stage it will be more important to develop a capacity for processing information than to devise channels for acquiring it.

In the world of the next twenty years, the capacity to generate information is likely to exceed the capacity to process and use it. As a by-product of the micro-electronic revolution, advances in communication technology will make transmission time and cost negligible, while advances in computer technology will make it possible to attain an intermediate stage of information processing rather easily, thus producing masses of data on almost any specific subject of interest to the techno-economic intelligence officer. An indication of this trend is the emergence of world-wide institutions specifically designed to interconnect information sources and networks (United Nations and other international agencies, multinational corporations and the scientific community, among others).

2. For a review of experiments giving evidence on this matter, see Eugene Garfield, 'It's a Small World After All', *Current Contents*, 22 October 1979, pp. 5–10.

In order to cope with the information environment of the future, a techno-economic intelligence group in a developing country will have to devise an opportunistic strategy and an eclectic approach to information gathering and processing. People will have to accept that it will be impossible to maintain secrecy, that exclusive or privileged information channels will no longer exist, and that most of the masses of data to be acquired will be irrelevant. In this new situation, the efforts of a techno-economic intelligence group should be directed towards building up data-processing and interpretation capabilities in order to discern trends, detect critical events, anticipate responses, identify opportunities and threats, and in general to use the increased amount of information to the developing country's advantage.

## Synthesists and Pattern Recognisers

Perhaps the most appropriate analogy to examine this new situation comes from science fiction literature. Stanisław Lem's novel, *Chain of Chance*,[3] explores the implications of a massive increase in the number of interactions in the social and material environments. So large a quantity makes it almost impossible to discern a pattern among the variety of small and large interconnected events and impedes the design of an adequate interpretation strategy. Extrapolating Lem's ideas, one could say that, regardless of the particular strategy to be followed in acquiring information, a techno-economic intelligence group would probably collect the data it needs, but it would find it difficult to process and interpret.

Another analogy could be drawn from John Varley's novel, *The Ophiuchi Hotline*,[4] where he describes the new profession of synthesist, as opposed to the 'analyst'. Varley's synthesist scans huge masses of data over a long period of time in order to choose that fraction which merits further study and which will be processed by specialists assisted by large electronic devices. The training of a synthesist is a complex and expensive undertaking, for a person of natural ability must be found and trained to establish interrelations, to assess relevance and, in general, to discern patterns among a seemingly incoherent mass of data.

3. Stanisław Lem, *Chain of Chance*, Harcourt, Brace, Jovanovitch, New York, 1984.
4. John Varley, *The Ophiuchi Hotline*, Berkley Publishers, New York, 1984.

Brian Aldiss identifies a similar profession, that of 'seeker', in his short story, 'An Appearance of Life',[5] and describes the training process as follows:

> To qualify as a Seeker, it is necessary to show a high serendipity factor. In my experimental behaviour pool as a child, I had exhibited such a factor, and had been selected for special training forthwith. I had taken additional courses in Philosophicals, Alpha-numerals, Incidental Tera-chotomy, Apunctual Synchronicity, Homo-ontegenesis, and other subjects, ultimately qualifying as a Prime Esemplastic Seeker. In other words, I put two and two together in situations where other people were not thinking about addition. I connected. I made wholes greater than parts. Mine was an invaluable profession in a cosmos increasingly full of parts.

In the information environment of the future, the techno-economic intelligence officer of a developing country should be, above all, a synthesist. No longer will he have to worry about devising ways and means of securing access to information, of building privileged channels, and of protecting the secrecy of his sources. He will be concerned with the processing of large amounts of data, with checking and comparing various sources to choose the most reliable and least expensive ones, and with establishing inter-connections among a variety of issues and events of particular relevance to his country's development.

Considering the time it takes to set up a well-run techno-economic intelligence unit and the changes in the information environment that are beginning to take place, developing countries would be well advised to undertake specific techno-economic intelligence tasks that could serve as training exercises for a selected number of professionals. Training should emphasise the synthesist approach to form a small and coherent group of individuals with skills in complementary disciplines. It is they who should act as a link between a developing country's policy-makers and the overloaded information environment of the future. They could articulate the acquisition and processing of information about the international situation and events taking place within the country, putting both in the perspective of the country's short-, medium- and long-term objectives. The developing countries' prospects will

5. Brian Aldiss, 'An Appearance of Life' in *New Arrivals, Old Encounters — Twelve Stories*, Ultramarine Publishers, Hastings on Hudson, New York, 1979.

depend to an increasing degree on the successful establishment of effective techno-economic intelligence groups, however improbable this undertaking may appear at present.

# CHAPTER 13

# Intelligence in Science and Technology Policy

## Pierre Piganiol

Keeping an ever-growing number of human beings prisoners of a scheme of things that now belongs to the past is the surest way to what has been called 'future shock'. The signs are already there in the crises that are breaking out all over our planet. Let us not be deluded by the 'islands' of advanced economies here and there among the developing countries. The lot of the population in a newly advanced country improves slowly and can sometimes deteriorate. The sudden creation of a modern enclave often leads to the exact opposite of the goal sought: unemployment increases, the economy becomes more dependent and the traditional bonds of solidarity gradually weaken.

This view may seem unduly pessimistic. In point of fact, I am convinced that the solution to these crises is within reach if a number of simple rules are followed, and scientific and technical knowledge is used judiciously. At the same time it is important to take advantage of the new opportunities offered by the latest scientific discoveries for a more subtle kind of development, the kind necessitated by our world's growing density of population which, in the absence of progress to offset the disadvantages, could quickly become intolerable.

But for this we need an intelligence of development and of the ways to achieve it. The word 'intelligence' is used here in its fullest sense: it is not only knowledge and learning, but also know-how, knowing how to adapt, how to innovate and how to adopt. The word implies complicity between man and the reality he is changing.

We are concerned here with the intelligence of science and technology in the interests of development and not with the intelli-

183

gence of development itself, though that will be discussed at the end of this introduction so as to serve as a subsequent guide. Let us start by noting — in the wake of Stevan Dedijer, who was a precursor in this field — that this intelligence must have a collective character. But the word 'collective' is ambiguous and needs to be clarified. In fact it means two things. First, this intelligence must be widespread, and therefore communicated, disseminated and shared. Second, the mechanisms that create and spread it must be national mechanisms.

The idea of a national or even regional intelligence implies that no one is left by the wayside of progress. While export-orientated industrialisation or agricultural development may be essential to acquire certain capital equipment, it is no less essential to develop a solvent domestic market, that is, to increase the resources and hence the productivity of the traditional sectors of agriculture and crafts, which in many cases employ over 80 per cent of the population.

These sectors have their own customs and values. Change cannot be imposed; willing acceptance and participation are what is needed. Progress is the outcome of two contradictory phenomena: competition and co-operation. But there will be no progress if all competition does is to trample down the weak, and if co-operation degenerates into organised bureaucracy.

Thus there can be no development without a vision of the future or rather a vision of human lifestyles in that future, and without a conception of the paths that will lead from the present to the future. The 'intelligence of development' is therefore, above all, 'intelligence of the future' and 'intelligence of society's evolution', with all the necessary innovations this implies.

But let us keep to science and technology and answer the following questions concerning the intelligence of science and technology in the furtherance of development: How is it to be acquired? How is it to be applied to the traditional sectors? How is it to be used in order to establish new activities? How is it to be used for further progress?

## How to Acquire Science and Technology Intelligence

Scientific and technical information is very widely available at a cost which is in no way prohibitive, even for a small country. (The example of Malaysia is discussed elsewhere in this volume.) That cost can be reduced or even eliminated by means of bilateral or

multilateral co-operation or through the efforts of world organisations like Unesco and the United Nations Industrial Development
Organisation (Unido).

But the information has to be passed on to all those individuals or
institutions whose role is to convert information into knowledge
and then intelligence. This involves the establishment of a national
or possibly regional centre which would collect information, if
necessary acquire the relevant documents and distribute them, after
having analysed, summarised, consolidated and duplicated them as
appropriate. We shall see later on that this centre is not usually the
only source of national information, but it is nearly always the main
source.

The processing of this information, which implies synthesis and
critical evaluation, can be done in part at the centre. But the bulk
will be done elsewhere, since knowledge is developed and assimi-
lated only through participation in its production, or at any rate
where its material implications are handled, which means in fundamental or applied research laboratories or even in the field.

But let there be no mistake. This does not necessarily imply
heavily endowed research programmes that will revolutionise science
or technology. In many cases, research would be on a modest scale,
done with and by young people and not necessarily original. Its
foremost aim would be to develop that complicity with reality
which, to my mind, is vital. Science policy must make ample room
for this kind of research. It will be doubly effective if it allows for
innovative research as well.

In many instances this sort of research stems from the educational
system, which is essential. In the industrialised countries that have
developed big research institutes, the amount of research done by
universities or engineering schools, far from decreasing, has increased considerably, since it is essential to the quality of education.
Without it, there can be no intelligence of science and technology.
But such research is done elsewhere, too, in varying degrees of
association with practical, goal-orientated research. Agronomic,
forestry and hospital centres are good examples.

I would also mention two other types of laboratory which I think
are vitally needed, even in a small developing country. First, test
laboratories. Even when very small, they render considerable services. Usually multi-disciplinary, they make standardised measure-
ments in mechanical engineering, electrical engineering, chemical
analysis, ageing and toxicity, among others. They are an important

185

locus of knowledge assimilation and pertinent questioning. Second, specialised laboratories in sectors like construction, civil engineering, ceramics, textiles and leather. It is a remarkable fact that in the industrialised countries, where big firms have their own well-structured laboratories, the latter have not meant the end of co-operative sectoral laboratories, which are often supported by the government. Even if these sectoral laboratories are restricted by their mandate to general research in areas of common interest where competition is not a factor, it is commonly acknowledged that they do a great deal to stimulate intelligence in the profession.

Is this enough? Certainly not. In many developing countries, the number of competent people who hold the knowledge and intelligence in a given field is very small: sometimes there is only one person. Deep understanding, which implies the posing of a great many questions, can be acquired only through discussions, exchanges and meetings. Creating the opportunities for these exchanges must be a key aim of science policy. There are two eventualities:

(1) A country is big enough for the community of scientists and technologists to reach its critical mass, at least in certain fields, and make it possible to establish and stimulate exchanges. Such a country can set up associations and organise symposia and conferences, thus providing occasions for discussions with foreign specialists;

(2) The critical mass is not attained, in which case other ways of letting in fresh air must be found. These could include internships abroad (sabbaticals, if necessary), international scientific associations, regional co-operation, invitation of foreign experts.

The university will have to play a leading role. Its action should not be confined to the student population but should extend to the whole country, and it should not limit its intelligence to the understanding of science but extend it to all the technologies that derive therefrom. It should even concern itself with traditional technologies, which will be discussed shortly, if necessary by officially broadening its mission. Correlatively, the university must have sufficient research resources to bring about the 'secret understanding' with physical and biological reality which often cannot be achieved by theoretical discourse alone.

The recent creation of an Association of African Mathematicians is an excellent initiative, though it alone is not enough. Specialists in the same field must be able to exchange their experiences and, in many cases, co-ordinate their work. It is also desirable that special-

ists in adjacent disciplines be able to meet: there are few development fields for which a uni-disciplinary approach will suffice. The
very recent creation of the African Association for the Advancement of the Sciences (AAAS) represents an attempt to meet this
twofold need. It is to be hoped that it will not confine its influence
to the development of pure science only.

Is that all? Nearly. It is worth noting that not all knowledge is in
written form, at any rate in serious science and technology journals.
A lot of information, with nothing secret about it, is passed on by
word of mouth or can be found in trade handouts or advertisements. Other information may appear in an economic article, in an
industrial firm's annual report to shareholders, and so on.

This information plays a considerable part in the evaluation of
reality and technological trends. It is important, therefore, to get
hold of it. This should basically be the task of scientific attachés in
embassies, all the more necessary for small and little-developed
countries but necessary for others, too.

Here some people have the idea that intelligence implies espionage. The very word 'intelligence', as in Britain's Intelligence Service,
suggests it. I hardly think that this idea is relevant in the majority of
cases. Experience proves that most of the necessary information is
available to the public. It is a question of being able to interpret it.
(This was even true in the case of the first Soviet satellite!) On the
other hand, secrecy surrounds ongoing research that should lead to
patented applications. But the patent itself constitutes disclosure
and sets a time limit on the legitimate profits which the inventor can
earn from his efforts. However, there are specific cases where it is
necessary to know how to pierce the veil of secrecy, which we shall
come to shortly.

## Applying Intelligence to Traditional Sectors

We have recently witnessed the birth of such new concepts as
intermediate technologies and adapted technologies, among others.
In fact these concepts are not properly understood: too often they
are seen as poor technologies with a small scientific content, merely
stepping stones to richer technologies that cannot be afforded until
later.

The truth is quite different, and much more complex. Let us try
to pin it down with the aid of an example: adobe construction. This

187

technique was once widely used and still is in many countries. In the French Alps, one can see multi-storey adobe buildings that are more than a century old. And there are mud buildings, or their ruins, that are veritable monuments in Morocco, Yemen and in the Andes. This kind of construction costs little — in that sense, it is a poor technology — it can be done by small teams without heavy mechanical equipment, it permits co-operation with neighbours ('I'll help if you can do the same for me one day'), and we all know how important this kind of co-operation is for society. But adobe construction also has its disadvantages, one of them being that the buildings are sometimes not durable enough, and that is why the advent of cement made it obsolete.

Let us inject science into this ancestral technology. Not just a bit of science, but all the knowledge that is relevant: granulometric studies, the study of the hardening properties of clays, knowledge of the effects of added lime and plastic binders, the high-temperature effect of blow torch techniques, the adhesive strength of protective plastic coatings, fibre reinforcement techniques, and so forth. When one knows the complexity of the soil sciences, and particularly of clays, there can be no underestimating the importance of all the knowledge that must be brought to bear. What else is needed? An intelligence of traditional building and of the links between a technology and an individual and social mode of life, as well as an intelligence of the scientific realities already taken into account intuitively or likely to be.

Let us assume[1] that we manage to improve the process significantly so as to obtain a better product more efficiently. We then have two eventualities:

(1) The improved process is still much inferior to cement. It nevertheless remains a process derived from an existing technology that is adapted to tradition, but which is an improvement over the latter thanks to science. It helps raise the standard of living appreciably but it will ultimately yield to another better technology. This is where we see the real meaning of the terms 'adapted technology' and 'intermediate technology'. The science used is nevertheless the most modern and the most sophisticated;

(2) The second, most probable, eventuality is that the process is

1. This in fact a certainty, as shown by the team of CRATERRE (Centre for Earth Research and Application), a French, Belgian and Peruvian team which has produced a remarkable work on adobe construction: *La Construction en Terre*, Editions Alternatives, Paris, 1980.

improved so much that the gap closes between its performance and that of modern processes. The comparison is not a simple one to make. It presupposes a whole range of criteria, not only physical and economic, but also psychological, emotional and social. The technology is then no longer intermediate. It is the point of departure for a new technology, which complements or is a substitute for modern technologies.

The same type of development could occur in traditional technology — ceramics, leather goods, textiles and, above all, agriculture. I propose to show, by way of somewhat simplified examples, that there is not enough intelligence of science and intelligence of tradition.

The scientist's intelligence is often sectoral, confined to his particular discipline. Most traditional processes cannot be correctly appreciated other than by means of a multi-disciplinary approach. It was to show this that I mentioned earlier seven possible fields of study, among many others, relevant to adobe construction. Similarly ceramics rests on chemistry (colloidal and crystal chemistry), on rheology (including thixotropy), on the science of the vitreous state, and on thermodynamics, among others.

Some scientists seem disinclined to concern themselves with traditional technologies. What may appear to be contempt for activities wrongly considered to have a low science content is in fact fear of the complexity of the multi-disciplinary approach, or an inability to handle it. Only when scientists turn their attention to these problems will they begin to acquire the real intelligence of science.

The intelligence of tradition is even more subtle. One must understand and distinguish between what is the result of observation and empirical experiment — in other words, of scientific intuition — and what is a transposal of habits and beliefs from one area to another. Tradition is very difficult to explain if it is regarded as something static, instead of a long, slow evolution marked by different stages.

The peculiarity of tradition is that it also takes into account, sometimes laboriously, natural constraints. Some have disappeared or can be overcome, and progress is easy. Others are still present but have not been identified: many of the unsuccessful attempts to introduce progress into agriculture are due to the fact that such constraints were not recognised. The disasters observed in Turkey, among other countries, where newly introduced tractors ploughed the land too deeply are examples of this kind of ignorance.

But tradition always combines production with social or even religious rites. Some deplore this and think that the ensuing obstacles to progress must be forcefully overcome. While this is sometimes necessary, albeit traumatic, it seems possible in most cases to reconcile objective intelligence of processes with intelligence of social traditions.

A successful experiment of this kind was carried out in Senegal. A modern experimental farm was set up in a village, and the peasants were invited to familiarise themselves with the techniques used. The farmers gradually came round, with characteristic prudence, adopting some techniques, modifying others and even eliminating a few. The intelligence of tradition and that of agronomic science were intermingled, became mutually complementary or were modified, and certain cultural attitudes were transformed while others were strengthened. What is certain is that this kind of experience gives birth to a new form of intelligence, one that is fully shared, elaborated by joint endeavour, remarkably efficient, and non-alienating.

Progress can go even further than the improvement of traditional techniques, combined with a few modern techniques; it can take on an entirely innovative character, as we shall see later on. But before that can happen, the new form of intelligence must be stimulated. This is perhaps the key function of the expert. He is making a mistake if he does nothing more than contribute his skills, for they must undergo a transformation on contact with the reality they are intended to improve.

## What Type of Intelligence is Needed for New Activities?

Let us now turn to activities that have become conventional in the industrialised countries, for the moment leaving to one side high-technology industries or those with a high content of recent innovation. These conventional activities are the very ones for which the concept of technology transfer was created, a concept which has not been sufficiently related to that of the intelligence of development or of technology. Early on, the transfer concept was often presented simplistically: 'Transfer your loss-making conventional activities to us; with the money we earn from our new exports, we will buy the high-technology products you alone are able to make. That will be a kind of division of labour.'

Expressed in such terms, the weaknesses of the concept show up. It is based on the existence of a wide labour–cost differential, which it is the precise purpose of development to eliminate. Moreover, it is disproved by facts: the most spectacular development has been in the subcontracting of electronics and photography. The concept can be expressed in more reasonable terms: 'Help us to set up the conventional basic activities for which we will strive to develop a solvent market, national or regional; to ensure this aid, try to envisage buying from us, at least to begin with, a part, that may perhaps dwindle progressively, of the goods we produce.'

Admittedly, unemployment in the industrialised countries and the progress made in automation — two facts that are partially related — constitute serious obstacles to this type of transfer. However, the prospect of a solvent domestic market may make them less formidable. What ought therefore to be discussed here — and the restricted scope of this paper prevents it — is the world structure of trade and modes of co-operation. I shall confine myself to the problem of intelligence of choices for a given activity for which there are local and international markets.

A choice must be made from among a number of technologies developed in different industrialised countries, and the right conditions must be created for their establishment and adaptation. I shall not discuss here the choice of the country of origin, which is a political choice and often a constraint. Let us stay in the sphere of technological intelligence.

First, the various technologies capable of generating an activity must be appraised. This appraisal — an operation typical of technological intelligence — encounters two kinds of difficulty. The first have been described in the first part of this paper, along with the means of surmounting them; the second are due to the incompleteness of published information. The fact that the necessary additional information is more or less secret makes it necessary to look more closely at the concept of intelligence.

Before buying a production plant, one wants answers to two questions. 'How reliably will it operate? What will the real costs of production be?' The answers to these questions are spelt out in the purchase contract that is negotiated. This is sufficient to prevent unwelcome surprises. Technological intelligence needs to be accompanied here by legal intelligence. The problem is not to forget anything. In this regard, the call for tenders followed by a comparison of bids constitutes a good guarantee — provided, of course, that the comparison is done properly.

But there are other ways of finding out the truth about projects: the selling firm's background and track record, its balance sheets and annual reports to shareholders, the nature and evolution of its advertising are all valuable sources of information. If an engineering consultancy firm is brought in, it will provide a list of the firms using the desired process. The activity of these firms must then be investigated. This, plus a few well-chosen questions at a convention or trade fair, will provide the intelligence of the industrial fabric of which the process concerned is a part.

These, then are the components of a strategy for acquiring industrial intelligence, which includes, but goes well beyond, technological intelligence, and which makes it possible, without industrial espionage, to pierce the veil of secrecy. But the understanding acquired and the resultant technology choice constitute only the first stage. The second is to find ways to integrate the purchased plant successfully into the country's social fabric. This entails several steps: studies to ascertain compatibility with existing or planned infrastructures (such studies are relatively easy); schemes for training the necessary personnel (always a difficult question and one which would warrant treatment at length); and adjustments that could be made to the plant which, without changing its basic technology, would change the human conditions of its operation.

This last point is crucial. It comes under the heading of social intelligence of industrialisation. By way of example, here are a few questions which show how subtle that intelligence is:

— Should certain features of the plant be demechanised in order to substitute labour for capital? There are very modern plants in which conveyor-belts are being replaced by wheelbarrows.
— Is it possible to decentralise the plant, setting up certain activities in villages, say, without sacrificing product quality? Textiles seems to be a good sector for this kind of experiment, though it is unfortunately made difficult by the influence of what the industrial countries have done. The size factor here needs to be analysed in detail.
— What systems should be adopted for the different levels of responsibility, for the transmission of orders, for the organisation of supervision? Taking psychological factors into account is a difficult but essential task. For example, in some cultures people react badly to the type of authority represented by a

typewritten office circular but are responsive to the spoken word. In other cultures, there is more of a sense of collective or group responsibility than of individual responsibility. Management systems must take this into account.

— Can traditional conceptions of authority be accommodated? Authority seldom derives from scientific ability and can often be hereditary, or even religious. It is often associated with the art of achieving a consensus, of identifying a common purpose. This art has been developed to a high degree in Japan. Amazing progress there is due in large measure to an original management intelligence, which has applied — one might say harnessed — all the traditional values to the pursuit of progress. Westerners do not yet fully appreciate how much Japan owes to the adaptation of its traditional system of responsibility and authority to modern production techniques. Here we have an example of a real intelligence in management problems combined with intelligence of the national culture.

— Can social innovations be injected into the industrial system so as to make it more compatible with tradition? A classic example is the replacement of individual wage-earners by collective work-contracts entered into by families or a village.

In other words, does the adoption of a technological system necessarily entail the adoption of an organisational structure patterned exactly on our own? These few questions are sufficient to pose, without solving, the general problem of the intelligence of social innovation.

It is not possible here to explore more fully the questions posed by the integration of modern industry into a traditional society, even if that industry has become conventional elsewhere, or is no longer evolving. Today, however, conditions are such that few industries can be regarded as static, even if they have progressed very little during the past twenty years, since the new constraints will prompt adjustments or developments that may well be rapid.

There is thus some danger in making technology choices without a very careful prospective analysis. The sale of an industrial plant that will be obsolete in five to ten years' time is not necessarily an act of conscious dishonesty. But its purchase without critical appraisal is always an act of utter naïvety. Today, much more than in 1970, there can be no policy of industrial development without intelligence of the future — in other words, without prospective analysis.

A last point to note — though this does not make the list exhaustive — is that the small size of many countries makes it necessary to think in terms of the region. Setting up an industry in one's own country may lead one to envisage economic agreements with a whole group of neighbouring countries. The development process then becomes part of an operation that extends beyond the nation's frontiers. This situation is frequent in Africa, but not specific to it.

It is perhaps this point which is currently the most obvious stumbling block in certain development endeavours. Creating the conditions for integrated development is a political task which must draw upon a highly acute intelligence of the future and a real determination to succeed.

## The Conditions for Endogenous Innovation

Our discussion has taken us beyond the confines of science policy, or rather has shown us its close links with a country's overall policy. The creation of an endogenous innovation potential would appear at first sight to be purely a matter for science policy. The problem is in fact more complex.

Obviously, there will always be plenty of discoveries to make for isolated researchers with few resources. This is true in the theoretical field, but it applies to some extent to the experimental field as well. Major discoveries can certainly be made in small, still poor countries. The important thing is not to stifle intellectual endeavours. But alongside this policy to create a favourable environment, there must be a goal-orientated policy. Here the constraints are more clearly evident: the existence of a critical threshold, the multi-disciplinary nature of the tasks linked to most of the goals, the cost of developing applications, and so on: these are some examples of the formidable constraints involved.

Choices have to be made, if science policy is to be something more than managing a dearth of resources. As a rule, there is little to be gained from tackling fields in which armies of researchers abroad have been working for years, unless the country has a particular advantage or a specific constraint. More often than not, the particular advantage will be a raw material, mineral or organic, which others have not thought of exploiting or known how to exploit. The specific constraint is more often than not climatic or geographic, such as transportation problems in the Andes, or the use of the region's rivers and lakes. The quality of science policy choices will in this case derive from intelligence of the physical environment.

But from time to time there may be new fields where a country may not be hard put to catch up. If they are judged promising, they should be entered right away. The typical example today is anything that has to do with biology: the use of biomass as a source of energy or raw materials, or the use of micro-organisms, possibly after genetic engineering, to produce medicines or even dyes.

Admittedly, this field of bioconversion is being eagerly explored by researchers in the industrialised countries, but this huge effort is quite recent, and there is still an enormous amount to be done. There is nothing to prevent a poor country from setting out on this road. It leads to successes which often, but obviously not always, can be achieved with limited resources. For example, the search for new plants from which proteins can be extracted requires little equipment, and there was nothing to prevent small African countries from discovering some micro-organisms that improve the protein content of cassava.

Here again, there is a need for a comprehensive intelligence of science in action. In the preceding example, of course, there is a favourable factor. Biological intelligence is widespread in most countries, owing to the existence of a medical and agronomic infrastructure, whereas technological intelligence is scarce.

A country that decided to enter the biomass and bioconversion field could also regionalise its effort through appropriate co-operation policies. Moreover, since there is little or no industrial experience in the field, production could be designed in the light of a prospective analysis of that society's evolution. Which activities could be decentralised to rural areas? Which should be concentrated and where?

But let us come back to the essence of science policy. By definition, information in a new field is insufficient; one would have to know about ongoing research programmes, to know what the first promising results have been and what has not worked. Ongoing research is always kept secret to a greater or lesser degree, even if economic agents are not involved. Scientists give top priority to intellectual property.

Where ground-breaking research is concerned, there is a great temptation to try to acquire the sort of intelligence that has connotations of espionage. In fact, it is easier than one thinks to know roughly what is going on. Although one cannot know what a rival laboratory is going to find, a study of its publications will at least reveal the main lines of its research. And, above all, secrets are exchanged. Experience shows that a visit to a foreign laboratory to which you bring something is always beneficial. In many cases this something is a researcher who will give of his best but will not come away empty-handed. He, too, will talk about his hopes and failures. Admittedly, these exchanges are easier in the framework of economic communities or under co-operation agreements. But experience has shown that this is not an essential condition. Although new fields like bioconversion are few, they do exist. Being able to detect them is decidedly an asset.

This chapter makes no claim to be exhaustive. Its sole purpose is to stimulate thought followed by action. It has stressed the links between science and technology in policy-making, the will to develop technologically, and the need for social prospective analysis and innovation. At a time when crises are hitting many developing countries, it is important to think about ways of cushioning the future shocks. At a time when research in the industrialised countries is often conducted with the aim of reducing a sometimes excessive interdependence, it is important to remind developing countries that by not innovating themselves, they run the risk of relapsing into a state of increased dependence, which might be irremediable.

It is therefore vital to know what obstacles might block the acquisition of indispensable intelligence. Some are institutional, others cultural. The word 'culture' should be understood here as meaning a representation of the physical, biological and human world, coupled with a system of values that stimulates and guides our thoughts and actions. Acquiring the intelligence of science and technology probably means first of all thinking about science itself and about the nature of one's own culture. This is an essential but much neglected task of cultural policies.

CHAPTER 14

# An Intelligence Model for Managers

## Thomas Lindberg

'What we are witnessing on every hand today is the beginning of the collapse of traditional industries, traditionally managed, and the rise of economies based on or assisted by new communications and information resources.'[1] Knowledge is changing from a precious asset possessed by a few into a commodity that can be exploited and developed through technical means until it permeates the very fibre of a nation. The 'knowledge game' will make or break both enterprises and nations in the decades to come.

The need for good economic, political, social and technological information is ever more pervasive. Some international corporations are already making systematic use of intelligence operations, while expanded trade missions and investigating committees show a corresponding effort on the part of governments.

A corporate intelligence model is particularly relevant to developing countries, which can draw lessons from what some of the more sophisticated industrial firms have done to build their own intelligence capability.

Generally speaking, the successful application of systematic intelligence within an institution depends upon a state of mind, which has far-reaching implications at the organisational level. To create this state of mind, there are a number of basic steps that can be taken to generate intelligence for strategic planning, crisis forecasting and issue analysis and monitoring, and to communicate this intelligence to decision-makers.

1. Oswald H. Ganley and Gladys D. Ganley, *To Inform or to Control?*, McGraw-Hill, New York, 1982.

## The Intelligence Process and Strategic Planning

As there is no recognised set of terms in the field of social, political
and economic intelligence, our discussion is based on the following
definitions: all data and information referred to are in the public
domain or are available commercially; 'information' is data that
have been evaluated for a specific purpose; 'hard' information is
information that can be verified, such as standard official data,
statistics or observed events; 'soft' information is information that
cannot be verified, such as uncorroborated accounts by individuals,
beliefs and the like; and 'intelligence' is information organised for
use in strategic planning.

By its very definition, hard information about the future does not
exist. It does, however, lend itself to search and selection by
computer. The softest pieces of information are political promises
and, though soft, they must be incorporated into forecasts. The
knowledge, experience and intuition of the intelligence researcher
or the issue analyst determine early on the end-quality of the
strategic intelligence (see Figure 14.1.).

A common complaint of intelligence officers in business and
government is that their reports go unread and unheeded. This
highlights an essential requisite of meaningful intelligence operations. If intelligence is ignored when operational directions are
being defined, it is wasteful and unjustified. The value of intelligence lies not only in its accuracy and timeliness, but also in the
degree to which it is and can be used by the constituents it is meant
to serve.

Figure 14.2. summarises the sequence of parallel actions taken by
an intelligence unit and, if the message is relevant and well-received,
by its constituents. The purpose of an intelligence unit is to keep a
constant watch on the environment, to identify key issues, to
analyse their relevance for the firm, to provide management with
strategic intelligence on issues and to propose directions for action.
Another task is to monitor important sources of information, some
of which may be the operations units of the firm itself. Here, the
intelligence unit will probably have to overcome initial scepticism
and a certain amount of territorial protectionism inherent in all
organisations. For example, sensitive 'competitive analysis' is often
performed by the marketing division and may not be immediately
available to the intelligence analyst. Marketing managers frequently
prefer to be the sole interpreters of information that could reflect

198

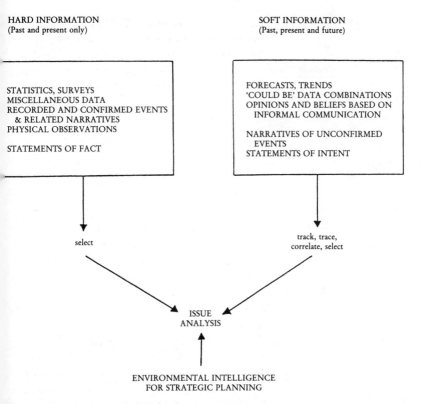

HARD INFORMATION
(Past and present only)

SOFT INFORMATION
(Past, present and future)

STATISTICS, SURVEYS
MISCELLANEOUS DATA
RECORDED AND CONFIRMED EVENTS
  & RELATED NARRATIVES
PHYSICAL OBSERVATIONS

STATEMENTS OF FACT

FORECASTS, TRENDS
'COULD BE' DATA COMBINATIONS
OPINIONS AND BELIEFS BASED ON
  INFORMAL COMMUNICATION

NARRATIVES OF UNCONFIRMED
  EVENTS
STATEMENTS OF INTENT

select

track, trace,
correlate, select

ISSUE
ANALYSIS

ENVIRONMENTAL INTELLIGENCE
FOR STRATEGIC PLANNING

**Figure 14.1.** The work flow of hard and soft information

upon their own performance.

In such a case, the intelligence officer can either ask management for extraordinary powers, which is the naïve approach, or he can slowly and painstakingly make his niche by providing the manager in question with important information. In this way, he can prove his maturity in handling sensitive internal issues, which is the creative approach. Effective intelligence rests upon constituency service and confidence. If the intelligence officer succeeds, a natural interaction can be established, based on an internal management communication system.

Paradoxically, this kind of give-and-take can be a source of frustration for intelligence officers. Once a certain environment-sensitive state of mind is created within a management group and a routine for communicating new environmental intelligence is estab-

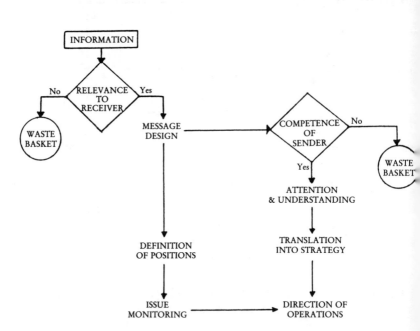

**Figure 14.2.** Intelligence justification by constituency approval

lished, managers tend to pick up new intelligence from the mass media, conferences and outside contacts. This may lessen the glamour attached to the job of environmental analyst. He may be met with more scepticism and contention as his constituents become increasingly better informed. But that is a sign that the intelligence unit has succeeded in creating effective interaction with the management system, not the opposite. (This interaction is schematised in Figure 14.3.)

## The Intelligence Professional and the Intelligence Window

Usually the intelligence professional has had no formal training for his job. He is often the odd man out in an organisation, the radical researcher in a peace institute or even a reporter. Increasingly, however, well-trained pragmatic company executives are turning up

200

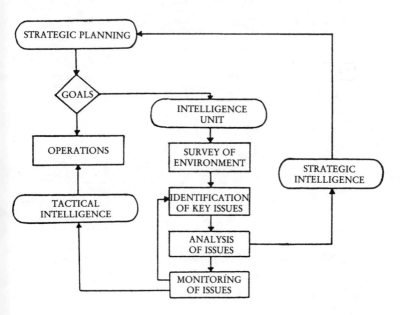

**Figure 14.3.** The interaction between intelligence unit, strategic planning and operations

in the profession, which signals the natural birth of social intelligence as a new vocation.

An ideal intelligence professional should be free from bias, have an analytical mind and a knack for synthesis, and be politically perceptive. He should also have knowledge appropriate to the company context and should remain distant from the decision process. He must be able to come up with clear messages and to break even bad news, regardless of the persons concerned.

Intelligence failures are liable to occur if one or several of these qualities are missing. According to one Belgian observer, the investments made by Swedish and Belgian steel companies during the early 1970s in all but obsolete technologies were cases where early, insistent intelligence literally bounced back on those transmitting it.

To use intelligence in a productive way, it is imperative to recognise not only its opportunities but its constraints. One of the latter is the intelligence window, situated at a point some two to three years hence, where the reasonably predetermined future ends. It marks the limit up to which strategic intelligence can be used for operational planning purposes, as shown in Figure 14.4.

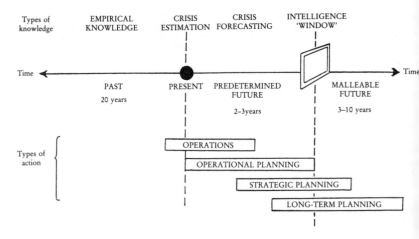

**Figure 14.4.** The intelligence window

## Crisis Forecasting and Estimation

To a certain extent, crisis forecasting is possible, but crisis esti-mation can be done only after the fact. This is because the depth and duration of a crisis are generally determined not by the underlying issues themselves but by the fact that most parties affected usually refuse to accept the imminence of a crisis and its true nature. They thus fail to act rationally. The 1973 oil crisis and the Iranian crisis are two cases in point: before a rational reaction could set in, a world recession and a change in geopolitics were permitted to come about.

Crisis estimation is the task of economists and statisticians, whereas crisis forecasting can be a major task for an intelligence unit, provided it is not blamed for being the bearer of bad news. During the 1981 French presidential election, for example, members of the business community forecast the victory of the Left but were consequently shunned by their outraged peers until the election results came in. Yet for many political analysts with access to unpublished surveys, the potential socialist victory was written on the wall.

Such classic neglect of a good intelligence evaluation of a potential event or crisis is commonly caused by the low credibility rating of intelligence units or of their sources. This can and should be avoided, because crisis forecasting can reveal not only exposure

202

areas but new opportunities as well. The solution lies in improving the transmission of intelligence evaluation to decision-makers.

## Issue Analysis

Underlying the environmental analysts' 'exposure and opportunity tracing' are the identification of key issues, as well as the processes of assessment and analysis. There is a point in time when a key issue comes to be perceived as such, but there is also a time when it ceases to be an issue, turning instead into a rigid, widely held concept. The period in between is one of dynamic opportunity to exploit the situation and to influence the outcome.

The initial perception of a new issue is always preceded by significant events. Rachel Carson's book *Silent Spring* marked the start of the present debate on our biological environment, just as the 1948 Hague Congress raised the issue of European federalism that was eventually to materialise as the European Community. As an issue passes into the public, political domain, a number of exogenous forces — mass-media exaggeration, political exploitation and the like — begin to work. They restrict a firm's operational flexibility relative to the issue.

It would seem that the time-frame within which a key issue moves from the level of perception to that of a concept — to broad political action or legislation — is from ten to fifteen years. For a firm, the critical questions are: to identify early on, out of a mass of issues, those that are relevant to its goals and operations; to assess their evolution correctly; to correctly perceive their ultimate effects, that is, the new concepts to which they will give birth; and lastly, to assess the impact of each new issue on the operational flexibility of the enterprise during the phase of evolution, as well as the level of constraints and opportunities in the final phase of conceptualisation.

## Monitoring Key Issues

A key issue usually touches on very basic concerns: health, happiness, liberty, equality, national security or scarce resources. Monitoring its evolution — continuous information-gathering — is a routine operation for any environmental intelligence unit, the prime sources being the mass media and published studies. It is amazing to see what patiently collected press clippings can reveal when viewed as a whole. A good file yields not only facts but also the evolution of public opinion, that is, the signals that have reached politicians and have conditioned their actions.

In building up a file, news should be evaluated for accuracy, breadth and immediacy. It is important to identify journalists with a reputation for high-quality news and analysis. Their names are readily available from institutions with data banks or document files in each subject area. In the field of political science, for example, several European universities co-operate in collecting subject files from a carefully selected set of papers and journalists. It is often possible to subscribe to these files or to obtain their selection criteria.

Public opinion polls and major studies are also important sources; not only do they approximate the state of affairs but their publication tends to influence public opinion. Subscriptions to political and economic risk-assessment services are available from specialised companies and some non-profit business organisations, though the quality of the inputs for their forecasts should be checked.

Governments issue a steady flow of reports which, if regularly and routinely scanned, will give indications of political direction, or the lack of it. Reports by intergovernmental organisations, such as OECD and the International Labour Office, are highly reputed. Even though United Nations committees and assemblies seldom reach agreement, some of the most controversial proposals can suddenly be unilaterally implemented by individual member countries. Some restrictive legislation on foreign investment and ownership in Nigeria and India strongly resembles certain features of the abortive discussion in the United Nations on technology transfer and codes for foreign investment in the Third World, for example.

Last but not least, direct personal contacts on the professional level can yield high-quality intelligence, provided the analyst is knowledgeable enough to have the confidence of colleagues and access to professional circles. Many companies encourage their specialists to participate actively in seminars, professional associations, trade associations and the like, for this is a highly effective way of ensuring a steady flow of basic intelligence.

Key analysts should be given company status so that they will be invited to top-level international seminars, such as business–government round tables and conferences arranged by international organisations. These events seldom yield factual news, but the trained listener can detect early signs of change in national and international politics.

## Defining Meaningful Action in Response to an Issue

Well researched and put into context by trained analysts, information from such sources should yield enough intelligence to delineate a meaningful field of action for management. It is the result of an intelligence equation that could be set down as follows: 'total scope of events' minus 'political imperatives' minus 'absolute economic constraints' equals 'meaningful field of responsive action'. The problem is then to present this to management in such a way as to be credible and digestible. The fact that this is not always easy is best illustrated by the classic disclaimers that frequently prefaced forecasts from 1975 to 1980, such as 'We assume that there will be no serious shortage of grains, raw materials or the like' or 'The assumptions for this forecast are that oil price increases will not exceed . . . '. Such common disclaimers rendered many corporate, national and international forecasts virtually useless. Why were they made? For the simple reason that computer simulation models cannot be designed like war games, but have to be based on fixed, stable conditions that can be expressed as algorithms.

Planners and policy-makers can overcome this severe constraint by giving serious consideration to deviations from standard forecasts — the more unpleasant scenarios — and by building alternative plans of action. To start with, the entrenched habit of calling a pleasant scenario 'the most likely' and the less pleasant one 'the worst-case scenario' will have to be changed; many large corporations now have to pay dearly for their lack of scepticism. That is why a company like IBM plans according to 'a base case' and a second case that presumes that some vital conditions in the base case will deteriorate. Should this happen, the company management can easily move at an early stage and in orderly fashion to the second case.

The technique for such multi-level planning is an offspring of the scenario technique. The future is sliced up into a number of co-existing 'worlds'. Forecasts for a shoe factory, for example, are broken down into a 'women's shoe world', a 'baby-shoe world', a 'leather world' and a 'financing world', among others. Within each, the most likely scenario is chosen for base-case planning and the worst-case scenario for fall-back planning.

The advantage of scenario development is that a company is fairly sure that it will not be seriously off track on important parameters. The mere study of scenarios sensitises management to environmental factors and operants. Top management wants planning scenarios to be presented in the form of strategic options, based on intelligence and business-requirement inputs.

## Integrating the Intelligence Staff in the Total Organisation

The intelligence staff should be kept apart from the final decision process. By remaining aloof from quantitative operations risk assessment, it can avoid being biased by what might seem to be more acceptable to management. This is important, because it is thanks to broad and unbiased curiosity that an intelligence unit, like any other research group, picks up the nuggets of its trade.

Moreover, operations risk assessment and strategic policy decisions are the responsibility of the financial, legal, operational and top-management staff of an enterprise. Diluting this responsibility by involving the intelligence unit would serve no purpose.

However, if the intelligence unit is functionally outside the management decision system, there must be another kind of link with management. It could be the concept of management by issue, that is, linking corporate objectives to key issues. This concept is simple in theory. The environment is scanned in the context of management's foremost objectives. Potential constraints on achieving these goals are designated as key issues. The intelligence unit works out an analysis of a strategic position on each of these key issues. These company positions are then used as strategic denominators in the operations-planning process.

For the sake of brevity, the process of identification and evaluation of key issues is given below in a series of questions:

— What are the company's prime objectives?
— What are the environmental constraints, that is, the key issues?
— What positions should the company take on these key issues?
— How should the company support these positions?
— How could the company influence the evolution of these issues?
— How should they be monitored?

206

— What would a course of no action cost the company?
— How much of this cost could the company reasonably avoid by acting?
— What will be the cost of such action, that is, the avoidance cost?

## Communicating Intelligence within the Enterprise

An intelligence unit has to gain the understanding and support of management for the issues it has identified as critical and for the company positions it recommends. Three questions can be asked in order to obtain a successful management communications process. What are the perceptional limitations of the management system? Its acceptance and rejection mechanism? This is the map-making approach. Who transfers his opinions most successfully within the management system? This is the gate-keeper approach. How can the whole organisation live up to, and/or support the company positions on key issues? This is the total communications approach.

The map-making approach is a concept of human communications based on the notion that there are limits to what a given audience can perceive and accept. Beyond these limits, any message is automatically rejected. For effective communication, a map of the target audience's mentality is needed. Thus, when trying to make a management system and its individual actors accept new intelligence, in particular early intelligence based on soft information, the communicator must have insight into their attitudes, policies, commitments, conditioned reflexes and the like.

The gate-keeper approach, on the other hand, assumes that the opinion of many is formed by a few. If members of the intelligence unit can get the gate-keeper to embrace a new idea, it will be diffused rapidly. In other words, to make intelligence work within an organisation, one must find the point of authority — the gate-keeper — whose backing will ensure that the new idea will become part of the mentality of those concerned.

This approach leads to the total communications concept, which entails using all the standard communications channels in an organisation to sensitise it to a specific issue and make it act out the related company strategy. This is what political organisations are good at.

## The Contribution of Business Intelligence Operations

Without an effective intelligence organisation, the units responsible for operations will receive only micro-signals from the part of the environment in which they operate — the market-place. They will tend to filter such signals and to reject anything that does not directly concern their short-term responsibilities. Their communication with management will take the form of conditioned responses to the objectives, incentives and disincentives imposed on them by the management system. For these reasons, a company that relies exclusively on imaginative management and good communications links to operations may not survive for long in a competitive and changing environment.

A number of enterprises and government ministries have now recognised the danger and have implemented long-term planning through a strategic planning unit. The unit has as its sole performance objective to make reliable forecasts of long-term business opportunities and constraints. But this fact in itself, plus the fact that a good forecaster normally has a very sceptical mind, can easily constitute another filter, through which only a limited set of macro-signals will reach senior management.

The business intelligence unit, which may or may not be part of strategic planning, will complement these two classical management-information sources. It will pick up the signals reaching both operations and strategic planning before they are filtered and edited. Above all, it will pick up signals from the environment which never reach, or which are rejected by, the rest of the organisation. It will structure, process and analyse all this information. In so doing, the unit can fill in the environmental map that should comprise all the elements relevant to the organisation. It can then serve as an early warning system by identifying new opportunities and constraints, which it communicates objectively and effectively to the management system.

In the course of these activities, the unit may identify trends that could change the environmental map. In so doing, it may sometimes challenge management's established concepts of reality. The resulting resistance will be overcome only if the intelligence is of high quality, structured to the needs of the organisation and properly communicated via the gate-keepers in the management system.

## Social Intelligence Systems for Developing Countries

'All the affairs of men hang on a slender thread', wrote Shakespeare. Today, this thread is information and knowledge. We are rapidly moving into an era in which those who possess superior knowledge will prevail over those who possess only capital or natural resources. The industrial nations have now acquired 'the art of being caught up with'[2] and will no longer permit their key industries to be caught sleeping. Their enterprises and governments, already developed into learning organisations, have installed expanding intelligence systems at home and abroad that keep track of developments in technology, industry, finance, trade, national politics and regulations, among others.

The developing countries, which have not yet fully converted themselves into production organisations, still have a long way to go to turn themselves into learning organisations. In order to match the development of social intelligence capabilities in the post-industrial world, they will have to create their own capabilities. However, the social intelligence structure they need will no doubt have to be closed from Western capability through political action. This could be brought about if OECD and the United Nations could expand their already ambitious information services to the developing countries. They could devise a programme for the implementation of social intelligence systems in developing-country governments and of managerial intelligence systems for their key industries.

Part of this programme could be devoted to making social intelligence a branch of academic research and education. It is a science in which the knowledge gap between North and South would be rather easy to bridge. Another part of the programme could be to make experts from the industrialised countries available to developing-country governments to advise on the implementation of a social intelligence centre. This small centre could be the nucleus for future expansion, eventually becoming part of an appropriate ministry.

To achieve this, developing country governments would have to grant their social intelligence organisation political immunity and keep it at arm's length from its military counterpart. Is such a scenario unrealistic? Is it not sufficient that the developing countries

2. John Pinder, 'Informed Communication', Policy Research Institute, London, 1976.

are receiving the support of OECD, the United Nations and the World Bank, among others, as well as the opportunity to hook into the expanding information networks of Europe and the United States?

A tentative answer is that intelligence is subtle knowledge and fine judgement, and that it therefore must be part and parcel of the culture it serves. What lies outside a company or a national culture are merely potential intelligence outputs. Processed from within, they become intelligence.

CHAPTER 15

# An Open Letter to Top Decision-Makers

## Yehezkel Dror

Heads of state are curiously neglected in much of the literature on development and decision-making. This is all the more regrettable since to a significant extent they share, and will undoubtedly continue to share, the fate of nations. Though their backgrounds, their mode of selection and their accountability, among others, may differ from one type of regime to the next, in democratic and non-democratic countries alike leaders represent a determining element in policy-making systems. In developing countries, they play an even more central role because of the frequent need to build new socio-political structures and to guide the development process. Any valid discussion of intelligence or development, therefore, cannot neglect this aspect of the question.

One of the prerequisites for improved policy-making — rarely mentioned but nevertheless true — is to upgrade the performance of national leaders. This can be done in a number of mutually complementary ways. Picking one of many possible approaches, this chapter presents a series of recommendations on intelligence for leaders, aspiring leaders and their advisers which, with minor adaptations, could apply to various governmental levels as well as to private firms.

### Improving Strategic Development Intelligence

Ostensibly, all decisions are based, at least in part, on facts and predictions of facts. This is an illusion, and an exceedingly dangerous one: no one can get at the facts. What one regards as facts are only images, often highly distorted, of reality. Understanding the limits of these images, reducing distortions as far as possible, and adjusting modes of decision-making to irreducible ambiguities and

211

doubts are imperative. Good intelligence, along with other aids, can help to do this.

Decision-making involves comparing the expected results of possible alternatives and choosing the alternative that should ensure the preferred future. Here, errors can crop up: the very ambiguity of predictions in a rapidly changing world can heighten image distortion and multiply propensities for error. The first step, then, is better intelligence of present realities, as well as their dynamics. To know and understand the present allows us better to face the future.

Recognising what causes image distortion is a daunting task. A leader may easily overreact by putting his faith in his own personal intuition, arguing that in any case intelligence is not to be relied upon. But unaided intuition is even less trustworthy. Even an exceptional human being is made of flesh and blood, though a person with outstanding intuitive gifts can often grasp complexities and sense connections better than a run-of-the-mill expert. Intuition is not a magic formula; it is itself weighted down with fallacies and cannot serve as a substitute for excellent intelligence.

A leader should therefore actively promote strategic development intelligence. Till now, nearly all intelligence efforts have been concentrated on national security, the rest being devoted to quantitative economic and demographic data collection and to sometimes doubtful social indicators. For development, this is inadequate: a country needs excellent intelligence on its principal development issues. To keep a country physically secure and on the right track, socioeconomic factors that affect development are more important than narrow defence intelligence, though the latter may be needed as well.

A highly advanced intelligence capacity can make a leader uncomfortable, for it forces him to discipline his thinking, leaves less leeway for exercising personal will and generally restrains his freedom of action. None the less, this is the best way to build up capacities and reduce errors. Subordination to verified knowledge will let a leader have more real impact on the future, even if it produces stress and strain in the present. Consequently, a leader should not place inordinate trust in his own innate superiority nor hesitate to accept the restrictions imposed by close contact with a top-notch strategic development intelligence unit. Benefits will far outweigh personal inconvenience.

## What Causes Image Distortion?

Recognition of what constitutes and what causes image distortion can help to reduce intelligence failures and can serve as the basis for establishing error-reducing systems. Indeed, sources of image distortion, and their related intelligence failures, are woven into the very fabric of social institutions, governments and individual mental processes. Even though military intelligence has been given high priority, grievous mistakes have frequently been made; Pearl Harbor, Barbarossa and Yom Kippur are classic examples of intelligence fiascos, no matter how much labour went into avoiding them. Comparable calamities in development, in which intelligence failures played a major role, are easy to identify in such fields as overall development strategies, economic and monetary policies, choices between heavy industry and agriculture or those concerning energy and national security.

Basic causes of image distortion can be found at all levels. Culture determines an individual's concepts and fundamental assumptions, which inexorably shape his views of reality, all the more insidiously since he and those around him undergo the same conditioning without being aware of it. Individuals tend to overinterpret new facts so that they fit their own opinions. They can misapprehend situations of risk and uncertainty, remain riveted to initial formulations of problems, and misperceive new situations, which are masked by historical and linguistic metaphors. Lastly, to reduce inner tension, individuals can distort or deny facts.

Groups, too, share a number of information-misprocessing propensities. They tend to seek agreement and mutual support rather than the closest approximation of the truth. Members of a group influence one another, and this can produce group judgements that often have little to do with the merits of the case. Needless to say, organisations have in-house doctrines, interests and habits.

Certain factors that often aggravate mistakes in military intelligence are usually less operative in civilian affairs: deliberate deception is less prevalent and secrecy less pervasive. But image distortion can permeate domestic questions through such factors as ideological commitments, political competition or conceptual ambiguity. In a country in the process of accelerated development, these factors can become especially intense. Moreover, a success in the past may insidiously reinforce adherence to outdated images. For example, a developing country's success in achieving independence and an

213

initial period of rapid growth may freeze world pictures and behaviour patterns for a long time, even after conditions have changed. Indeed, the more successes one has had in the past, the greater the risk of failure when conditions are undergoing rapid change. This warning is particularly applicable to intelligence: images proven correct in the past easily become sanctified, and the sense of reality is lost.

Leaders can aggravate the tendency to hold fast to false fact-images by motivating those around them to proffer only those suggestions that will meet with approval. Meanwhile, they themselves are overloaded with work and consequently have difficulty in absorbing new inputs and benefiting from them. They also tend to be oversure of themselves, which lessens their learning capacity. All this means that the images held by leaders are prime targets for others' manipulation.

The picture is a harsh one indeed: leaders are condemned to make decisions on the basis of distorted fact-images. Their decision-making can best be seen as fuzzy betting — gambling against largely unknown odds and with undetermined rules for high stakes. When the future of a country is at stake, this may give a better sense of the utilitarian and moral imperative for leaders to make the maximum effort to improve strategic development intelligence.

True, there are times when incorrect images may be useful, especially when facing the real facts may lead to despair and paralysis. A leader attempting a mission impossible may in some ways be better off not thinking constantly of the real facts and his slim chances of success. He may otherwise give up, thereby reducing his achievement probabilities to zero and losing his chance of a self-fulfilling prophecy. But this is an unusual situation, which cannot justify weaknesses in development intelligence.

To sum up: leaders face a real danger of being trapped in a cocoon of myth and half-truths, nourished by their entourage with illusion- and delusion-breeding information. To break out, they must build up strategic development intelligence and personally conduct themselves in such a way as to get the maximum benefits from it. The following recommendations may be of help.


### Establishing a Small Unit for Strategic Development Intelligence

Leaders may need in their personal entourage a small group in charge of strategic development intelligence. Six to ten highly qualified professionals headed by a development intelligence adviser will do. This unit could assure the production of high-quality intelligence and its supply for decision-making. In particular, such a unit's functions could include the following:

— Developing intelligence for broad policy decisions: for instance, by diagnosing a situation as either on a downward or on an upward path.
— Monitoring development-intelligence production to ensure coverage of all the leader's information needs: among other things, by communicating his interests and his agenda for taking decisions on issues to the appropriate agencies.
— Linkage analysis which interrelates different sectoral intelligence estimates to arrive at integrated assessments, with special emphasis on the fusion of domestic and external intelligence.
— Upgrading intelligence production to ensure its quality and format.
— Co-ordinating various intelligence-producing agencies, to avoid lacunae and to reduce conflict.
— Processing and re-evaluating all material and preparing it for a leader's perusal in a form that will save him time but will not suppress or oversimplify content.
— Developing a proper interface between intelligence and decision-making by introducing relevant estimates and conditional predictions into the decision process and checking estimates against what actually occurs.

A delicate function of the strategic development unit, and especially its head, is to blast a leader's pet illusions and help him get rid of fixed ideas. A clinical relationship between the leader and his unit, marked by complete frankness and avoidance of emotionalism, is essential.

The head of the unit should be a senior member of the leader's inner circle of advisers. His staff should have close ties with the policy-analysis and planning staff (another requisite for leaders, not discussed here) but should not be an integral part of it, so as to avoid the bias that can come from direct responsibility for policy advice. Before strategies and structures become too rigid, one of a leader's first steps should be to appoint a suitable development-intelligence adviser and let him build up his unit as quickly as possible, but not so fast as to compromise quality.

## *Encouraging Sectoral Intelligence and an Allocation of Priorities*

A government's effectiveness can be heightened by better fact-images. By encouraging intelligence, a leader cannot only meet his own decision-making needs but upgrade the performance of the government as a whole. To conserve resources and prevent information overloads, priorities should be set. Social problems and processes, which are a key to successful development, are often neglected, compared with defence and economics.

## *Insistence on High-Quality Intelligence Products*

As the leader is the ultimate client of much of strategic development intelligence, he should personally insist on high-quality intelligence products. Among other things, he should demand clear indications of the reliability of various estimates and the probability of predictions. Terms such as very probable, possible, and so forth should be clearly defined, and the use of question marks to indicate uncertainties should be encouraged.

The leader should also be presented with the complete gamut of opinions, and conclusions should carefully indicate the range of uncertainty and ignorance. There should be standard sets of intelligence products that go far beyond present practices, such as short- and long-range estimates; trends analyses, with special attention to possible discontinuities; integrated alternative futures; studies of possible surprise events; and conditional estimates of alternative consequences of the main options.

Good intelligence supplied too late is worthless, so strict time-tables should be drawn up. An overload of unreadable good material is just as bad as hastily drawn, one-sided conclusions. While gadgetry should generally be shunned, a carefully designed interactive computer system may be of great help to make better use of intelligence. A leader should not hesitate to devote time to learning about the system, so he can use it alone. Benefits will quickly make up for the time spent.

## *Institutionalising Failure-Reducing Intelligence Systems*

To handle complex problems, complex systems are needed to re-

216

duce image distortion. Unless specifically requested by the leader, such systems will not be established. But if a leader does not overview them, their complexity will rapidly become obfuscated.

In the more critical domains of strategic development intelligence, a leader should insist on some combination of the following systematic arrangements:

— Positive redundancy, that is, various independent units that compete in studying intelligence issues. To reduce the tendency to have identical biases, these units should be in different locations and should have different intellectual orientations, methodological bases and internal cultures.

— Institutionalised devil's advocates: special teams to work out and defend positions contrary to those supported by the main intelligence outfits.

— Organisational short-cuts to permit those with unconventional opinions to have access to the leader. This is difficult, as the leader can easily become swamped with esoteric proposals while essential hierarchical structures become eroded. None the less, intelligence professionals with unconventional opinions should be allowed direct access, if only to prevent the leader from becoming a captive to self-appointed mind-keepers.

— Mixed methodologies, including estimates based on hard facts and on intuition. Interdisciplinary knowledge and varied life experiences are a must for good intelligence.

— High-quality staff, with turnover and lateral entrance. This sounds simple but is in fact a radical departure for intelligence units, since many bureaucracies traditionally move staff up the hierarchy, which can freeze doctrines and close minds. To put political cronies in charge of intelligence is to court disaster. The only sound advice is to use qualified professionals.

— Due attention to new problems which should be given new units and new professionals. A good example is that of scientific intelligence in the United Kingdom during the Second World War, which got off to a weak start and ended up with brilliant successes.

— Use of external intelligence and estimation capacities that can be found in research institutes, universities, think-tanks, and the like. Only in such places can in-depth studies be done.

— Use of international material: it should be reanalysed by

217

capable staff and applied to the leader's needs. This is an important point for developing countries, comparable to other fields of knowledge-production and import.

— Intelligence units must be close enough to decision centres to be aware of needs and to be able to input data, estimates and sometimes proposals for decision-making. At the same time, intelligence units must be excluded from the responsibility for and over-involvement in decision-making to reduce biases and vested interests.

— Even harder to attain is the most essential of all intelligence-system features, namely an innovative and sophisticated atmosphere. A leader can do much to encourage this by his choice of a strategic development intelligence adviser and his influence on the selection of the principal heads of intelligence units. One of the main duties of the adviser and his aides is to help a leader build up the necessary characteristics of the intelligence system as a whole and to monitor its operations.

## Avoiding a Monopoly on Intelligence

The tendency to monopolise information in order to preserve power is to some degree unavoidable, though it should be bridled as much as possible. All those who are to participate in major decisions should have full access to salient intelligence, including background material.

As for the public at large, sharing information has both ethical and political implications. An enlightened public opinion is basic to democracy. Moreover, it improves the quality of intelligence, thanks to open debate. On the other hand, revealing some types of intelligence may impair a leader's capacity to govern, demoralise the public and hurt chances for development. Indeed, secrecy can be both a tool and a weapon and must consequently be used only after careful consideration. Needless to say, under no circumstances can intelligence leaks be tolerated.

## Respecting the Needs of Good Intelligence

The recommendations set out above may prove hard to follow even if a leader understands their importance. But there is no excuse for either repressing good intelligence or misusing it. This is difficult for leaders because they are generally prone to a number of weaknesses.

Among them are an intolerance of uncertainty and ambiguity, a strong attachment to images proven to have been effective in the past and an overwhelming faith in their own judgement. Leaders also show a strong aversion to tension and tend to distort unpleasant information to render it less stressful.

Leaders tend to keep their thoughts too much to themselves, which makes it difficult, if not impossible, for intelligence to serve their needs. As leaders generally carry too great a load, they become impatient. This slows down learning from intelligence, which can take time and energy. They therefore choose to remain ignorant, if not disdainful, of intelligence and decision methods. This is a near guarantee that they will make serious blunders. It is also a standing invitation for others to try to manipulate them. To demand that leaders avoid making such blatant mistakes is less than useless. One of the main tasks of intelligence is precisely to educate leaders to use intelligence correctly. If they do not want to learn or are incapable of doing so, they cannot be helped.

## Starting from Scratch

In some countries, strategic development intelligence may have to be built from the ground up. The best way to start is to establish an island of excellence around the leader, in the form of a first-class policy-analysis and planning unit. Within this unit, a distinct strategic development intelligence group can be formed, until the time is ripe to set it up as an independent unit.

The main functions of this initial group could then include the following institution-building activities: establishing a set of priorities to build up the development intelligence system in accordance with the country's main problems and the leader's policy agenda; setting up an infrastructure for a phase-by-phase build-up of development intelligence, including training at home and abroad, as well as selective imports of relevant knowledge and experience; and training senior decision-makers so they can use intelligence correctly, with special attention to the country's specific problems, needs and distorting effects.

By starting from scratch, it may be possible to bypass some intermediate stages, moving directly to a compact, advanced intelligence system for development. But leaders must be very careful not to become trapped on the way by too much emphasis on hardware, rather than on sophisticated professionals and self-education.

## A Reading List for Leaders

Much can be learned about strategic development intelligence from intelligence failures in defence. Outstanding introductions to this subject are Roberta Wohlstetter, *Pearl Harbor: Warning and Decisions*, Stanford University Press, Stanford, Calif., 1962, and Barton Whaley, *Codeword Barbarossa*, MIT Press, Cambridge, Mass., 1973.

The ubiquity of intelligence incapacities is strikingly demonstrated, of all places, in medical diagnosis. An enlightening though depressing book is Arthur S. Elstein, Lee S. Shulman and Sarah A. Sprafka, *Medical Problem Solving: An Analysis of Clinical Reasoning*, Harvard University Press, Cambridge, Mass., 1978. Some of the technical analysis may be skipped without losing the main findings.

Nearer to the concerns of national leaders is Robert Jervis, *Perception and Misperception in International Politics*, Princeton University Press, Princeton, NJ, 1976.

The three following items will suffice to explore the main causes of operational failures in security and external affairs intelligence, which can also apply to strategic development intelligence: Roberta Wohlstetter, 'The Pleasures of Self-Deception', *Washington Quarterly*, vol. 2, no. 4, Autumn 1979, pp. 54–63; Richard K. Betts, 'Intelligence for Policy-Making', *Washington Quarterly*, vol. 3, no. 3, Summer 1980, pp. 118–29; Thomas L. Hughes, *The Fate of Facts in a World of Men — Foreign Policy and Intelligence Making*, Foreign Policy Association, New York, 1976.

Moving to even more insidious causes of intelligence failures, cultural factors in action are brought out by Mary Douglas and Aaron Wildavsky, *Risk and Culture: An Essay on the Selection of Technological and Environmental Dangers*, University of California Press, Berkeley, Calif., 1982.

Dangerous group processes are presented in Irving L. Janis, *Victims of Groupthink*, Houghton Mifflin, Boston, 1983. Organisational information misprocessing is treated in James G. March and Johan P. Olsen, *Ambiguity and Choice in Organisations*, Universitetsforlaget, Bergen, Norway, 1976.

An understanding of psychological dynamics, which distorts images and produces incorrect conclusions from intelligence, is essential. Good introductions to various aspects of the subject can be found in Irving L. Janis and Leon Mann, *Decision Making: A*

*Psychological Analysis of Conflict, Choice and Commitment*, The Free Press, New York, 1977; and in Daniel Kahneman, Paul Slovic and Amos Tversky (eds.), *Judgement Under Uncertainty: Heuristics and Biases*, Cambridge University Press, Cambridge, 1982.

PART IV

# General Conclusions

CHAPTER 16

# General Conclusions

Nicolas Jéquier and Stevan Dedijer

One of the common themes running through the proposals made by the authors of the four preceding chapters is the importance of what might be called an 'intelligence culture'. Such a culture is not so much a system of accepted values shared by a community as a sensitivity to, and awareness of, the complex and ill-defined factors which account for good intelligence. When Sagasti writes about the need for pattern recognisers or synthetists, for instance, he is thinking less about a clearly defined profession than about a state of mind and a set of attitudes which do not fit easily into a classic job description. When Lindberg talks about the perception of new issues or the distinction between hard and soft information, he is referring not to formal structures or well-defined classification systems, but to qualitative factors which are difficult to formalise yet crucially important in the process of information acquisition and evaluation. In the same way, Piganiol's idea of the intelligence of development — which is not the same thing as intelligence for development — reflects a quasi-artistic perception of problems rather than formal organisation principles. Dror's precepts on image distortions, failure-reducing mechanisms or institutionalised devil's advocacy epitomises the same sort of sensitivity to the qualitative factors that account for good intelligence.

This intelligence culture, or sensitivity, is one of the crucial elements in an organisation's ability to acquire, evaluate and use information. The authors also suggest, implicitly or explicitly, that this intelligence culture is not only an internal quality of specialised information or intelligence units (for example, an industrial firm's long-range planning group, a government's national security agency or a minister's policy-analysis group), but a state of mind and set of attitudes that should be shared by all decision-makers and managers in a firm, government agency or country.

General Conclusions

## Information Infrastructure and Information Environment

Nurturing this intelligence culture is one of the important dimensions in an intelligence policy, and more generally in the effective utilisation of information and knowledge. Another important dimension which was touched upon by several authors in the first two parts of this volume — notably El Kholy in his analysis of Egypt, Tell in his comparison between Sweden and Malaysia and de Grolier in his discussion of governments and the information industry — is the role of a country's information infrastructure and its general information environment. In Sweden, for instance, information of any kind is easily accessible either from abroad or within the country, there is a very good network of libraries and data banks, the telephone system functions well, personal contacts are easy, there is a thriving publishing industry, and the general attitude towards information is one of openness and transparency rather than secrecy. This general environment makes it relatively easy for an industrial firm, or indeed for any organisation, to find the information it needs and carry out its intelligence work. It is also vital to good functioning of the country's knowledge industry: with good libraries, easy access to data banks and no restrictions on foreign contacts, the research centres of universities and private industry (which are among the main producers of scientific and technological knowledge) can operate much more effectively than would be possible without such facilities.

In a country like India, by contrast, the information environment is much less favourable, and the information infrastructure is generally poor. The publishing industry — a basic element in the transmission and storage of knowledge and information — is hampered by permanent paper shortages; the libraries of universities and research centres contain a very high proportion of outdated books and cannot afford subscriptions to more than a limited number of important foreign periodicals; photocopying machines are scarce; the internal telephone system functions rather poorly; foreign travel by Indian businessmen and scientists is costly and subject to time-consuming bureaucratic procedures; and industrial firms have great difficulties in importing machinery that could be used for 'reverse engineering' (that is, disassembling a piece of machinery, reconstituting its blueprints and copying it), or foreign technology which could help to update their production methods.

Even so, India has a rather good knowledge industry. It has

226

hundreds of thousands of scientists and engineers, some very good research laboratories both in the private and public sector, a good nucleus of world-class researchers, a large network of higher education institutions, a large number of literate people (the overall literacy rate is around 37 per cent), an emerging computer industry and a good telecommunications equipment manufacturing industry.

This contrast between a rather good knowledge industry on the one hand, and a poor information infrastructure and unfavourable information environment on the other, is characteristic of a number of other countries, developing or semi-industrialised, which in the last thirty years have made very significant investments in education and research. Such a situation suggests that one of the major challenges facing these countries is not so much to increase the overall size of their knowledge industry — important as this may be in the long run — as to help create a more favourable information environment and develop the information infrastructures without which the knowledge industry, and in particular the research and innovation sytem, cannot operate effectively. Creating this better environment and building up the information infrastructures is a major task of an intelligence policy, and one of the conditions for the effective mobilisation of knowledge for development purposes. It is also one of the keys to what several authors in this volume have called social intelligence, namely the intelligence of a society or country.

Some of the means for improving the information environment are simple and fairly inexpensive, while others are much more complex and costly. Some require major changes in attitudes and values, and belong to the field of culture, while others require no more than money, and belong to the field of physical infrastructures. Some finally may appear rather trivial, while others, which are seemingly more important, may in fact be rather minor.

## Secrecy and Transparency

One of the first ways to improve a country's information environment is to reduce the level of secrecy and increase transparency. The importance of this issue has been clearly underlined by O.A. El Kholy in his analysis of Egypt in Chapter 8 of this volume: he shows that the pervasive atmosphere of secrecy, which was motivated in large part by national security considerations and sanctioned by strict legal dispositions, turned out to be highly detrimental to the country's development effort. His story raises three important points. The first is that such a general atmosphere of secrecy is to a large extent the result of social and political structures, and reflects a style of government based on generalised distrust. In this sense, it is the expression of a system of values, and not a simple side-effect of a method of government. The second is that secrecy works for the benefit of the strong, and to the detriment of the weak: those who are strong enough and prepared to devote the necessary resources (for example, a large multinational corporation or an enemy beyond the borders) can almost always obtain the information they really need, whereas those who are weak and poor (the ordinary citizens, the small corporations, and so on) cannot obtain the information they need, despite the fact that its security value to the state is non-existent, or at least extremely tenuous. The third point is that the obsession with secrecy tends to overshadow the value of secrecy in specific well-defined circumstances: by considering all potentially important information as secret, a government tends to debase the secrecy of what should legitimately remain secret. In fact, there may well be a Gresham's Law of secrecy: just as 'bad money drives out good money', 'bad secrecy' (that is, excessive secrecy) 'drives out good secrecy' (the secrecy which attaches the truly important information about national security matters).[1]

If excessive secrecy is detrimental to a country's development effort, or indeed to the day-to-day operations of any social institution, be it an industrial firm, a trade union, a government department or a citizen's association, some degree of secrecy is nevertheless necessary, and secrecy should be viewed as an important information resource. The great problem in managing secrecy is to draw the line between its value as a resource and its negative effects on operations.

This concept of secrecy as a resource which must be managed, nurtured and controlled can perhaps best be illustrated with the help of two concrete examples. Take a commercial bank, for instance: in order to operate effectively, it must be in a position to

1. Sir Thomas Gresham, adviser to Queen Elizabeth I of England, was asked to inquire into the causes of the debasement of the coinage. His conclusion that 'bad money drives out good', since known as Gresham's Law, reflects the fact that when a debased currency and a good currency circulate together in a country, people tend to hoard the good and pass on the bad in repayment of debts or for the purchase of goods.

protect, within the limits of law, the identity of its customers and the details of the transactions it conducts with them. The degree of secrecy which it is able to maintain *vis-à-vis* outsiders (the general public, a political party or the country's tax authorities, for example) conditions to a large extent its effectiveness as a bank, and is one of its main intangible business assets. Were it only to confirm this, one can observe that the countries which harbour the largest and most successful international banks are most generally those where bank secrecy is closely enforced by the law, and not those where bank transactions are more transparent to tax authorities. In the world competition between banks, secrecy is in fact a much more important determinant of success than either the bank's efficiency as an organisation or the level of remuneration it offers to its depositors.

Banking, like national security, is one of the areas of human activity where secrecy is governed by precise legal prescriptions. In many other cases, secrecy is a matter of judgement left to the individual or the organisation concerned. Take the case of a negotiation between the government of a developing country and a foreign corporation about a major industrial development project. In this process, it is vitally important for the government and its authorised representatives to have as much information as possible about the firm's intentions, its technological capabilities, its long-range plans and its financial soundness, not to speak of its psychological dispositions and its reputation as a partner in joint ventures. In the same way, it is extremely important for the firm to know as much as possible about the country in which it is proposing to invest: how stable is the government? What is its financial situation? What is likely to be the rate of exchange in the next few years? Both partners will thus engage in a certain amount of intelligence work about each other prior to negotiation, and this work continues once the negotiations are under way. At the same time, both of them will be using secrecy as an instrument of negotiation. This can be done in two ways. The first is for partner A (the multinational firm) to prevent partner B (the government representatives) from gaining certain types of information about A, and vice versa. The second is for partner A to keep partner B in the dark about the extent of his knowledge concerning B. In the first instance, each of the negotiators is trying to protect or restrict the information about itself; in the second instance, each partner is trying to conceal the depth of its information about the other. In both instances, secrecy is a resource for the partner using it (and both generally use it) and an obstacle to the opponent. This secrecy can be preserved to some extent by strict security rules, and enhanced with the help of deception, misinformation and disinformation.

Secrecy is an essential component in the social interactions between individuals, between institutions and between the citizen and the state. At the level of the individual, one of the major policy issues posed by the expansion of the knowledge industry and the development of information technology is that of personal privacy, that is, the legitimate right of an individual to maintain a certain degree of secrecy about himself *vis-à-vis* other individuals or the state. The problem of privacy, or rather secrecy, at the level of a government or a nation-state is equally important. How much should individual citizens be entitled to know about the actions of a government authority?[2] In the democratic industrialised countries, the trend has generally been one of greater openness and transparency, and less secrecy. This trend has been reinforced by legal dispositions (such as the Freedom of Information Act in the United States), the jurisprudence of the courts, and perhaps even more by the investigative abilities, or intelligence capability, of individual citizens, social groups such as consumers associations or professional associations, and the press. In many other countries, however, Francis Bacon's famous dictum — 'knowledge is power' — is very much the norm, and the retention of information is used as an instrument of government. Secrecy is a key political resource, but what is often overlooked is that it can also be a major liability in the long run, since it is a source of great rigidities in a country's information infrastructure and an obstacle to the development of the knowledge industry. Any national policy for the improvement of the information environment and the use of intelligence as an instrument of development must take into full account the secrecy factor and gain better appreciation of the economic and social value of greater transparency.

## The Transmission of Information and the Time Element

In the intelligence-system model presented in Chapter 1, an im-

2. On this point, see, for instance, James Michael, *The Politics of Secrecy*, Penguin, Harmondsworth, 1982. On the more general problem of government secrecy, see Itzhak Galnoor (ed.), *Government Secrecy in Democracies*, Harper Colophon

portant function which was covered only very cursorily was the communication or transmission function, that is, the set of mechanisms, institutions, networks and infrastructures that ensure the timely transfer of data, information or knowledge between the different actors in an intelligence system. People carry out this transmission function for the most part with the help of physical infrastructures such as the telecommunications sytem, the mail or the transportation system, and by machines (for example, computers) which use this same physical infrastructure. The efficiency and speed with which information is transferred is conditioned to a large extent by the quality and density of the infrastructure. It is also influenced in no small measure by such immaterial elements as attitudes towards secrecy, social values, personal relationships, cultural traditions and structures of authority.

The value of information depends not only on its intrinsic importance, its relevance or its veracity, but also on its timeliness. Information which arrives late is often of little use, however complete and reliable it may be. Conversely, the value of incomplete or partially incorrect information can be greatly enhanced if it is the first to arrive, and one of the central problems in any intelligence effort, or indeed in any activity dealing with information, is the trade-off between timeliness and reliability.

One of the elements of the physical infrastructure of information which has contributed most directly to the emergence of an information economy in the highly industrialised countries is the development of the telecommunications network, and in particular of the telephone system. At the same time, it is interesting to observe that very little attention is given to this transmission medium in national information policies. Part of the reason could be that the telephone is a comparatively old, and therefore unglamorous technology (it was invented in 1876) which is taken for granted as a feature of our information landscape. The size of this information infrastructure is enormous: its value represents a cumulative world-wide investment of some $700 billion while annual world-wide investment in this sector is in the region of $80 billion. By far the largest part of these investments has been made in the highly industrialised countries of the OECD area: these countries have some 84 per cent of the world's telephones and other telecommunications infrastructures,[3]

---

Books, New York, 1977.
   3. On this point, see, in particular, *Telecommunications, Pressures and Policies for*

as against a little more than 8 per cent for all the developing nations, and some 7.5 per cent for the socialist countries. The gap between industrialised and developing nations is even more striking if one compares not absolute figures, but the density of telecommunications networks — the number of telephones relative to total population: in the OECD area, the average density is a little over 50 telephone lines per 100 inhabitants, whereas in the developing nations taken as a group, it is slightly more than two, that is, less than one-twentieth.

By virtue of the density, quality and diversity of their telecommunications infrastructure, the highly industrialised countries benefit from an enormous advantage in economic efficiency, and this infrastructure in turn is one of the important elements in the good functioning of their knowledge industry and the speed with which information can be transmitted throughout society.

While it would probably be futile to try to determine the extent to which a good telecommunications infrastructure is a cause or a consequence of a high level of economic development, or even try to measure the overall impact of telecommunications on the functioning of the knowledge industry, it is not unrealistic to assume that better telecommunications facilities would allow the developing countries to use information in a much more efficient way and would greatly enhance the effectiveness of their emerging knowledge industry.

The difficulty facing developing countries is that investments in telecommunications are very costly, and have to be balanced against public investments for rural development, urban housing, health, education and national security. In the political competition for increasingly scarce funds, telecommunications generally fare very poorly, and this explains to a large extent why, with a few notable exceptions (Brazil, several oil producing countries with a low population density, and the newly industrialised countries of South-East Asia), telecommunications infrastructures in the developing world have been growing rather slowly in the last two decades. In some regions, this growth has not matched the rate of population increase, and the result is that the density of the telecommunications networks has actually declined, as is the case, for

*Change*, OECD, Paris 1983; Gérard Blanc, *The Impact of Telecommunications on Employment*, ITU, Geneva, 1983; and Robert Chapuis, 'Some Basic Reflections on the Economics of Telecommunications', paper presented at the World Communications Year Seminar in Lomé, Togo, August 1983.

instance, in sub-Saharan Africa.

The value of an investment, however, is not determined simply by its cost, but by the relationship between cost and direct and indirect benefits. Traditionally, telecommunications investments have tended to be appraised on the basis of their financial profitability, that is, the ratio between total costs and the total income accruing to national telecommunications authorities. The economic benefits, direct or indirect, which take the form of increases in economic activity, better uses of information or greater transparency in a national economy, were generally not taken into account, largely because of the methodological difficulties involved in measuring them.

A recent research project, sponsored by the International Telecommunication Union (ITU), tried to solve this problem and develop methodologies for measuring direct and indirect economic benefits of investments.[4] The methodologies developed can serve to measure both the macro-economic benefits of telecommunications (such as increases in gross national product or improvements in the efficiency of public services) and the micro-economic benefits (for example, reductions in individual travel expenditures or improved access to important information). The application of these techniques shows that these direct and indirect economic benefits are considerably larger than the more narrowly defined financial benefits. The results of this research help place telecommunications investments in a new perspective: they show indirectly that such investments contribute to major increases in economic efficiency as a result of the faster and more fluid flow of information, and that they are also immensely more profitable from a purely economic point of view than had previously been assumed. The implications for a national intelligence policy are equally clear: investments in telecommunications infrastructures must be viewed not only as an expenditure which has to be balanced against other political and social priorities, but also as one of the most cost-effective ways of building up an efficient information infrastructure.

Building up a good telecommunications network is a long-term undertaking. It is also one of the largest investments in the field of information and knowledge. One should not overlook the fact that the process of information transmission within a society does not

4. The results of this project are summarised in William Pierce and Nicolas Jéquier, *Telecommunications for Development*, ITU, Geneva, 1983.

depend exclusively on the quality and density of the telecommunications infrastructure. It is also linked with other infrastructures such as a good transportation system, and with adequate supplies of goods like paper which serve as the material support in the transmission and storage of information.

The fluidity and efficiency of information-transmission processes within a society are also determined by a number of less conspicuous but equally important immaterial elements. One of these is the way in which expenditures on information transmission are treated in the budgetary process of government departments, industrial firms and research institutes. In most institutions, it is felt that expenditures on travel, telecommunications or publications should be kept to a minimum since budgetary resources are limited. Indicative of this type of attitude is the case of a developing country in South Asia where all imports of foreign scientific publications were suspended for two years as a result of foreign-exchange difficulties. Or take the case of a leading chemical laboratory in a neighbouring country where budgetary limitations make it practically impossible for its researchers to attend scientific conferences abroad: on average, each researcher in this laboratory stands one statistical chance in two of making one trip abroad during the thirty-odd years of his working career.

Expenditures on communications should more rightly be considered as investments which can be subject to the same sort of cost–benefit analysis as investments in new machinery, scientific equipment or buildings. Intuitively, one can sense that a $50 phone call to an overseas colleague to solve a particular technical problem or acquire an urgently needed piece of information is intrinsically different from say a similar expenditure on cleaning, in the same way that $10,000 spent on foreign scientific publications or travel abroad does not fit in the same category as a $10,000 expenditure on a company car.

Modification in accounting procedures alone cannot, of course, change attitudes and culture: like all social norms — from building codes to technical standards — accounting rules are the expression of a society's culture and values, rather than one of their causal factors. In the same way, the lack of fluidity in a society's patterns of communication and information transmission reflects a society's values and traditions, and for this very reason is generally not perceived as a weakness or failing. It tends to be accepted as a normal feature which is seldom put into question, and it usually takes an outsider (such as a foreigner or a foreign-educated national) to realise how important the problem is, and how much more efficient the country's knowledge industry could be if communications within the country and with the outside world were not so difficult. What further reinforces this normality of poor communications is the fact that societies, institutions and individuals tend to adapt to the ecology of poor communications: the usual response to such a situation is not an effort to improve things, but rather a gradual reduction in the need for communication — a situation which, of course, further reduces the demand and opportunities for communication. In the same way that people simply cease to use the telephone when the quality and density of the network is too low or too poor, societies reduce their needs for communication when these needs cannot be satisfied under normal circumstances.

Another major factor accounting for the lack of fluidity of communications is the system of authority within a society or an institution. When hierarchical structures are governed by authoritarian power — and this usually means that secrecy is used as an instrument of domination and control — information generally circulates very poorly. Those people who have the information keep it to themselves as a protection against their superiors and as a means of controlling their subordinates, and those who do not have it spend considerable amounts of time acquiring what to them might be a vitally important resource. Those who should or could transmit information act in effect as barriers or filters in the transmission process. This role can be performed by delaying transmission times, for instance by passing on information only once it has lost much of its timeliness, by withholding selected pieces of information, by acting as information black holes (attracting vast amounts of information without letting any of it escape to other interested parties) or by swamping the opponent with large quantities of trivial and irrelevant information.

In this sense, creating an information-efficient infrastructure is not so much an organisational problem as a question of attitudes, confidence, motivation and state of mind. For instance, setting strict organisational rules about the flows of information within an institution can help to increase in a marginal way the fluidity of the transmission process, but the ways in which decision-makers receive truly important and timely information from subordinates and colleagues depend much more on the patterns of authority and the networks of mutual trust within an institution.

General Conclusions

## The Computer Revolution and the Business Intelligence Explosion

One of the major components of an information-efficient infra-structure is, of course, the computer. In his chapter on Sweden and Malaysia, Björn Tell raised the idea that computers, along with all the hardware and software of the knowledge industry (libraries, telecommunications infrastructures, institutional memories and patterns of communication within a society) formed what might be viewed as the social brain of a nation. In an earlier chapter, Eric de Grolier suggested that the highly industrialised societies are now only at the beginning of the information revolution, or computer revolution, and will have to face in the coming decades a set of entirely new social, economic and political problems resulting from this explosive growth of computer technology.

This information revolution has already transformed beyond recognition both the structure and the end products of a number of well-established manufacturing industries — the motor-car industry and the telecommunications industry are good illustrations of this — as well as of service industries such as banking, insurance, air transportation or power distribution. It is giving rise to entirely new industries and new services; and it is transforming, perhaps less visibly but no less deeply, the ways in which governments operate, and the relations between citizens and the state.

Unlike political revolutions, this revolution has no master plan. It is a long and complex process, extending over decades, rather than a single event taking place at a clearly identified point in time, and its leaders are not a few charismatic figures, but tens of thousands of innovators, entrepreneurs, researchers, industrial firms, social scientists, public servants and educators working for the most part in the highly industrialised Western countries. This revolution is initiating a tidal wave of change, to use Stevan Dedijer's expression,[5] and the strength of this wave lies not only in its sheer mass but also in the inner momentum resulting from the interactions and synergies between all its actors.

As Philip Abelson observed,[6] 'With the revolution in computers

5. Stevan Dedijer, 'Social Intelligence for Self-Reliant Development, Basis for Government Policy in the Intelligence Revolution', paper prepared for the United Nations University project on the emergence of new social thought, Lund University, March 1985.
6. In the introduction to the special issue of *Science*, 12 February 1982, on

and electronics, to the ancient tensions between the rich and the poor will be added the tensions between those with high intellectual capacity and the less gifted, and between the well educated and the untrained'. What is true of a given society — Abelson was thinking here essentially of the United States — is even truer of world society, and notably of the relations between rich and poor countries, or industrialised and developing countries. Control over information and knowledge is gradually adding an entirely new dimension to the traditional political confrontations over territory, population or natural resources.

Precisely because of its extraordinarily diffuse nature and the very large number of actors involved in it, this revolution cannot have a master plan, let alone an imperial design. But the absence of imperial design or grand strategy does not mean that it is without imperial consequences. The most important of these imperial consequences, at the international level, is the growing gap between those countries and societies which master this information revolution, and those which do not or cannot, or in other terms, between those societies which have the greatest intelligence — in the psychological and social sense of the word — and those which are still less developed in this respect.

One of the great difficulties in dealing with this issue at the international level — be it bilaterally or in the framework of international negotiations — is that it tends to be perceived very differently by the various actors involved in the game. For the highly industrialised Western countries, the intelligence competition is essentially a competition between these countries themselves — the United States against Japan, Europe against America, France against West Germany — and between the different economic, scientific and technological actors in this same group of countries. And in the military sphere, this intelligence competition is taking place for the most part between the superpowers. This competition between the industrialised countries and between East and West is one of the driving forces behind the information revolution, and the developing nations, with the exception of a few newly industrialised countries, are largely absent from it.[7] This

computers and electronics.

7. It should be noted here that in some specific areas, the newly industrialised countries are in fact ahead of the 'old' highly industrialised nations. Thus Brazil for instance, which has been using computers to process incoming passengers in its international airports since 1973, whereas in 1985, the United States, one of the

explains in large part the lack of interest of the highly industrialised countries in the growing information and intelligence gap between them and the developing nations and, more serious, their lack of sensitivity to the fact that this issue is increasingly perceived by the developing nations as a major problem, and perhaps even as the manifestation of some grand imperial design.

This perception by many developing nations of the information revolution as a new imperial design is further reinforced by the fact that some of the most conspicuous actors in this revolution are the big multinational firms. These firms are important not only as sources of technological innovations — in the computer industry, in telecommunications hardware, in microelectronics, in artificial intelligence or in new types of software — but also, and perhaps even more, because they are today at the forefront of the intelligence field, just as government agencies were at the forefront of this field during the Second World War.[8] Business intelligence, or rather the intelligence efforts and capabilities of large multinational firms, is one of the least well-charted aspects of the information revolution.[9] This intelligence, systematically nurtured and developed by the big multinationals themselves as a major instrument in their competition against other multinationals, is an instrument of power and a factor of inequality. As such, it is a political problem, even if it is not perceived in this way by the major actors concerned.

As suggested earlier on this book by such authors as William Colby and Francisco Sagasti, the crucial issue facing the developing countries is not so much to negotiate a better deal with the industrialised countries (what the object of the negotiation might be is still far from clear) as to develop their own intelligence capability in the social sense of the word. This capability obviously implies computer literacy, which will be as important in the world of tomorrow as ordinary literacy is in the world of today. But it is much more than the mere ability to use, or even manufacture, certain particular

---

world leaders in computer applications, was still using old manual methods to do this work. And it may be recalled here that when the summer 1976 drought struck the United Kingdom, technical assistance was requested from Israel, the world's leading country in terms of computerisation in the field of water resources management.

8. For a first introduction to the business intelligence explosion, see Stevan Dedijer's documentary notes, 'What is Your Enterprise Intelligence?', Lund University, Lund, December 1985 (mimeo). One of the best histories of government intelligence in the Second World War is R.V. Jones, *Most Secret War*, Hamish Hamilton, London, 1978.

9. See Dedijer, 'What is Your Enterprise Intelligence?'.

pieces of hardware. It is also a frame of mind, a set of attitudes, an understanding of what information and knowledge really are, and the perception that a society's ability to develop and grow depends first and foremost on encouraging and deploying the intelligence of all its citizens.

## The Emergence of Social Intelligence

One of the positive results of the innumerable studies on the knowledge industry and the information economy carried out during the past fifteen years has been to sensitise policy-makers in the industrialised countries to the importance of information as a productive force and pave the way for more coherent policies in the field of information. These efforts to quantify employment, investment, production and trade in the knowledge industry are similar in some respects to one of the great survey works undertaken several generations ago in practically all the emerging nation-states, namely the compilation of a first dictionary of the national language.[10] Aside from their obvious political and cultural function in creating a sense of national unity, dictionaries help to unify one of the basic instruments of information, namely language; they also serve as the memory and history of a people's language, and always show that a language is immensely richer and more diverse than commonly thought. What a dictionary does not tell us, however, is how to use the language. In the same way, surveys of the knowledge industry have helped to unify our basic concepts in the field of information and knowledge, creating a common information culture and bringing to light the unexpectedly wide range of activities in the field of information, but they do not tell us much about the ways in which this new language of information can be used.

One of the assumptions underlying the various chapters of the present book is that intelligence is perhaps the most adequate instrument for using this new language. In this sense, intelligence might be viewed as the capacity of a society and its institutions to identify problems (the identification of a problem being primarily a

10. Examples include the seventeenth-century *Dictionnaire de l'Académie Française* (which has yet to be completed!), and, in the second half of the nineteenth century the dictionaries of Finnish, Russian, Hebrew, Polish and Serbo-Croatian, to name but a few.

239

request for information), to assemble the relevant information about these problems, transmit, process and evaluate it and finally use it for action. Intelligence includes the production and creation of knowledge, but is also much more than that: it involves the memorisation of knowledge, the ability to retrieve it from the collective memory, and the ability to make judgements about its value, timeliness and relevance.

This concept of intelligence in the social sense, or social intelligence, is still far from being fully operational. At this stage, what we can propose is an intuitive set of potential applications and some general directions towards the future, rather than concrete proposals or a systematic view. The exploration of the intelligence function carried out by the authors in the first part of this volume should not be viewed as the final word on the subject, but as a preliminary approach to what is still largely uncharted territory. The case-studies presented in the second part have tried to show some of the ways in which intelligence is used by nations to meet their development challenges, or by corporations in pursuit of their growth objectives, but do not purport to present a comprehensive picture of intelligence applications. In the same way, the practical suggestions and general principles outlined by the contributors to the third part of this volume should be viewed as broad indications of the ways in which to proceed, not as well-tested recipes for action.

An impressionistic inquiry of this nature necessarily leads to equally impressionistic conclusions, which could be summarised in the following statements:

— The knowledge industry and information networks within a society form what could be called a social brain and the way in which this brain functions could be called social intelligence.
— The ability of a society to survive and develop, to adapt to new challenges and modify its environment depends to a large extent on its social intelligence, much in the same way as an individual's ability to operate successfully in a society depends on his intelligence, as psychologists define the term.
— In the developing countries, the effective utilisation of this social intelligence is essential if these countries are to meet the political, economic and social challenges facing them in their fight against poverty, inequality, underdevelopment and foreign domination; one of the critically important instruments in the

mobilisation of social intelligence for development purposes is a
development-orientated intelligence policy.

— All societies and all institutions are involved in intelligence
work, but these activities are generally not acknowledged as
such; this failure to recognise the intelligence function for what
it is often means that it is not used as effectively as it might be.

— The effectiveness of a society's social intelligence is conditioned
to a great degree by the size of that society's knowledge industry and by the density and quality of its information networks.

— A society's social intelligence, or for that matter the intelligence
of any organisation, is also conditioned by attitudes, values,
patterns of authority and systems of social relations.

— A nation that has a small indigenous knowledge industry and
relatively underdeveloped information networks can to a large
extent overcome this disadvantage with the help of intelligence,
and an effective intelligence policy can enable it to acquire from
outside most of the knowledge and information necessary for
its development purposes.

— Building up an intelligence capability for development is not
necessarily very costly, and could in fact be among the most
profitable long-term investments for a poor country.

# About the Contributors

**Wilhelm Agrell** held various positions in Swedish intelligence and has been associated since 1978 with the Research Policy Institute at the University of Lund. He is the author of several books on security, military technology and national intelligence.

**Gérard Blanc** is a graduate of France's Ecole Polytechnique. Before joining the Institute of Advanced Studies in Public Administration at the University of Lausanne, he worked at the OECD Development Centre where he co-authored several books on appropriate technology. He is also the editor of the French-language quarterly, *CoEvolution*.

**Jan M.M. van der Broek** is the director of the Centre for Integrated Studies, set up jointly by the Institute for Aerial Studies and Earth Sciences (ITC) and Unesco. A Dutch citizen, he has worked as a consultant in a number of developing countries to help establish information systems for development.

**William E. Colby** was director of the US Central Intelligence Agency from 1973 to 1976. He is currently an attorney with the firm of Reid & Priest and an international political and economic consultant with International Business-Government Counsellors Inc. in Washington, DC.

**Stevan Dedijer** is the former director of the Research Policy Institute at the University of Lund, and is now resident consultant in business intelligence at the School of Business Administration. Born in Yugoslavia and presently a Swedish citizen, he studied physics and worked for several years in nuclear research, and has carried out numerous missions throughout the developing world.

**Yehezkel Dror** is a professor of political science and Wolfson Professor of public administration at the Hebrew University in Jerusalem. His publications include studies on policy-making, strategic planning and the redesign of governments. He has served with the Israeli Ministry of Defence, has acted as adviser to a number of heads of state, planning ministries and administrative reform agencies in the developing world, and worked with the Rand Corporation in the United States.

**O.A. El Kholy** was formerly the adviser to the Minister of Education and Science in Egypt and assistant director-general for science and technology of the Arab League Educational, Scientific and Cultural Organisation (ALESCO). He is at present senior adviser to the Kuwait Institute for Scientific Research and is actively involved in science and technology policy and industrial development in the Arab region.

**Eric de Grolier**, a specialist in information systems, directed the research bureau of the International Council for the Social Sciences and was secretary-general of France's National Institute for Documentation Techniques. He has taught in North America and Africa and served as a consultant to Unesco in the Middle East. He is the author of numerous publications, notably in the field of organisation of information systems.

**Nicolas Jéquier** is a professor of public administration at the Institute of Advanced Studies in Public Administration at the University of Lausanne. A Swiss citizen, he worked for several years at the OECD Development Centre, and is the author of several books on appropriate technology, technology policy, telecommunications, the electronic industries and financial institutions.

**Thomas Lindberg** worked for more than ten years as an environment analyst with the IBM Corporation in Europe. In 1982, he founded his own consulting firm which deals with strategic planning, environment analysis and foreign business risk assessment.

**Jan J. Nossin**, a Dutch geo-morphologist, is vice-rector of the Indian Photo-Interpretation Institute in Dehra Dun, India. He is a specialist in earth sciences, remote sensing applications and survey integration, and has participated in many seminars organised by international agencies on these subjects.

**Frank T. Pearce** is a British economist, statistician and management scientist who practises as an independent consultant. He was awarded a national prize for his numerous writings on intelligence questions.

**Pierre Piganiol** was formerly the Délégué Général à la Recherche Scientifique et Technique to France's Prime Minister. He now works as a consultant on development questions for several international organisations, and is a board member of L'Air Liquide and the Banque Privée de Gestion Financière et Foncière in Paris.

**Francisco R. Sagasti** is associate director of the Development Analysis Group (GRADE), professor at the Universidad del Pacífico and member of the board of Peru's National Council for Science and Technology. He has published twelve books and over eighty articles on science and technology policy, industrialisation, planning and systems theory. In 1980, he was awarded the United Nations Peace Medal and the Paul Hoffman Award for outstanding contributions to development.

**Björn Tell** is director of the National Lending Library at the University of

Lund, Sweden. He served for ten years as member of the OECD information policy group and was rapporteur of the OECD *ad hoc* group on scientific and technical information.

**Arnaldo K. Ventura,** former chairman and executive director of Jamaica's Scientific Research Council, is a virologist by training. He has served as scientific and technological adviser and consultant to several developing countries, international agencies and national institutions. At present, he is a senior consultant to the World Association of Industrial and Technological Research Organisations.

**Michael J. West** is a director of the economics division of the Economist Intelligence Unit Ltd. in London. He has published a large number of articles, as well as two books on Britain and Europe and the Commonwealth and Europe.

# Index

# Index

# Index

209, 237
Garfield, Eugene, 81f., 179f.
gatekeeper approach in intelligence, 207
gatekeepers, 108, 129, 208
gateways to information systems, 137
General Agreement on Tariffs and Trade (GATT), 11f., 47
General Organisation for Industrialisation, Egypt, 106
generation of information, 179
of knowledge, 175
genetic engineering, 195
resources, 148
Geneva, 143
geo-information, 163
geological structures, 159
geology, 163
Germany, Federal Republic, 36, 37, 38, 81, 87, 207, 237
Gesellschaft für Information und Dokumentation, Germany, 87
glass packaging industry, 67, 68, 69
*Gmelin Handbook of Inorganic Chemistry*, 84, 87
Götze, Dietrich, 79f.
government
laboratories, 68
publications, 68, 69
governments, role in information industry, 79–92
grain
cartel, 147
intelligence, 148, 153–7
intelligence policy, 153–7
intelligence unit, 155
seeds, 148
trading corporations, 95, 96, 139–57
Gray, Fred, 9f.
Greece, 132
Grennes, Thomas, 141f.
Gresham's Law, 228
grey information, 18–21
Grey Literature, System for Information on, 19f.
Grolier, Eric de, 28, 236
Gross, Bertram, 4f.
ground stations for satellites, 156
groupthink, 220
Guinea, 115
Guyana, 6, 9

Hague Congress (1948), 203
Haiti, 115

*Handbücher*, 83
Hanis, Edward H., 92f.
hard information, 56, 148, 172, 198–200
*see also* soft information, quantitative information
hardware, 35, 49, 125, 132, 236
Harris, W., 4f.
harvest forecasting, *see* crop forecasting
heads of state, 121, 172, 213–19
health, 203, 232
heavy industry, 105, 213
Helvetica, 80
Her Majesty's Stationery Office, 69
heuristics, 221
high-fructose corn syrup, 7
high-technology industries, 190
Hill, V.G., 112, 113f.
Hitachi-IBM espionage affair, 59, 92
hobby magazines, 69
Honeywell Corp., 133
hot spots in intelligence, 72f., 91
Hughes, Thomas L., 220
Huff, A., 4f.
human
intelligence, 23, 34
resources in intelligence, 123
sources in intelligence, 33, 34
Hungary, 144
hunger, 139
hybrid seeds, 153

IBM Corp., 10, 11, 59, 92, 133, 205
identification
capability, 17
function, 16, 198
of problems, 16, 17, 198
ideology, 213
ignorance, 95, 113, 115, 219
illiteracy, 80
illusions in policy making, 215
image distortions, 213–14
imaging radar, 160
imperfect information, 74
Imperial Group, 59
imperialism, 40, 47
income level and link with secrecy, 91
independence, economic, 1
indeterminacy, 54
India, 10, 67, 155, 166f., 204, 226
Indian Institute for Remote Sensing, 166f.
indigenous technology, 104
individuals

*Index*

# Index

negotiation, 175, 229, 237
  intelligence, 11, 12, 106, 111, 112
  with multinational firms, 5, 6, 10,
    107, 112, 142
  preparation, 5, 106
  role of information, 114
  role of secrecy and transparency, 95
Nepal, 10
Netherlands, 36, 97, 166
network of networks, 87
networks, 67, 70, 96, 178, 235
neutron bomb, 44
New Information Order, 45
*New Scientist*, 149f.
New York, 144
*New York Times*, 17
newspapers, 32, 43, 44, 69, 81, 146
Nigeria, 160, 204
Nobel Prize, 17
non-existent information, 20, 91
non-proprietary information, 110
Nossin, J.J., 97
nuclear
  balance, 33
  deterrence, 33
  weapons, 42, 44

obsolete information processing
  methods, 80
obstacles to intelligence, 117
October War (1973), 35, 104, 107
OECD countries, 39, 231
office automation, 80
official development assistance, 44
offshore resources, 9
oil
  crisis, 37, 202
  demand for, 5
  producing countries cartel, 40
Olsen, J., 220
Olympic Games, 39
omissions as sources of intelligence, 69
open door policy (Egypt), 109
open information, 17, 18, 19, 20, 21, 22
open skies, 150
open sources of information, 32, 33,
  34, 68, 69, 70, 107, 108
open trade, 47
openness
  of information, 63, 226
  in intelligence, 27
  of society, 135, 226, 230
operational planning, 202
operations intelligence (in

management), 53–5
operations research, 57, 61
opinion polls, 99, 204
optic fibres, 7
Organisations for Economic
  Co-operation and Development
  (OECD), xi, 39, 44, 85, 131, 204,
  210, 232f.
organisation function (in management),
  50
Organisation of Petroleum Exporting
  Countries (OPEC), 116
organisational intelligence, 15
organisational problems of
  intelligence, 28
organisational structures, 193
Orwell, G., 92
Ottawa, 147

packet-switched networks, 130, 132
Palestine Liberation Organisation, 44
Panama, 144
panels of experts, 76
parties, political, 104, 114, 120
patents, 187
Paterson, T.T., 51f.
pattern recognition and recognisers,
  171, 180, 225
patterns in intelligence problems, 71,
  74
Pearce, Frank T., 4f., 13f., 28
Pearl Harbor, 31, 37, 213, 220
Penang, Malaysia, 133
Pepsi Cola Corp., 8
perishability of information, 143
personal contacts and relations, role in
  intelligence, 28, 70, 108, 204, 226
Peru, 175, 188f.
Peruvian Center for Higher Military
  Studies, 188f.
Philippines, 153
photocopying machines, 226
photography, 158, 191
Pierce, William, 233f.
Piganiol, Pierre, xi, 171, 225
pilot projects in intelligence, 77
Pinder, John, 209f.
pitfalls in decision-making, 172
planners, 177
planning, 101, 219
  and information, 138
  ministry, 8
  and remote sensing information,
    164

# Index

resource information, 102, 154
responsibility, link with authority, 51
retrieval of information, 21, 73, 240
revolution, Egypt, 100
Revolutionary Government of the
  Armed Forces, Peru, 176
rice, 140, 145, 152
risk, 28, 53, 54
  analysis services, 204
  assessment, 206
  and culture, 220
  intelligence, 75
  management, 145, 150
Robert, Jean, 153f.
Rohde, Eric, 79f.
Royal Institute of Technology,
  Sweden, 132, 133
Royal Library, Sweden, 130
Rowat, Donald G., 90f.
rubber production, 135, 152
rules of behaviour, 46
rumours, 111

saccharin, 7
Sagasti, Francisco R., 171, 225, 238
Sahara, 156
Sahel, 42
Sains University, Malaysia, 131, 134–7
sampling techniques, 56, 57
sapiential authority, 51
satellite intelligence, 33
satellites, 6, 12, 33, 39, 44, 123, 149,
  156, 158–67, 186
Saudi Arabia, 65
Scandinavian Council for Applied
  Research, 133
Scandinavian countries, 130
SCANDOC, 130
SCANNET, 130, 133
scanning of data, 180
scenarios, 54, 205
schizophrenia, institutionalised, 174
*Science*, 152f.
*Science Citation Index*, 89
science fiction writers, 171, 180, 181
science and technology
  journals, 187
  links with intelligence and warfare,
    33
  policy, 3, 171, 183–96
scientific
  aspects of intelligence, 36
  conferences, 234
  publications, 2, 79, 82, 234

publishing, 79
traditions, 119
scientific and technical information
  (STI), 128–38
scientific and technological
  developments, intelligence on, 33
scientists and engineers, shortage of,
  171
search
  methods, 132, 133
  for technical information, 113
Searle Corp., 8
Seasat, 160
Second Civilisation, 174
secrecy
  danger of, 95
  in general, 64, 104, 111, 115, 187,
    191, 213, 226, 230
  need for, 58, 102–3, 120, 165, 178,
    180
  and privacy, 27, 28
  role in intelligence, 36, 37, 45, 139,
    142, 146–8, 171, 177, 218, 228, 229
  and transparency, 29, 90–2
secret
  agents, 177
    *see also* spies
  information, 18–22, 47, 63, 64
  methods in intelligence, 37
secrets, exchange of, 196
sectoral intelligence, 216
security, 15, 31, 203
  agencies, 3, 16, 17, 22, 23
  conceptions of national, 36, 37, 175,
    176
  forces, 125
  national, 6, 27, 103, 150, 175–6, 212,
    227, 229, 232
  problems in remote sensing, 162, 165
seed distribution industry, 146
seeds, 153
self-deception, 219
self-education in intelligence, 219
self-fulfilling prophecies, 214
self-sufficiency in data bases, 87
Senegal, 190
sensitive information, 107, 150
Seoul, Korea, 143
sequences in management intelligence,
  57
Service de Recherche de la
  Bibliothèque de la Législature,
  Québec, 82
service industries, 236

# Index

Surinam, 115
surprise events, 216
superpowers, 39, 237
supply intelligence, 65
surveys of information resources, Egypt, 100
Sweden, 36, 95, 96, 128–38, 201, 226, 236
Swedish Council of Environmental Information, 136
Sweeney, Gerry, P., 79f.
synthesists, role in intelligence, 171, 180, 225
Syria, 104
System Development Corporation, 89, 134
Système Probatoire d'Observation de la Terre (SPOT), 161
systems analysis, 4, 57, 58, 172
systems of authority, 235

tactical intelligence (in management), 53–5, 201
Taiwan, 5
Tanzania, 8, 9
tax authorities, 229
technocrats, 102
technological
   development and intelligence policy, 105
   forecasting, 22, 54
   trends, 187
technology
   appropriate, 187, 188
   acquisition process, 95
      see also access to technology
   choice, 193
   traditional, 125, 172, 186
   transfer, 105, 190, 204
techno-economic intelligence, 173–82
technostructure, 50
telecommunications, 80, 132, 148, 177, 233, 233f., 238
   infrastructures, 2, 236
   investments, benefits of, 233, 234
   manufacturing industry, 227
   networks, 14, 15, 21, 155, 231
   systems, 7, 231
teleconferencing, 129
telegraph, 142
telephones, 2, 21, 130, 226, 231, 235
television, 129
telex, 134
Tell, Björn, 96, 226, 236

territory, 237
testing laboratories, 172, 185
text processing, 80
textiles, 189, 192
think-tanks, 82, 96, 217
Third Civilisation, 174
Third Industrial Revolution, 9
Third World, 38, 39, 103, 112, 121, 165, 204
   information output, 39
   see also developing countries
Thorndyke, E., 4f.
Thursby, Marie, 141f.
time element in intelligence, 230
timeliness of information, 231
timetables, 216, 237
tobacco, 152
tomato paste canning industry, 99
topographic mapping, 160
Tracking and Data Relay Satellite System, 162
Tradax Corp., 143
trade associations, 204
trade magazines, 71, 147
trade promotion, 63
Trade Union Research Centre, Jamaica, 126
traditional technology, improvement of, 125, 172, 186
traditions in information collection, 130
Trager, James, 147f.
training, 46, 58, 60, 77, 181
   of decision-makers, 219
   of development leaders, 44
   of intelligence specialists, 77, 181
   in remote sensing, 97, 166
transborder data flows, 80
transfer
   of knowledge, 15, 41, 46
   of technology, 204
translation of foreign publications, 43
transmission
   channels, 16
   of information, 14, 226, 232, 233
      see also telecommunications
transnational corporations, see multinational firms
transparency, 27, 29, 38, 39, 90–2, 96, 135, 136, 171, 178, 226, 227–30, 233
transparency gap, 39
transportation system, 231
treason, 4
trend extrapolation, 209, 210

262